"If evangelicalism is to have a coherent future, it needs to understand not only its own past but also the past of the church catholic. In this collection of essays, Ken Stewart brings his typical combination of insight, conviction, charity, and catholicity to bear on evangelicalism's relationship to history. You do not have to agree with all of his conclusions to agree with his basic thesis—we need history—and to be challenged by the range of interlocutors he chooses—from the ancient church fathers to Cardinal Newman and beyond. This collection should provide professors and pastors with much food for thought."

Carl R. Trueman, Westminster Theological Seminary

"This remarkable book seeks to trace the deep roots and determine the DNA of evangelical Protestantism. Using his considerable and profound knowledge of a vast terrain, Dr. Ken Stewart digs deep to show that evangelicalism is firmly rooted in Scripture, the early church, and historical Christianity. His archaeology of doctrine and liturgy argues against the recent loss of confidence and self-identity of evangelical Protestants who may be tempted to seek more 'stable' pastures or to wander with historical amnesia into cul-de-sacs. Instead, evangelical Protestants are urged to share the confidence of their Protestant-era forebears who knew their ancient pedigree and stood on sturdy ground. This is an important and timely book."

Robert M. Solomon, bishop emeritus, The Methodist Church in Singapore

"Ken Stewart's *In Search of Ancient Roots* is a panoply of well-argued, well-documented, and well-written chapters centering on evangelicalism's engagement with its own pre-Reformation past. He provides a compelling case not only for the deep roots of evangelical movements throughout history but also for evangelicalism's attention to its historical Christian roots as the norm rather than the exception. Stewart also provides exceptional discussions on important practical matters facing evangelicals as they begin to engage with church history—matters like the frequency of the Lord's Supper, the apostolicity of infant baptism, the interpretation of Scripture, and justification by faith. In the process, Stewart also takes on many of the exaggerated claims made by evangelical converts to Roman Catholicism and Eastern Orthodoxy regarding the historical priority of those ancient traditions. Any evangelical should read this book before abandoning the orthodox, Protestant, evangelical faith for traditions that claim to be more authentically connected to Christianity's ancient roots. In all of these cases, Stewart's work becomes a conversation-starter rather than a conversation-ender. He is refreshingly irenic and candid. I enthusiastically recommend this book to anybody interested in the Christian past and evangelical identity as well as those who need to reflect deeply on the vital questions Stewart raises for today."

Michael J. Svigel, chair and professor of theological studies, Dallas Theological Seminary, author of *RetroChristianity*

"'To be deep in history,' said John Henry Newman, 'is to cease to be a Protestant.' But Ken Stewart begs to differ. In this learned and eminently readable volume, Stewart conducts a constructive assessment of the evangelical identity crisis currently facing the church. His informative and evocative reflection upon the ecclesial drama argues persuasively that instead of a wilting cousin of the 'Great Tradition,' evangelical movements are poised to flourish by extending their roots into the soil of pre-Reformation Christianity—that is, providing they do so with integrity. *In Search of Ancient Roots* provides such insight, enabling readers to give a clear answer for their evangelical hope."

Chris Castaldo, senior pastor, New Covenant Church, Naperville, Illinois, author of *Talking with Catholics About the Gospel*

"Present-day evangelicalism has a strange relationship with history. On the one extreme, there are those who endorse a 'gap theory' whereby their experience of the Christian life has little if anything to do with any sense of historical continuity. On the other extreme, recent fascinations with romantic and selective appropriations of 'tradition' show how easy it is to uncritically embrace beliefs and practices that are idiosyncratic with regards to Scripture. What is at stake is the historical nature of evangelicalism as such. As a learned historian and acute theologian, Kenneth Stewart helps the reader come to terms with the diachronic dimension of evangelicalism that runs through church history, taking different shades and colors but ultimately responding to the same principles of biblical faithfulness and spiritual involvement. This book is a vigorous and rigorous rebuttal to John Henry Newman, according to whom 'to be deep in history is to cease to be Protestant.' Stewart is convinced that to be deep in history one does not need to turn to Rome (becoming Roman Catholic) or to Antioch (becoming Orthodox). His case is convincing. A must-read for every person struggling with the question, 'What does evangelicalism have to do with history?'"

Leonardo De Chirico, pastor, Breccia di Roma, lecturer in historical theology, Istituto di Formazione Evangelica e Documentazione, Padova, Italy, director of Refomanda Initiative

"This book shakes us free from naive and romantic notions that Roman Catholicism and Eastern Orthodoxy are the best expressions of early Christianity. For evangelicals attracted by that fantasy, it is an urgent wake-up call to examine the full facts and rediscover the deep historic roots and spiritual riches of their own tradition."

Andrew Atherstone, Latimer Research Fellow, Wycliffe Hall, University of Oxford

IN SEARCH OF ANCIENT ROOTS

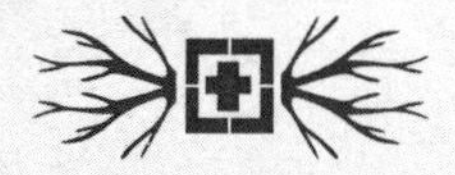

THE CHRISTIAN PAST *and the* EVANGELICAL IDENTITY CRISIS

KENNETH J. STEWART

An imprint of InterVarsity Press
Downers Grove, Illinois

InterVarsity Press
P.O. Box 1400, Downers Grove, IL 60515-1426
ivpress.com
email@ivpress.com

InterVarsity Press® is the book-publishing division of InterVarsity Christian Fellowship/USA®, a movement of students and faculty active on campus at hundreds of universities, colleges, and schools of nursing in the United States of America, and a member movement of the International Fellowship of Evangelical Students. For information about local and regional activities, visit intervarsity.org.

Cover design: David Fassett
Interior design: Jeanna Wiggins
Images: © Quentin Bargate / Getty Images

ISBN 978-0-8308-5172-0 (print)
ISBN 978-0-8308-9260-0 (digital)

Printed in the United States of America ♾

InterVarsity Press is committed to ecological stewardship and to the conservation of natural resources in all our operations. This book was printed using sustainably sourced paper.

Library of Congress Cataloging-in-Publication Data
A catalog record for this book is available from the Library of Congress.

P 23 22 21 20 19 18 17 16 15 14 13 12 11 10 9 8 7 6 5 4 3 2 1
Y 36 35 34 33 32 31 30 29 28 27 26 25 24 23 22 21 20 19 18 17

TO THE MANY FRIENDS AT

Lookout Mountain Presbyterian Church,

Lookout Mountain, Tennessee,

who by their shared concern for this subject and

by personal encouragement have helped

move this book toward completion.

Contents

Acknowledgments

THIS SUBJECT HAS BEEN ON MY MIND for more than a decade. Such is the profusion of literature bearing on the subject of how and why we ought to appropriate from ancient Christianity that I have often described my situation to friends as that of a man chasing a moving train that has already left the station. At some point, one simply has to be content with what one has read and stop reading.

Across this decade or more, various parts of this book have first seen light as essays and conference papers. Chapter five was delivered in the 2007 Wheaton Theology Conference and then appeared in the *Evangelical Quarterly* (80, no. 4 [2008]: 307-21). Chapter seven first saw light as a contribution to a festschrift edited by Ian Clary and Steve Weaver, *The Pure Flame of Devotion: The History of Christian Spirituality; Essays in Honor of Michael A. G. Haykin on His Sixtieth Birthday* (Joshua Press, 2013). Chapters ten and eleven began as short essays in *Books and Culture* (May–June 2003 and March–April 2011) and have been expanded here. Chapter twelve appeared in *Themelios* (39, no. 2 [2014]: 268-80). The Evangelical Theological Society has provided a venue for the presentation of drafts of six chapters (6, 7, 8, 12, 13, and 15). Thank you, various auditors, for help along the way!

Various friends have commented on parts of this project. Among these are Leonardo De Chirico, Cameron Fraser, Ernie Manges, Michael Svigel, and Jack Whytock. I am indebted to the two Covenant College student assistants who assisted me at various stages: Sarah Grace Kaye and A. J. Millsaps.

I especially want to acknowledge the kindness of my wife, Jane, who has proved to be my indefatigable and thorough editor.

INTRODUCTION

The Situation from Which We Begin

Evangelical Christianity's Current Self-Doubt

EVANGELICAL CHRISTIANITY IS NOW a surging global phenomenon. Such writers as Philip Jenkins, David Martin, and David Aikman have reported that Africa, Latin America, and Southeast Asia's Christian future looks increasingly "evangelical" in the sense of embracing Biblicist, Christ- and cross-centered, conversionist, and Holy Spirit–oriented Christianity.[1] But in western Europe and North America (the regions from which pietistic and evangelical expressions of Protestant Christianity were transmitted to the global church), the current era is one of increasing introspection and self-doubt.

This introspection and self-doubt has not to do with any sheer loss of momentum, for church planting goes on apace in western Europe and in North America, and the evangelical "knack" for adaptation to emerging circumstances and cultural change is still alive and well. No, the introspection and self-doubt are the result of three principles still being worked out.

[1]Philip Jenkins, *The Next Christendom* (New York: Oxford University Press, 2002); David Martin, *Tongues of Fire: The Birth of Latin American Protestantism* (Hoboken, NJ: Wiley-Blackwell, 1993); and David Aikman, *Jesus in Beijing* (Chicago: Regnery, 2003).

THREE PRINCIPLES

The run-down factor. These are, *first,* the increasing distance of space and time from the period of evangelical origin and a resulting "run-down."[2] Original ideals and guiding principles can lose their edge over time. I hold that today's evangelical movements are the linear descendants of the popular late-medieval religious movements that eventually gave rise to the various Protestant movements of the sixteenth century (Anabaptist, Lutheran, Reformed, Anglican). Many of the early Protestants had first been agitators for spiritual religion in the years before Luther's protest of 1517. These initially regional movements (not all of which entered Protestantism at its emergence) were both diffused over wider regions than those they initially affected and in turn were modified through adaptation to new cultures and contexts. In the early modern period, evangelical Christianity went "global." But this gradual and natural adaptation, when combined with a gradual loss of momentum, also provoked second thoughts about the need to recover earlier evangelical ideals.

Thus, by the closing decades of the seventeenth century, Dutch and German Pietists as well as the Puritan inhabitants of New England were noting and lamenting the "running down" of evangelical religion and praying for its recovery; this in fact occurred in waves beginning in the 1680s and 1690s on both sides of the Atlantic.[3] The better-known period of the eighteenth century, which we have come to call the Great Awakening or Evangelical Revival, extended this recovery of momentum until the dawn of the next century.

The nineteenth century, especially, witnessed Protestant attempts to recover afresh the original purity of apostolic Christianity. The emulation of the Christianity of the Acts of the Apostles became all the rage circa 1830; whatever had happened *since* the death of the apostles was something that

[2]I use this in the sense defined by Merriam-Webster, as with a wound clock, "the exhaustion of motive power." It should be plain that the various expressions of Christianity are all subject to this loss of momentum.

[3]See the essay of Thomas S. Kidd, "Prayer for a Saving Issue: Evangelical Development in New England Before the Great Awakening," chap. 6 in *The Advent of Evangelicalism*, ed. Michael G. Haykin and Kenneth J. Stewart (Nashville: B&H, 2008). The volume was first released as *The Emergence of Evangelicalism: Exploring Historical Continuities* (Leicester, UK: Inter-Varsity Press, 2008). See also Douglas Shantz, *An Introduction to German Pietism* (Baltimore: Johns Hopkins University Press, 2013), chaps. 1-2.

could be "let go" in these movements called "Restorationist."[4] It was apostolic practice that mattered most. Such movements took a dim view of the Protestant evangelical "status quo," which seemed to them to have become very comfortable with the world as it was.

The early twentieth century was also an especially tumultuous period for evangelical movements in the Western world as there arose a great crisis of confidence in the Scriptures as a reliable record of divine revelation earlier given, and in the Christian gospel as a message of salvation for the entire globe. All Christianity in the West was affected by this period of crisis. In the same decades, there arose another "Restorationist" movement: that variant of evangelicalism now known as global Pentecostalism. In a way akin to the just-named movements of Christianity in the preceding century, Pentecostalism saw itself as remedying a defect in evangelicalism. It believed that evangelical Christianity had left the Holy Spirit under-recognized.[5] Yet given the theological tumults of the early twentieth century, all forms of evangelical Christianity (Restorationist included) tended to navigate in this era by "lightening the ship"—that is, by insisting on fewer essentials of the faith in the interests of defense and propagation.

The lateral factor. But this crisis-driven process of "lightening the ship" went hand in hand with a *second* difficulty that I will call the "lateral factor." In the early twentieth century, ever-larger portions of evangelical Christianity came to be located outside the denominations that had traced their lineal descent from the Reformation movements. This migration of believers happened chiefly because the historic Protestant denominations were not able to satisfactorily resolve fundamental questions about the historical reliability of the Scriptures and the unique saviorhood of Jesus Christ. Inasmuch as the churches of the Reformation had themselves, at their foundations, provided an understanding of the relation in which they stood to the preceding 1,500 years of Christian history (an understanding entailing appropriations of the church fathers, early liturgy and the sacraments, and early

---

[4]Movements such as the Christian Brethren and Churches of Christ hail from this era. Representative histories of the origins of these movements are H. H. Rowden, *The Origins of the Brethren* (London: Pickering and Inglis, 1967) and D. M. Thompson, *Let Sects and Parties Fall: A Short History of the Churches of Christ in Great Britain and Ireland* (London: Berean, 1980).

[5]See, for example, Vinson Synan, *The Holiness-Pentecostal Tradition: Charismatic Movements in the Twentieth Century* (Grand Rapids: Eerdmans, 1997).

ecumenical councils and creeds), those strands of evangelical Christianity that moved in the nineteenth and twentieth centuries *beyond* the historic churches were unwittingly put at the disadvantage of being twice-removed from Christianity pre-1500.

Thus, evangelicals who remained within historic denominations viewed the pre-Reformation centuries more favorably than did those who aligned themselves with Holiness or Bible or independent churches. After all, Anglican, Presbyterian, and Methodist congregations continued to bear the names of pre-Reformation saints (such as St. George, St. Andrew, St. Columba). Now, these distinguishable stances of the historic Protestant churches compared to independent church movements were also transmitted through crosscultural missions to the non-Western world.

Thus, when the twentieth century dawned, one would find Presbyterians in Africa and also plenty of African independent churches. There were Anglicans in India (along with most other Europe-rooted churches) along with commendable efforts to establish indigenous Indian-led churches. Baptists and Lutherans, Presbyterians and Anglicans were in China founding churches that were aligned to their stance regarding pre-Reformation Christianity. Yet Hudson Taylor, founder of the China Inland Mission, determined to establish an indigenous Chinese church that did not take over these loyalties. Each stream of evangelical Christianity held, at least informally, a distinguishable perspective on the pre-Reformation Christian past. To speak in general terms, offshoots of Europe's historic Protestant churches were more likely to find things of value in pre-Reformation Christianity, while the more independent type of evangelical Protestants were less inclined to seek things of value in what came before the Reformation era. It was easily supposed that there was little of value until Luther came on the scene. But there was also a *third* factor.

The thaw in Protestant-Catholic relations. Global evangelical movements could not have anticipated how their varied but established ideas about pre-Reformation Christianity would be called into question by the Second Vatican Council of the Roman Catholic communion and what has followed it. In autumn sessions held annually from 1962 to 1965, this gathering of bishops and theologians from Catholic communions around the globe adopted a number of stances that made Protestants sit up and take notice. Instead of being anathematized (as had been the case at the Council of Trent [1545–1563]), Protestants were now termed "separated brethren." While the division of Western Christendom into Protestant and Catholic was still lamented, Vatican II laid on Roman Catholicism some of the responsibility for this permanent rift. Instead of insisting that only clergy and the church hierarchy could safely interpret the Bible, rank-and-file Catholic believers were now encouraged to own and study the Bible in an accurate translation—of which several were rapidly produced directly from the original languages. Church services, formerly conducted in Latin, were now encouraged in the vernacular of the population.[6]

Not only the Protestant observers who had been invited to be present but the wider Christian world began to sit up and take notice that the Roman communion was in earnest about discussions and collaboration with the wider Christian community. Catholicism was gradually transformed in the mind of Protestants from a monolithic, foreboding, and unfriendly expression of Christianity to one that stimulated curiosity. And besides, this expression of Christianity unashamedly claimed for itself an unbroken succession from the apostles and from earliest Christianity. A succession of modern popes—John Paul II (1920–2005), Benedict XVI (1927–), and Francis (1936–)—two of whom showed interest in and entered discussions with evangelical Protestants, strengthened the impression that Catholicism was no longer "forbidden territory." Roman Christianity, now viewable in an improved light, proved to be especially of interest to two types of evangelical Protestants: (1) those whose lateral distance from the classical Protestant movements had left them quite unprepared for understanding the 1,500 years of Christianity before Protestantism and who easily felt a kind of "allure" toward Rome's claims to antiquity and unbroken succession, and (2) beleaguered Christians in the historic Protestant churches who believed that they were witnessing a retreat from biblical authority and the unique role of Jesus Christ as only savior, for which their historic Protestant churches had been known.

---

[6]These changes and the perceptions of them formed by evangelical Protestants are helpfully surveyed and analyzed in David Wells's *Revolution in Rome* (Downers Grove, IL: InterVarsity Press, 1972).

A CURRENT EVANGELICAL IDENTITY CRISIS

These three factors—the "run-down" factor, which is the outworking of distance of time from evangelical Christianity's rise; the "lateral" factor by which more and more evangelical churches stood in no direct relation to the churches that first stood apart from Rome; and the striking of a new and daring posture by Rome since 1965—have combined to engender an evangelical identity crisis. One is made to wonder, what *is* evangelical Christianity in relation to the "Great Tradition" from which it chose to stand apart? Along with the identity crisis has come a loss of nerve; many wonder if perhaps evangelicalism is, after all, only the threadbare cousin of a nobler "Christianity of the ages."

The symptoms of this identity crisis and loss of nerve may be observed all around. Not only is there a steady flow of reports of evangelical Christians who have undergone "conversion" to Rome (and also to Eastern Orthodoxy), but there is also, among those whose Christian allegiances do not shift so dramatically, a steady tendency to appropriate devotional practices, religious art, and forms of discipleship from the pre-Reformation churches. One observes that such appropriating is too often taken up with the kind of relish that supposes such treasures have been "hidden" from evangelical Christians as if by some determined conspiracy by our Protestant forebears. For persons driven by such concerns, the burden of proof necessarily falls on the evangelical movement rather than the movement from which evangelicalism has stood apart. There exists an inchoate drive to press "behind" the Reformation in the supposition that there has been a misrepresentation or at least neglect of issues that deserve another answer. There is also manifest in many who depart for Catholicism and Orthodoxy an attitude of what I can only call "loathing" toward the forms of evangelical Christianity they leave behind. For these, evangelical Christianity has in hindsight appeared to be a cul-de-sac, a blind alley.

Personally, I can identify to a high degree with much of this ferment. My own spiritual journey has entailed a search for a Christianity with deeper roots than were locatable in the pietistic evangelicalism in which I grew up. The Reformed tradition, in which I now stand, has offered a wealth of resources not originally available to me. I certainly understand this determination to have access to a Christian past that has, at the very least, seemed to be ignored.

Thus, this book cannot hope to argue successfully that *all* such reaction against evangelical Christianity's current situation is ill-founded (yet some certainly is) or that *all* such reaction is unwarranted (though some certainly is). The book aims instead to address two fundamental issues that, like a thread, run through these manifestations of what I will call the "evangelical identity crisis." I identify and deal with these in the conviction that only when these matters are faced can evangelicals confront their current crisis with integrity and guided by principle. What are these two issues?

TWO FUNDAMENTAL ISSUES

In brief, this book will argue *first* that too many evangelicals today are failing to grant that evangelical movements are perennial and recurring. Evangelical Christian churches and movements could decide today to merge with other expressions of Christianity and yet emerge again within a very short time. This recurrence of evangelical tendencies would happen because evangelical movements have always been those that sought *more* in the way of the call to conversion, *more* honoring of Jesus Christ, *more* holiness of life, and *more* Bible knowledge than what prevails in the Christian mainstream. I acknowledge that such a claim is easier made than supported; yet I *will* aim to support it. If evangelical Christianity's existence were to be accepted as something perennial and recurring, we would feel less of an inclination to apologize for its continued existence and expansion. But such evangelical resilience is in short supply just now. Instead we observe a widespread evangelical "inferiority complex" rooted in the misconception that evangelical Christianity is a latecomer—a flash in the pan or, perhaps, just an expression of some age that is now behind us.

The book will argue *second* that appropriation from the pre-Reformation Christian past is both acceptable and welcome provided that it is done according to some agreed principle. I can assure readers that there has in fact been no evangelical "cover-up," no conspiracy to deflect curious evangelical believers away from "neutral" pre-Reformation liturgies, devotional practices, and forms of discipleship. What there *has* been is a range of approaches (some much more defensible than others) by which pre-Reformation Christianity was "weighed" on scales that yielded the judgment that some elements of earlier Christianity were defective. Readers will be impressed, I think, to learn just how very familiar, how adept, and how well-versed numerous evangelical Christians of past centuries were at assessing earlier Christianity. We will need to remember again and again that evangelicals had learned to consciously "stand apart" from the Christian mainstream just because they were upholding a conviction not universally shared: that Jesus Christ fully intended to guide his church by the Holy Spirit speaking in Scriptures entrusted to the whole people of God.

Thus, an extensive chapter will be devoted to an exploration of the standards by which pre-Reformation Christianity has been and still needs to be evaluated. In a subsequent chapter, we will take up the difficult but rewarding subject of the development of Christian doctrines over the centuries. The question is not so much one of whether this development has happened but of what determines whether such developments are legitimate or illegitimate.

And with that having been clarified, we will go on to examine examples of *three* kinds. We will first see that the last five hundred years offer us examples of skillful Protestant interaction with and appropriation of the pre-Reformation Christian past. Next we will take note of examples of what can only be called evangelical gullibility—the too-quick embracing of points of view that suppose evangelical Christianity to have been foolish or misguided. Finally, we must look at some weighty, lingering questions that require our further attention. My firm conviction is that resolution will be found to these questions by the application of our two foundational principles: the perennial character of evangelical movements and the evangelical understanding of supreme authority.

PART I

SETTING THE STAGE

Our Evangelical Identity Crisis

1

Only a Latecomer in Christian History?

The Evangelical Identity Crisis

"'BIBLE ANSWER MAN' CONVERTS TO ORTHODOXY" read the startling headline of *Christianity Today*'s April 2017 story.[1] The center of the story's attention, Hank Hanegraaff, had been a highly influential evangelical apologist and cult-watcher since 1989. Hanegraaff is the author of many books and a popular radio broadcaster; the periodical *Christian Research Journal*, published by the broadcast's parent organization, the Christian Research Institute, has a wide following. In the days following the news of Hanegraaff's realignment with Orthodoxy, reactions were swift and frequently critical.[2]

As well, I have taken up an interesting devotional book, *The Daily Office*.[3] It was not quite what it seemed. I was intrigued to find that this guide to

[1]Sarah Eekhof Zylstra, "'Bible Answer Man' Converts to Orthodoxy," *Christianity Today*, April 12, 2017, www.christianitytoday.com/gleanings/2017/april/bible-answer-man-hank-hanegraaff-orthodoxy-cri-watchman-nee.html.

[2]Art Moore, "'Bible Answer Man' Converts to Eastern Orthodoxy," *World Net Daily*, April 13, 2017, www.wnd.com/2017/04/bible-answer-man-converts-to-greek-orthodox-church.

[3]Peter Scazzaro, *The Daily Office: Remembering God's Presence Throughout the Day* (Barrington, IL: Willow Creek Association, 2008).

disciplined prayer, issued in association with the Willow Creek Association of Barrington, Illinois, attempts to use the cycle of daily prayer as set out in the ancient monastic Rule of St. Benedict (ca. 480–547) as a guide for modern believers. Paradoxically, the publisher—the Willow Creek Association—has come to be identified among evangelical Christians as a kind of epitome of "big box" generic Christianity that has sought to shun tradition in the attempt to reach the unchurched with the gospel. So, Willow Creek now keeps company with St. Benedict?

I am certain that readers who are now taking up *In Search of Ancient Roots* can relate similar observations. On the one hand, we can see men and women shaking the dust off their feet (so to speak) and exiting evangelical Christianity for something Roman or Eastern; on the other hand, there is the smorgasbord-style sampling of a little bit of this and a little bit of that from beyond evangelical Christianity. There is, to say the least, an unsettledness with things as they are.

Though vignettes like this are far from being the whole story (by book's end, we will see that the flow *into* evangelical Christianity exceeds the trickle of those leaving), let's be frank. In recent times, it has grown fashionable for a fair number who were reared in evangelical churches or are indebted to evangelical movements to express the sentiment that, like the proverbial mist, evangelical Christianity will soon evaporate. We hear of "post-evangelicals" as well as "ex-evangelicals."[4] Now these terms by themselves do not indicate that the individuals employing them have left the Christian faith, but they do mean that they have distanced themselves from the evangelical movement—a global network linking together churches and believers. Evangelicals seek to uphold a scriptural Christianity emphasizing that salvation is appropriated by a personal faith in Christ, is demonstrated in subsequent holy living, and supports world evangelization.

Of course, no one is obliged to be included in this movement against their wishes. But in our time, people are leaving evangelical Christianity for a relatively new reason: their conclusion is that—in the big picture of things—

[4]See, for example, the 1995 work of Dave Tomlinson, *The Post-Evangelical* (London: Triangle; American rev. ed., Grand Rapids: Zondervan, 2003) and the rejoinder volume it generated, Graham Cray et al., eds., *The Post-Evangelical Debate* (London: Triangle, 1997). A contemporary example of the ex-evangelical genre is Christian Smith's *How to Go from Being a Good Evangelical to a Committed Catholic in Ninety-Five Difficult Steps* (Eugene, OR: Cascade, 2011).

this movement is an upstart and a latecomer. The Christian tradition has survived without evangelical Christianity during most of its existence (so goes this argument); why should not the Christian tradition survive without it now? From this perspective, evangelical Christianity was either merely the descendant of the Protestant Reformation of the sixteenth century *or* a child of the modern period, especially the Enlightenment era. With these eras of world history now well behind us and exerting a diminished influence, evangelical Christianity has, on this understanding, been orphaned; it is now only a kind of flotsam and jetsam left from an earlier time. Despite whatever dominance it may admittedly have exerted in past centuries, it will (on this view) steadily surrender its place to some other expression of Christianity. What that "other" expression of Christianity might be varies with the one leaving the cause.

For some, that other expression of Christianity is found in Roman Catholicism or one of the expressions of Eastern Orthodoxy.[5] Such communions as the Roman Catholic and Orthodox are transnational; they exemplify the *opposite* of a kind of provincialism displayed within portions of the evangelical world. And they are also expressions of Christianity that are pre-Enlightenment.

Yet there are at the same time those who—responding to the influences of postmodernity—want to find an expression of Christianity that is *less* tethered to the past, *less* focused on transmitted dogma, and more socially conscious. These say farewell to certain forms of evangelical Christianity, not (like those already described) because of evangelical Christianity's perceived tenuous connection with the Christian past but because its "best before" date has arrived. As one who wrote in support of saying such farewells to evangelical Protestantism put it, each five-hundred-year period of

[5]This body of literature is extensive and growing. Among the narratives consulted here, published by those leaving evangelical Protestantism for Roman Catholicism, are Tom Howard, *Evangelical Is Not Enough: Worship of God in Liturgy and Sacrament* (San Francisco: Ignatius, 1984); Scott and Kimberley Hahn, *Rome Sweet Home* (San Francisco: Ignatius, 1993); and Smith, *How to Go from Being*. Similar literature authored by those leaving evangelical Protestantism for forms of Eastern Orthodoxy includes Peter Gillquist, *Becoming Orthodox*, rev. ed. (Ben Lomond, CA: Conciliar Press, 1992); Charles Bell, *Discovering the Rich Heritage of Orthodoxy* (Minneapolis: Light and Life, 1994); Michael Harper, *The True Light: An Evangelical's Journey to Orthodoxy* (London: Hodder & Stoughton, 1997); and Frank Schaeffer, *Dancing Alone: The Quest for Orthodox Faith in the Age of False Religion* (Brookline, MA: Holy Cross, 1994).

Christian history requires a "rummage sale" in order to be "reconfigured" for the next phase of Christianity; that "sale" and "reconfiguration" are under way right now.[6]

LEAVING EVANGELICAL CHRISTIANITY MEANS LOSING WHAT?

Now, if a person leaves the evangelical movement for one alternative or the other, what is it that is left behind? The person departing from this stream of Christianity for Roman Catholicism or Orthodoxy is convinced that he or she is leaving a movement that is frivolous and "lite" and embracing instead another that, because it is rooted in Christian antiquity, is substantive. The one leaving this expression of the faith for an emergent, postmodern expression of Christianity believes that he or she is jettisoning a stream that is compromised by an undue stress on the rational defense of Christian dogma and on the importance of numerical indicators of success. Such seekers believe they are gaining a movement characterized by community, consensus building, and room for mystery.

But are these views of gains and losses rooted in a sober assessment of things? We can admit that evangelical Christianity is *not* monochromatic; some forms of it are very "lite," and numerous expressions of it *do* have features that are off-putting and even extreme. Even so, such ways of calculating the reasons for which evangelical Christianity deserves to be jettisoned are problematic for at least two reasons.

First, those departing (especially from sectarian expressions of evangelical Christianity) are very prone to attribute the perceived defects of their own somewhat raw and imbalanced evangelical past to the whole of the evangelical movement. It does not necessarily follow that the emotional outbursts, speculation about end times, or legalistic tendencies that some who depart lament about *their* backgrounds were ever universal evangelical traits. Yet such extrapolation is widespread among disconcerted evangelicals who are eyeing the exits. Second, such approaches about the poverty

---

[6]Phyllis Tickle, *The Great Emergence* (Grand Rapids: Baker, 2008), 26-27. See also Brian McLaren, *A Generous Orthodoxy* (Grand Rapids: Zondervan, 2004). An insightful volume named above, Dave Tomlinson's *The Post-Evangelical*, should be thought of as belonging to this same genre; it seeks to accommodate Christianity to the postmodern situation.

of evangelical Christianity entail the embracing of an estimate of evangelical Christianity's origins, habits of thought, and expanse that is at odds with this movement's self-understanding. The evangelical movement does *not*, in fact, conceive of itself as utterly cut off from Christian antiquity; nor does it understand itself to be merely a child of the Enlightenment. The person contemplating abandoning evangelical Christianity should therefore be more careful to weigh this movement according to its actual self-understanding rather than one that is only surmised.

But having insisted on this, it is only proper to acknowledge that evangelical Christianity has more than one way of viewing its own origin and expanse. There are three identifiable perspectives on this.

A time-honored view of evangelical origins. Since the Reformation era, there has been a widely accepted opinion within evangelical Protestantism that entails viewing the movement as the continuation of an earnest Christianity characterized by strong loyalty to Christ, submission to the central authority of the Bible, and the necessity of a living, personal faith, extending far back in the Christian centuries. One finds the conception expressed by Protestants as long ago as 1546, the year in which Martin Luther died. His colleague, Philip Melanchthon, eulogized him by linking him with "greats" from many preceding centuries:

> After the apostles comes a long line, inferior, indeed, but distinguished by the divine attestations: Polycarp, Irenaeus, Gregory of Neocaesarea, Basil, Augustin, Prosper, Maximus, Hugo, Bernard, Tauler and others. And though these later times have been less fitful, yet God has always preserved a remnant; and that a more splendid light of the gospel has been kindled by the voice of Luther cannot be denied.[7]

The English chronicler and contemporary of Melanchthon, John Foxe (1516–1587), had the same objective in mind when he gathered martyr stories from all the preceding Christian centuries up to and including his own in the multivolume *Acts and Monuments* (1559).[8] In the eighteenth century, John Wesley (1703–1791) encouraged the early Methodists to think

[7]Philip Melanchthon, "Funeral Oration over Luther" (1546), reprinted in Lewis W. Spitz, *The Protestant Reformation: Major Documents* (St. Louis: Concordia, 1997), 70.

[8]The 1559 edition of *Acts and Monuments* was published in Latin. An expanded version in English followed in 1563. Modern readers rely on the eight-volume Victorian edition, often reprinted.

in such terms by incorporating material from second-century Christianity as well as extensive excerpts from Foxe's *Acts and Monuments* in his multivolume series *The Christian Library*.[9] This perspective—which viewed evangelical Protestantism as standing in clear continuity with vigorous scriptural Christianity of earlier ages—was still alive and well in the second half of the twentieth century and received clear articulation by well-known evangelical leaders such as John Stott (1921–2011), who wrote in 1970,

> One would even dare to say that, properly understood, the Christian faith, the catholic faith, the biblical faith and the evangelical faith are one and the same thing. . . . If evangelical theology is biblical theology, it follows that it is not a new-fangled "ism," a modern brand of Christianity, but an ancient form, indeed the original one. It is New Testament Christianity.[10]

J. I. Packer, whose career largely paralleled Stott's, wrote that evangelical Christianity is

> the Christianity, both convictional and behavioral, which we inherit from the New Testament via the Reformers, the Puritans, and the revival and missionary leaders of the eighteenth and nineteenth centuries. . . . The reason why I call myself an evangelical and mean to go on doing so is my belief that as this historic evangelicalism has never sought to be anything other than New Testament Christianity, so in essentials it has succeeded in its aim.[11]

One could readily find this essential viewpoint, stressing evangelical Christianity's longevity, being articulated in the mid-1990s. Alister McGrath

---

[9]Wesley's series, The Christian Library, was originally published in fifty volumes commencing in 1750. An improved edition of 1821 appeared in thirty volumes, and of these, the first four were concerned with ancient Christianity and a condensed treatment of Foxe's martyrology. I am indebted for these details to Northwest Nazarene University, accessed August 29, 2012, available at wesley.nnu.edu/john-wesley/a-christian-library/.

[10]John Stott, *Christ the Controversialist: A Study in Some Aspects of Evangelical Religion* (Downers Grove, IL: InterVarsity Press, 1970), 33. Stott was still sounding this note in his *Evangelical Essentials* (Downers Grove, IL: InterVarsity Press, 2000). Non-Anglican evangelical writers had also argued the same case for Evangelicalism's doctrinal continuity with strands of earlier Christianity. See, for example, E. J. Poole-Connor's *Evangelicalism in England* (London: Henry Walter, 1966), esp. chap. 8.

[11]James Packer, "The Uniqueness of Jesus Christ: Some Evangelical Reflections," *Churchman* 92 (1978): 102. The Packer essay had been delivered as an address the year previous in the annual Islington, London, Church of England pastoral conference. This writer heard Packer espousing identical statements to those quoted here: "A Personal Retrospective on the Conversation Between Evangelicals and Catholics," delivered April 11, 2002, at the Wheaton College (Illinois) Theology Conference.

was then insisting that this expression of Christianity "had its origins in the later European Renaissance, especially in France, Germany, and Italy." This perspective goes on being articulated at the present day by Gerald Bray.[12]

A more recent view of evangelical origins. Even so, in the last decades a distinguishable viewpoint has arisen, urging that whatever doctrinal continuities may be shown to exist between evangelical Christianity as it has been passed down to us today and older expressions of the faith, nevertheless something *new* happened within Protestant Christianity early in the eighteenth century.[13] On account of strong seventeenth-century differences of opinion as to whether a Protestant state should ally itself with a single expression of Protestantism and legislate favorably in support of that church (to the exclusion and disadvantage of those not persuaded about the terms on which religious comprehension was offered), rival forms of Protestantism began to inhabit a single territory. Thus, in addition to Catholic-Protestant division (traceable from the Reformation era forward) one now found both Protestants loyal to their state churches *and* Protestants committed to independent forms of Christianity within those same territories.

In England the rigid imposition of religious conformity after 1662 provoked the continuance of what has since been called "dissent" or "nonconformity." After religious uniformity was legislated in 1662, non-Anglican Protestants (whether Baptist, Presbyterian, Congregationalist, or Quaker) had no guaranteed right to preach or to assemble for religious services until 1689. And in Scotland, the same Restoration period saw the resurgence of

---

[12]Alister McGrath, *Evangelicalism and the Future of Christianity* (Downers Grove, IL: InterVarsity Press, 1995), 26. McGrath had begun to elucidate this contention earlier (19-20), making explicit reference to movements among Italian Benedictines and aristocratic elites. See also Gerald Bray's provocative essay, "Evangelicals: Are They the Real Catholics and Orthodox?," in *Evangelicals and the Early Church*, ed. George Kalantzis and Andrew Tooley (Eugene, OR: Cascade, 2012), chap. 9.

[13]The case for distinguishing between Protestantism pre- and post-1730 has nowhere been argued more persuasively than by David Bebbington in his *Evangelicalism in Modern Britain: A History from the 1730s to the 1980s* (London: Unwin Hyman, 1989). An American edition followed in 1992 from Baker Books. The same disjunction between pre- and post-1730 is also maintained by Mark Noll in his *The Rise of Evangelicalism: The Age of Edwards, Whitefield and the Wesleys* (Downers Grove, IL: InterVarsity Press, 2003). Noll is quite ready, however, to discuss numerous "antecedents" of the age of Evangelicalism. See his second chapter. There is a similar readiness to acknowledge pre-1730 antecedents of Evangelicalism in *Dictionary of Evangelical Biography*, ed. Timothy Larsen (Downers Grove, IL: InterVarsity Press, 2003), 1-2.

an existing "Covenanter" movement on account of royal attempts to direct the governance of the national Church of Scotland (after 1662 made subject, as earlier in the century, to royally appointed bishops). In Scotland, the period up to 1690 saw an intensification of earlier persecution culminating in what came to be called "the Killing Times."[14]

While reasoned cases were made in England and Scotland both on behalf of religious comprehension within a state church *and* of religious nonconformity extending beyond it, it is hard to avoid the conclusion that the work of the gospel suffered materially through the repression of preachers and the harassing of congregations. The net effect of this Restoration period was the fragmentation of Protestantism and the polarizing of some preachers and congregations from others with which they were in considerable agreement about the gospel and godly living.

Now, according to this recent view, Evangelical*ism* (as distinct from the evangelical *faith*, which admittedly was older) unfolded in the period we now call the Great Awakening or Evangelical Revival (commencing circa 1730) as a transdenominational and cooperative movement emphasizing the proclamation of central gospel themes, the work of evangelism, and (in due course) world mission and the reform of society. This movement that emerged in western Europe, in the United Kingdom, and in North America in that era was one that promoted a higher degree of transdenominational collaboration than had ever prevailed earlier.

No one embodied this transdenominational impulse more than the Anglican evangelist George Whitefield (1714–1770), whose travels across the United Kingdom and the American colonies and his preaching in churches of various denominations (as well as out of doors) furnished sinews for this renaissance.[15] Whitefield, when called on by members of the Anglican clergy at Boston to defend his preaching in the pulpits of non-Anglican churches, his treating non-Anglican ministers as his equals, and his participating in Communion services with the same, gladly confessed himself guilty of all such practices.[16]

---

[14]K. M. Brown, "Covenanters," in *Dictionary of Scottish Church History and Theology*, ed. Nigel M. de S. Cameron (Downers Grove, IL: InterVarsity Press, 1993), 218-19.

[15]Mark Noll aptly describes Whitefield's transcolonial role in his *A History of Christianity in the United States and Canada* (Grand Rapids: Eerdmans, 1992), 91-95.

[16]Noll, *Rise of Evangelicalism*, 14.

And, in the nineteenth century, this transdenominational movement found expression in umbrella organizations like the first mission, Bible, and tract societies and the World Evangelical Alliance—many of which efforts still continue today.[17] Through such efforts (especially world mission), evangelical Christianity reproduced itself on continents remote from western Europe or North America.

While this view of an Evangelicalism only emerging in the eighteenth century does not deny demonstrable continuities of evangelical faith and action with the era preceding and of commonalities of devotion and piety between older Protestantism and the movements of the eighteenth century,[18] it has placed the greater emphasis on the things that distinguished the evangelical Christianity of the eighteenth century from the evangelical Protestant Christianity that preceded it.[19]

Another view: modern Evangelicalism is essentially the fundamentalism of the twentieth century. However, there is yet another perspective on this question. Diverging just as truly from the traditional view of evangelical Christianity's longevity is an outlook we can associate with the names of the late Ernest Sandeen, Richard Kyle, D. G. Hart, Michael Svigel, and Matthew Sutton.[20] Such writers have taken the view that evangelical Protestantism has undergone such radical transformation since the nineteenth century that it became something more sectarian, more anti-intellectual, and more belligerent than any conservative Protestantism that preceded it.

---

[17]The consolidation of evangelical efforts in such cooperative enterprises as the eighteenth century gave way to the nineteenth and has been described in such works as R. H. Martin, *Evangelicals United* (Metuchen, NJ: Scarecrow, 1983); Charles Foster, *An Errand of Mercy: The Evangelical United Front, 1790–1837* (Chapel Hill: University of North Carolina Press, 1960); and Ian Randall and David Hilborn, *One Body in Christ* (Carlisle, UK: Paternoster, 2001).

[18]On this subject, consult Tom Schwanda, ed., *The Emergence of Evangelical Spirituality: The Age of Edwards, Newton, and Whitefield* (Mahwah, NJ: Paulist Press, 2015).

[19]The adequacy of this view of Evangelicalism's origin, introduced by Bebbington in 1989, has been assessed by Kenneth J. Stewart, "Did Evangelicalism Predate the Eighteenth Century?," *Evangelical Quarterly* 77, no. 2 (2005): 135-53, and in the essays gathered by Haykin and Stewart, *Emergence of Evangelicalism*. An American edition of this volume appeared under the title *The Advent of Evangelicalism* (Nashville: B&H, 2008).

[20]Ernest R. Sandeen, *The Roots of Fundamentalism: British and American Millenarianism, 1800–1930* (Chicago: University of Chicago Press, 1970); Richard Kyle, *Evangelicalism: An Americanized Christianity* (New Brunswick, NJ: Transaction, 1996); D. G. Hart, *Deconstructing Evangelicalism* (Grand Rapids: Baker, 2004); Michael Svigel, *Retro-Christianity: Reclaiming the Forgotten Faith* (Wheaton, IL: Crossway, 2012); Matthew Avery Sutton, *American Apocalypse: A History of Modern Evangelicalism* (Cambridge, MA: Belknap, 2014).

On this view, so great were the modifications introduced in the period following 1860 that any discussion about how long evangelical Christianity has existed is deemed to be beside the point. Evangelical Christianity as we know it, according to such authors, is a fairly "oppositional" movement[21] with roots in the nineteenth century that entered into open conflict with other expressions of Christianity late in the nineteenth and early in the twentieth century.

Now, while there is some considerable basis for the view that deep and significant shifts took place within evangelical Christianity across the last century and a half, there is not (in my opinion) a sufficient basis for arguing that utter discontinuity exists between this expression of evangelical Christianity and what preceded it. Quite a wide swath of Protestantism used the term "evangelical" late in the nineteenth century; by the early twentieth century, this movement had settled into two stances. Some supporters went on to style their movement "liberal Evangelicalism," while others were determined to employ the adjective "conservative."[22] The terminology of "evangelical" and "Evangelicalism" was thus not purely the preserve of the conservative and belligerent.

Moreover, belligerent and anti-intellectual evangelical leaders could certainly be found across the nineteenth century as well as in the early twentieth.[23] Besides, it is generally agreed that an intentional reaction took place against this sectarian tendency in what is now known as the neo-evangelical era commencing around 1940. Those at the head of this movement were

---

[21]This useful descriptor originated with Martin Marty and is used by Alister McGrath in *Evangelicalism and the Future of Christianity*, 30.

[22]In the North American context, this bifurcation is referenced in Matthew Bowman, *The Urban Pulpit: New York City and the Fate of Liberal Evangelicalism* (New York: Oxford University Press, 2014). For the UK context, see David W. Bebbington and David Ceri Jones, eds., *Fundamentalism and Evangelicalism in the United Kingdom During the Twentieth Century* (New York: Oxford University Press, 2013), esp. chaps. 1 and 2. Liberal evangelicalism's heyday is reflected in Vernon F. Storr, *Freedom and Tradition: A Study of Liberal Evangelicalism* (London: Nisbett & Co., 1940). A retrospective of the movement is provided in A. E. Smith, *Another Anglican Angle: Liberal Evangelicalism; The Anglican Evangelical Group Movement, 1917–1967* (Oxford: Oxford University Press, 1991).

[23]An example of early nineteenth-century belligerence would be the London preacher Edward Irving (1792–1834). For a description of the rise of a belligerent evangelicalism in the Napoleonic era, see Ian S. Rennie, "Fundamentalism and the Varieties of North Atlantic Evangelicalism," in *Evangelicalism: Comparative Studies of Popular Protestantism in North America, the British Isles and Beyond, 1700–1900*, ed. Mark Noll, David W. Bebbington, and George Rawlyk (New York: Oxford University Press, 1994), chap. 16.

determined to reconnect with less-belligerent forms of evangelical Christianity in the nineteenth century and earlier.[24]

So, to return to our question, which "profile" of evangelical Christianity is it that our contemporaries have determined to abandon? I admit that they will not have thought about this in precisely these terms. Nevertheless, it is a question worth pressing on them and on others beginning to follow their paths. Is it the belligerent and pragmatism-oriented evangelical movement of the last century and a half that they would find it so easy to live without? Or will it be the "fusion" of older Protestantism with some appealing aspects of Enlightenment thought in the eighteenth century that they discard because it is lacking in antiquity and wedded to modernity? Perhaps they would have the greatest amount of difficulty in dismissing evangelical Christianity as reckoned by the still older view, which is that it transmits to us—by way of the Protestant Reformation—ideals and emphases traceable to the apostolic age and the New Testament. We will return to these important questions later.

QUESTIONS FOR DISCUSSION

1. Do you know an individual or individuals who have left evangelical Christianity for Roman Catholicism, Eastern Orthodoxy, or post-evangelical Christianity? Did that person explain their reasons for the change?
2. Do you agree with the suggestion that evangelical Christianity is currently facing an identity crisis? If you agree, what evidence or example would you point to in confirmation?
3. The author has proposed three contributing factors to the current identity crisis (distance from origin, lateral movement away from the original movements of protest, the thawing of Catholic-Protestant

[24]On this seminal period commencing around 1940, see Joel Carpenter, *Revive Us Again: The Reawakening of American Fundamentalism* (New York: Oxford University Press, 1999); George Marsden, *Reforming Fundamentalism: Fuller Seminary and the New Evangelicalism* (Grand Rapids: Eerdmans, 1995); and Garth Rosell, *The Surprising Work of God: Harold Ockenga, Billy Graham and the Rebirth of Evangelicalism* (Grand Rapids: Baker, 2008). Developments of this period, portrayed from the Boston vantage point of Ockenga, have recently been provided by Owen Strachan, *Awakening the Evangelical Mind* (Grand Rapids: Zondervan, 2015).

relations).[25] Does any one of these explanation prove more helpful to you than another? Does an additional explanation for the identity crisis come to mind?

4. In your opinion, which explanation of evangelical origins proves most convincing: that evangelical origins lie in earliest Christianity, that these origins lie in the eighteenth century, or that these origins lie in the more recent liberal-fundamentalist controversy of a century ago?

[25]See these elaborated in the preface to this book.

2

Evangelical Movements as a Perennial and Recurring Feature of Christian History

IN THE PRECEDING CHAPTER, we acknowledged that some thoughtful persons are abandoning evangelical Christianity and writing about their "pilgrimages" into Roman Catholicism, Eastern Orthodoxy, or (alternatively) a general "post-evangelicalism." In point of fact, the movement is more deeply rooted in the Christian past than they suppose.

Now we must give closer attention to something mentioned in passing: that is, those very claims that have been made to assert that evangelical Christianity both preceded the era of the Protestant Reformation and manifested itself in most of the centuries following the apostolic age. Surely it is because this assertion has not been taken with sufficient seriousness that we today face the claim that the early centuries of Christianity somehow "belong" to the Roman Catholic and Orthodox families and to no other expression of the Christian faith,[1] or that the Christianity of the eastern

[1]This precise argument is used by Christian Smith in *How to Go from Being a Good Evangelical to a Committed Catholic in Ninety-Five Difficult Steps* (Eugene, OR: Cascade, 2011); his thirtieth step

Mediterranean represents the actual "original" from which other expressions (including the Roman) have somehow declined.[2] Let us consider the evangelical claim to a share of Christian antiquity. We will find that this claim is anything but recent; it has, in fact, been asserted by Catholic as well as Protestant writers.

A CATHOLIC AS WELL AS PROTESTANT CLAIM

R. A. Knox (1888–1957), himself a convert to Catholicism in 1922 from an evangelical Church of England family (his father, E. A. Knox, was the evangelical bishop of Manchester), made a kind of backhanded acknowledgement of Evangelicalism's long pedigree in his provocative 1950 book, *Enthusiasm*. One might say that in this book Knox disparaged his evangelical Protestant upbringing, for he claimed that the book was the fruit of thirty long years of reflection.[3] We do not need to agree with Knox's loaded terminology. (By "enthusiasm" he clearly meant to imply something unsavory and excessive.) Yet we may find suggestive his linking of various movements from the early Christian centuries (such as the Montanists) with others such as the Anabaptists of the sixteenth century, Quakers and Jansenists of the seventeenth, and Methodists of the eighteenth.[4]

At bottom, the book sought to demonstrate that from the early Christian centuries forward, certain tendencies have regularly resurfaced,

---

entails the claim that the early church ecumenical councils (which evangelical Christians claim to uphold) were creedal definitions composed "by leaders of the Catholic church" (63). Not only are evangelical Christians treated like squatters by this approach, so also are the various branches of Eastern Orthodoxy and of global Anglicanism. The latter, more than any other Protestant body, explicitly claims continuity with English Christianity of all centuries. Smith's claim might simply have been that the ecumenical creeds are the product of the early, undivided church—to this no one could take exception—but his "proprietary" claim is anachronistic and indefensible.

[2]See this perspective especially in Michael Harper, *The True Light: An Evangelical's Journey to Orthodoxy* (London: Hodder & Stoughton, 1997), 118: "The Eastern Church, frequently threatened by Islam, was almost unaffected by the great religious, political and cultural changes which have happened in the West: the Renaissance, the Reformation, and the commencement of the Enlightenment."

[3]R. A. Knox, *Enthusiasm: A Chapter in the History of Religion* (Oxford: Oxford University Press, 1950), v.

[4]Knox may be said to have been reviving an argument first used in the sixteenth century, when Catholic authorities asserted for polemical purposes that Luther and his co-Reformers were reviving ancient heresies. Knox used the argument after having adapted it so as to present post-Reformation evangelical Protestantism as the continuator of excessive tendencies locatable in earlier Christian centuries.

though always under different names. He considered that one might as easily call this tendency "ultra-supernaturalism" because this kind of Christian believer

> expects more evident results from the grace of God than others. He sees what effects religion can have, does sometimes have, in transforming a man's whole life and outlook; these exceptional cases (so we are content to think them) are for him the average standard of religious achievement. He will have no "almost-Christians," no weaker brethren who plod and stumble, who (if truth must be told) would like to have a foot in either world, and whose ambition is to qualify, not to excel. He has before his eyes a picture of the early Church, visibly penetrated with supernatural influences; and nothing less will serve him for a model.[5]

Knox saw this tendency at work in second-century Christianity among the Montanists in what is now northern Turkey. The Montanists practiced ecstatic prophecy at a time when prophecy was in decline in wider Christianity. They utterly forbade remarriage after bereavement or divorce; they also gave considerable weight to visions received by their leading women. The mainstream church that the Montanists sought to "outflank" by such measures was a church still subject to sporadic persecution in the second century—and was hardly the indolent church that many allege came into existence after imperial toleration was granted in AD 313.[6]

Knox found the same tendency among the Donatists of the fourth century. After the cessation of imperial persecution, they stood apart from the Christian mainstream by claiming that the ministry and sacraments of the mainstream church were weakened due to its failure to reprimand clergy who had compromised the faith under persecution. In due course the same tendency to outmaneuver manifested itself in later Catholic movements such as the Waldensians of the twelfth century. It was no part of Knox's argument that, having passed into Protestant Christianity, this "enthusiasm" ceased in what is now Roman Catholicism. Indeed, one of the major sections of the book is given over to a treatment of the

---

[5]Knox, *Enthusiasm*, 2.

[6]Ibid., chap. 3. A helpful investigation of the issues at the center of the Montanist controversy is provided by David F. Wright, "Why Were the Montanists Condemned?," *Themelios* 2, no. 1 (1976): 15-22.

seventeenth-century French Jansenists (Catholics deeply loyal to St. Augustine and his teaching).[7]

But the book, having pursued this conception of recurring traits of the ultra-supernatural type of Christian into the post–Martin Luther era, also claimed to find the tendency alive and well in the English Quaker George Fox (1624–1691), the radical French Huguenot faction known as the "prophets of the Cévennes" (whose activity followed the repression of Protestantism following the revocation of the Edict of Nantes in 1685), and supremely in John Wesley and the Wesleyans after 1730. From the Montanists of the second century through to Wesley and his societies in the eighteenth,[8] Knox claimed always to find a readiness to expect divine communications or impressions extending beyond conventional revelation; a high expectation that God's dealings with humans are of a kind that will be sensed, felt, and observed (including some of a disorderly kind); and a tendency to a somewhat preening self-consciousness (of an individual's sense of special importance in God's purposes).[9]

Knox's design, then, had been to focus on these expressions or symptoms that, by their very recurrence, convinced him that all such expressions of Christianity were essentially one, spread over time. He did not adequately explain why, for all intents and purposes, his survey of "enthusiasm" terminated in the age of Wesley.[10] Both his argument and his method are open to

---

[7]I raise this point deliberately here, as I think it wise to consider that a good number who have written about their pilgrimages from Evangelicalism into Catholicism and Orthodoxy were, and still are, what Knox would call "enthusiasts" or "ultra-supernaturalists." They have simply taken this outlook with them into different environs.

[8]It was only after the death of John Wesley in 1791 that the societies themselves were formally recognized as being other than affiliated with the Church of England. Some Wesleyan meeting houses had been registered as nonconformist chapels as early as 1787. See A. Skevington Wood, "Methodist Churches," in *New International Dictionary of the Christian Church*, ed. J. D. Douglas (Grand Rapids: Zondervan, 1974), 653-54.

[9]Knox, the former evangelical Protestant, takes a stance as a rather fastidious Catholic (he had briefly been a High Church Anglican) that all such tendencies, running beyond what might be called "institution-centered" Christianity, are to be regarded as frivolous. For a protest against this latter category of self-consciousness, made within the Methodist tradition, see John Kent's *Wesley and the Wesleyans* (Cambridge: Cambridge University Press, 2002), chap. 1. Kent uses the term "primary religion" to describe this notion of the individual believer being at the center of things in terms of God's dealings with the world.

[10]For a book published in 1950, we should expect more than the passing references to Irvingism (circa 1830) and the early twentieth-century African American figure "Father Divine" supplied in chapter 12.

question. Is passionless, other-than-fervent Christian faith (free from the excesses of ultra-supernaturalism) *indeed* to be preferred? He made it seem so. Did he not engage in undisciplined pearl-stringing by linking groups across vast centuries that he considered to be similar? Yet his claim to detect ongoing commonalities did have the effect of depicting—at least such examples of Protestantism as he highlighted—continuity with forms of pre-Reformation Christianity.[11] Even though he posited an *unsavory* continuity, the notion of continuity itself is very germane to our discussion.

But Knox, writing in 1950, was hardly the only person to have explored the question of evangelical Protestantism's long pedigree. We find as we proceed that Protestant investigators of this question have, while agreeing on the concept of evangelical longevity, tended to pursue the concept of Evangelicalism's long *reach* in several ways of their own devising.

A SUCCESSION OF FAITHFUL WITNESSES

We have already noted that at Martin Luther's death, his associate, Melanchthon, linked him to heroes of the faith in preceding centuries. His chief contention (shared by others who have since argued for a similar succession) is that there have all along been champions of fervent personal faith in Christ, of the supreme authority of the Scriptures, and of the need for the purification of the visible church. Luther stood in that already existing line.[12] Of many persons in the centuries before the Reformation who are said to have prefigured the protesting activity of Luther, two stand out: John Wycliffe (1329–1384), an Oxford scholar and preacher, and John Hus (1372–1415), a fiery preacher of Prague. Both exalted biblical authority and emphasized the limits of papal power.

Luther himself had come to accept some such idea of evangelical succession after he tangled with an opponent in controversy. In the Leipzig debate of June–July 1519, he came to the assistance of his colleague Andreas

[11]I find it especially significant that Knox made no real effort to depict the magisterial Reformers or the Puritans of the Tudor and Stuart period as part of this succession story. Despite whatever fervency they displayed in their own time, Knox did not fault them with the extremes he found in others in those centuries. Anabaptists and Quakers are included.

[12]See the preceding chapter. Melanchthon had defended Luther against the charge of departing from the teaching of the church fathers as long before Luther's death as in his *Defense of Luther Against the Paris Theologians* (1521), which may be seen in Leander Flack and Lowell J. Satre, eds., *Melanchthon: Selected Writings* (Minneapolis: Augsburg, 1962), 74.

Bodenstein von Karlstadt (1477–1541), who at Leipzig was facing the Catholic controversialist Johann Eck (1486–1543). Eck insinuated that by Luther's denying both that the papacy existed by God's express intention and that there existed a necessity of submitting to this pope's authority in order to be saved, he was repeating the errors of a condemned heretic of the preceding century, John Hus. Luther did not repudiate the parallel being drawn.[13] Of course, there was only a partial overlap of concerns between Luther and Hus, and Luther would later take pains to distinguish his views from those of the earlier leader of protest.[14] But those who have pursued this approach of "successionism" have been satisfied to point out that what matters is that the Luthers of the Christian world possessed a *consciousness* that they were building on precedents laid by known persons of an earlier time. This is important for demonstrating that issues for which Protestants contended were not just fabricated by them, without any previous existence.

It would be possible to multiply these examples many times over. We have already mentioned the Reformation chronicler John Foxe, whose *Acts and Monuments* related martyr stories of faithful Christians from the era of the early Roman persecutions right up to the mid-sixteenth century. When his account came to the fourteenth century, Foxe was eager to include the likes of Wycliffe and Hus not only to augment his compilation of those who had suffered indignities and death for their Christian faith but to show that they stood in a succession leading to the eventual Reformation of the sixteenth century.[15]

This quest to identify a succession of Christian leaders from the pre-Reformation period who anticipated the stances of Protestants of a later time was especially popular in the eighteenth and nineteenth centuries—both on the Continent and in Great Britain. Erasmus Middleton (1739–1805) began his *Biographia Evangelica* (1779) with those same late-medieval advocates of

---

[13]James M. Kittelson, *Luther the Reformer* (Minneapolis: Augsburg, 1986), 140.

[14]See the discussion of this point in Heiko A. Oberman, *Forerunners of the Reformation* (London: Lutterworth, 1967), 10.

[15]In the 1846 eight-volume version of the *Acts and Monuments* edited by George Townsend, Foxe began his treatment of the precursors of the age of Reformation in volume 2 (book 5) and extended it through volume 3 (book 5). The possibility of the transmission of doctrinal themes from the age of Wycliffe to the later age of Reformation has more recently been explored by Donald Dean Smeeton in *Lollard Themes in the Theology of William Tyndale* (St. Louis: Sixteenth Century Journal Publications, 1986).

reform, John Wycliffe and John Hus, as well as Jerome of Prague (1371–1416) and John of Wessel (1420–1489) before proceeding to outline the lives of sixteenth-century Reformers, the Puritans of the seventeenth century, and the evangelicals of his own age.[16] Much the same approach was followed by late eighteenth-century evangelical historian Joseph Milner (1744–1797), whose *History of the Church of Christ* showed a determination to locate the "real Christians" in the discouraging centuries prior to the Reformation. He focused on Thomas Bradwardine (1290–1349), former archbishop of Canterbury, as well as the above-named persons.[17]

Early in the nineteenth century, German church historian Karl Ullmann (1796–1865) prepared a two-volume study, *Reformers Before the Reformation* (1841), which investigated those of the fifteenth century who paved the way for the eventual Reformation in Luther's time.[18] Ullmann, knowing that Wycliffe and Hus had already received their due from other Protestant writers, concentrated on lesser-known figures such as John Pupper of Goch (d. 1475), John of Wessel, and the Brethren of the Common Life.[19] One could find the same essential approach being followed at century's end by the English Methodist historian H. B. Workman in a two-volume work, *The Dawn of the Reformation* (1901). Wycliffe and Hus, reckoned by Workman to be precursors of the eventual Reformation, received one volume each.

We need to admit, however, that all these efforts to locate Christian leaders who anticipated the Reformation in certain ways have suffered from serious weaknesses. Most obviously, we must face up to the fact that all these named individuals lived in the three centuries immediately prior to Martin Luther. If these individuals form a kind of succession, it is a succession of too-limited

---

[16]I have consulted the 1816 edition published in London by William Baynes in four volumes. In his preface to volume 1, Middleton makes plain his indebtedness to the preexisting accounts of John Foxe.

[17]Joseph Milner, *History of the Church of Christ*, 6 vols. (1794–1809; repr., London: T. Cadell, 1827). See the reference to "real Christians" at 4:63, where a study of the fourteenth century begins. Bradwardine is treated extensively between pages 77 and 106.

[18]Karl Ullmann, *Reformers Before the Reformation*, 2 vols. (1841; English trans., Edinburgh: T&T Clark, 1863). The approach of Ullmann was subjected to searching criticism by Heiko Oberman in his *Forerunners of the Reformation*, chap. 1.

[19]The Brethren of the Common Life were Christian men and women living a communal life in houses segregated by gender. They were not bound by vows. Residents worked at various trades and promoted biblical literacy, sound learning, and the cultivation of piety. The most famous person associated with the Brethren was the author Thomas à Kempis (1380–1471), famous for his devotional work *The Imitation of Christ*.

duration to prove that the evangelical faith has been a hardy perennial. At best, it would show roots extending back only into the high medieval era. Still more seriously, these efforts have neglected to accept that the eventual Reformation (which these figures are believed to have anticipated) was a contingent event that could as easily *not have happened* as happened. We need to acknowledge that efforts to locate anticipations of an event that might not have happened have banked too heavily on a supposed inevitability of the Reformation's eventual dawning. *If* Luther's early protest had been met with welcome and honest dialogue, *if* the terrible abuse of the sale of indulgences had been addressed, and *if* Pope Leo X had not issued his bull of excommunication of Luther in 1521, would these writers of the last four centuries have been so industrious in seeking to locate Luther's precursors? But these medieval Christian leaders would have taken their bold stands in any case.

Also, if it is allowed that the eventual Reformation had such precursors or forerunners, is it safe to assume that they paved the way *exclusively* for Luther and other Protestants? There were, after all, contemporaries of Luther—also eager for the reform of the church, who never broke with Rome. Persons such as Lefèvre d'Étaples (1455–1536), Erasmus of Rotterdam (1466–1536), and John Colet (1466–1519) went to their graves just as keen for the restoration of scriptural Christianity but still in communion with the Roman Catholic Church. Who is to say that figures like Wycliffe and Hus were precursors to Luther but not these others?[20] Did they anticipate those who remained Catholic, those who broke with Rome, or both?

And yet, with these major caveats admitted, there is something still to be considered in these centuries prior to Luther's protest—something substantial enough that it is not difficult to show that the Reformers of the sixteenth century were continuators of appeals that had been made for centuries beforehand. It is not so much the names of those who raised their voices earlier but the recurrence of their concerns that interests us here.

A SUCCESSION OF RECURRING CONCERNS

What impresses one far more than the mere recital of the names of those who are claimed to have been Luther's precursors is the frequency with

[20]This is a point for which I am indebted to the clear survey of this issue in Oberman, *Forerunners of the Reformation*, 37-40.

which the Reformers could spell out the views of individuals spread over many preceding centuries in support of their own protests. We can see this most clearly through a series of concrete examples that illustrate the Protestant approach to more than a thousand years of the Christian past.[21]

John Jewel:* An Apology for the Church of England *(1562). John Jewel (1522–1571) had the good fortune to be a university student of real promise at Oxford in the early 1540s—a time when England was open both to Renaissance learning (which stressed familiarity with ancient Greek and Latin literature) and some of the currents of the early Reformation (which stressed a renewal of biblical and theological study using ancient Christian sources). After the death of King Henry VIII in 1547 and during the short reign of Henry's son, Edward VI, Jewel was privileged to become closely associated with an important Reformation theologian, Peter Martyr Vermigli (1500–1562). This Italian humanist-theologian had been invited into England from Strasbourg by then archbishop of Canterbury, Thomas Cranmer (1489–1556). Jewel's (and Martyr's) service to the Reformation of England was interrupted by the death of young Protestant Edward VI in 1553 and the accession to the throne of his Roman Catholic half sister, Mary Tudor (1516–1558).

Yet at Jewel's return from a European exile in 1559 (a return warranted by the accession of the Protestant Elizabeth Tudor to the throne), he came immediately to prominence. This rapid promotion came about by reason of his ability to effectively articulate in voice and in print the relationship of continuity in which the reformed Church of England meant to stand to the pre-Reformation church and the church of antiquity.

Pressed into the leadership of the English church as bishop of Salisbury, Jewel performed two services that were impressive for their boldness and effectiveness. First, he accepted the assignment of giving public sermons in November 1559 at St. Paul's Cross, London (a venue favored for the delivery of sermons of potential national significance). In these sermons, he sought to make the case for the English parliament proceeding to enact legislation in favor of the Reformation (and thus repealing legislation of an opposite

[21]This theme will also be highlighted in chapter 5, where we will survey five hundred years of Protestant appeals to pre-Reformation Christianity.

kind introduced under the previous monarch, Mary Tudor).[22] In his Paul's Cross sermons (there were three in all), Jewel named practices common under Marian Catholicism that he characterized as either of doubtful authority or plainly unscriptural. These included the doctrine of transubstantiation (the belief that appearances notwithstanding, the bread and wine of the Communion had been altered by consecration into the body and blood of Christ), the practice of multiple Masses offered on behalf of the dead, the insistence on prayers and liturgies recited in Latin, the withholding of the Bible from the common people, the worship of images in the church, and the insistence that the bishop of Rome held universal sway over the entire church.[23] Regarding these, Jewel hurled the challenge:

> If any learned man or all our adversaries, or if all the learned men that be alive, be able to bring any one sufficient sentence out of any old catholic doctor or father or out of any old general council or out of the holy scriptures of God, or any one example of the primitive church, whereby it may be clearly and plainly proved [that current practices were in use in the early centuries of the church] I promise that I would give over and subscribe to them.[24]

Jewel was confident in making this challenge—not because there were already laws in place that would penalize anyone who tried to contradict him, but because as a Christian humanist who had one of the best grasps of Christian antiquity in all England, he knew of what he spoke. The practices and policies against which he protested were the products of medieval Catholicism, *not* of early Christianity.

In time, Jewel would expand on this kind of argument in composing his *An Apology for the Church of England* (1562). In this literary work, written—like the earlier public sermons—with a view to affirming the doctrinal legitimacy of the national Protestant church, Jewel went on the offensive. Rather than daring his theological opponents to come forward in defense of medieval Catholic practices and beliefs, he positively appealed to the Scriptures and

---

[22]Jewel's task was not to convince Parliament to take this course but to prepare the populace for the coming legislative change that would reintroduce Protestantism. He would show that the doctrines and practices about to be reintroduced were well-supported by Christian antiquity. W. M. Southgate, *John Jewel and the Problem of Doctrinal Authority* (Cambridge, MA: Harvard University Press, 1962), 49-51.

[23]Ibid., 50.

[24]John Jewel, *Works*, 1:20-21, quoted in Southgate, *John Jewel*, 50.

many church fathers in support of the doctrines and practices of the Church of England, as it now stood reformed by acts of Parliament.[25]

Was the supreme authority of Scripture challenged by critics in judging matters of doctrine and practice? Jewel summoned Augustine, Jerome, and Ambrose as affirmers of scriptural supremacy.[26] Ambrose was quoted thus: "Let the Scripture be asked the question; let the Apostles be asked; let the prophets be asked; and let Christ be asked."[27] Was utter submission to the bishop of Rome urged or required? Jewel also drew from Cyprian of Carthage (d. 258) in support of equality among the original apostles of Christ: "All the apostles as Cyprian saith were of like power among themselves, and the rest were the same that Peter was; it was said indifferently to all 'Go into the whole world'; indifferently to all 'teach ye the gospel.'"[28] And further, referring to the papacy, "Tell us I pray you good holy father . . . which of all the holy fathers have at any time called you by the name of the highest prelate, the universal bishop, or the head of the church?"[29]

Further, Jewel raised the question of what is the right conception of the Lord's Supper, and affirmed

> that the bread and wine are holy and heavenly mysteries of the body and blood of Christ, and that by them Christ himself being the true bread of eternal life, is so presently given unto us, as that by faith we verily receive his body and his blood. Yet say we not this so, as though we thought that the nature of bread and wine is clearly changed and goeth to nothing; as many have dreamed in these later times, which yet could never agree among themselves of this their dream.[30]

Jewel then went on to cite opinions in support of this guarded position from Ambrose, Augustine, Origen, Chrysostom, and Cyprian.[31]

I stress that we take Jewel purely as a representative example of the many Renaissance-era Christian humanists who became Protestant

---

[25]Principally the Acts of Uniformity and of Royal Supremacy (1559).

[26]John Jewel, *Apology for the Church of England,* in *English Reformers*, ed. T. H. L. Parker (Philadelphia: Westminster, 1966), 18-19.

[27]Ambrose, *De fide* Lib. I, cap. vi 43, as cited in Jewel, *Apology*, 19.

[28]Cyprian, *De Unit. Eccl.* (PL 4.502), as cited in Jewel, *Apology*, 22.

[29]Ibid., 42-43.

[30]Ibid., 28.

[31]Ibid., 28-29.

Reformers.[32] A background in humanistic studies of antiquity gave them—Cranmer, Ridley, Calvin, Bullinger, Melanchthon, Martyr, and Oecolampadius—a ready facility in mining the church fathers so as to use them as a kind of plumb line in determining what were legitimate and what were illegitimate understandings of Holy Scripture.[33] With such an acquired ability, Jewel and his kind were able both to discern doctrinal drift or deterioration over the millennium that separated them from the age of the Fathers *and* to recall the church of their age to purer expressions of the Christian faith.

Philip Schaff:* The Principle of Protestantism *(1845). Philip Schaff (1819–1893), the important Swiss-American church historian, popularized the view that the Protestant tradition, rather than being a repudiation of what came before it, was in fact an organic extension of it:

> He [Luther] gave utterance to what was already darkly present to the general consciousness of his age, and brought out into full view that which thousands before him, and in his own time, had already been struggling in various ways to reach. Genuine Protestantism is no such sudden growth, springing up like a mushroom of the night, as the papist, and certain narrow minded ultra-protestants, would fain have us believe. Its roots reach back to the day of Pentecost. In all periods of the Church, in connection with the gradual progress of Romish corruption, it has had its witnesses, though not always fully conscious of their own vocation.[34]

This interesting notion had, however, nationalistic or civilizational rivalries embedded within it. Schaff believed that the march of civilization entailed the northern (and Germanic) peoples throwing off the yoke of Europe's Latin south. On this approach, Luther, along with contemporary

---

[32]It is important that we acknowledge that not *all* Renaissance humanists did.

[33]The attention paid by the Protestant Reformers to Christian antiquity is developed further in chapter 5.

[34]Philip Schaff, *The Principle of Protestantism* (Mercersberg, PA: German Reformed Pub. House, 1845), 37. Schaff, while standing within the Reformed tradition, was of broad sympathies. He was associated early in his career with Mercersberg colleague, John W. Nevin, in advancing what came to be known as the "Mercersberg Theology"; this was a kind of protest against the Americanization of Protestantism. But Schaff, later in his career at Union Seminary, New York, also learned to relate to the wider evangelical Protestant world, as is evidenced by his support for the creation of the Evangelical Alliance. See Gary K. Pranger, *Philip Schaff (1819–1893): Portrait of an Immigrant Theologian* (New York: Peter Lang, 1997), esp. chap. 7.

German writers such as Ulrich von Hutten (1488–1523) became the cultural and religious liberators of the northern peoples.[35] Schaff continued, "Such a nationality is fitted constitutionally for a deep, inward apprehension of the Christian system; while the Roman and Romanist spirit, as naturally, was led to embrace it prevailingly in a more outward way, as a body of mere rules and statutes."[36]

But it was not only southern European religious dominance that was broken in the age of the Reformation; no, the former decadent medieval cultural dominance was also broken—as both the cultivation of the literary study of antiquity and the study of art in the same had led to a cultural renewal. Erasmus, Calvin, Beza, and Reuchlin had been deeply involved in the recovery of ancient learning.

But whatever we may think of Schaff, the Swiss-American, pinning so much hope for the future of Christianity on the "northern races,"[37] we must not miss the idea of Christian development implicit in his theory. That developmental idea is not racial or geographical but chronological:

> The Church, not less than every one of its members, has its periods of infancy, youth, manhood, and old age. This involves no contradiction to the absolute character of Christianity; for the progress of the Church, outward or inward, is never in the strict sense creative, but in the way only of reception, organic assimilation and expansion. In other words, all historical development in the Church, theoretical and practical, consists in an apprehension always more and more profound of the life and doctrine of Christ and his apostles, an appropriation more full and transforming always of their distinctive spirit, both as to its contents and its form.[38]

To sum up, Schaff's approach to the burning question of how evangelical Christianity related to early and pre-Reformation Christianity is one that asserts that evangelical Protestantism is a fuller expression of the power and genius latent in the Christian gospel from the time of its origin.

---

[35]Schaff, *Principle of Protestantism*, 41.

[36]Ibid., 39.

[37]Paradoxically, now in the twenty-first century, we see the brightest future for Christianity in southern latitudes.

[38]Schaff, *Principle of Protestantism*, 51.

Now Schaff, who went on to build a formidable reputation as a church historian and editor of patristic works,[39] was fully aware that the Reformers (as in the case of Jewel) showed themselves highly competent interpreters of early Christianity for a later time. But writing in 1845, he did not think it sufficient to merely reiterate the approach used by apologists in the age of the Reformation. He extrapolated from that demonstrable continuity of conviction toward something else: an assertion of progress and advance.

Taken by themselves, neither the approach of a Reformation apologist such as John Jewel or the approach of a nineteenth-century historian like Schaff are fully satisfactory to us now. Since Jewel's time, all sides have come to admit that appeals to the statements of individual church fathers are surrounded with a greater degree of complexity than was recognized at that time.[40] And Schaff's view—tinged with a kind of idealism that has since gone out of fashion—will sound somewhat overblown to our ears.[41]

But we have another Protestant attempt to consider before we lay this question down, and this is one that represents attempts to demonstrate that the grievances aired against the late medieval church by both the advocates of reform *within* Catholicism and those who aligned themselves with the nascent Protestant movement were one and the same as those earlier raised at intervals over the preceding millennium. This is to say that the Reformers were the repeaters of complaints that had been voiced repeatedly by others in the centuries beforehand.

G. R. Evans:* The Roots of the Reformation *(2012). At the current time, this kind of argument has been renewed and extended much further by the demonstration provided in G. R. Evans's *The Roots of the Reformation.*[42] According to the wide-ranging survey provided by this historian, the medieval period—which we can reckon broadly to have extended from the withdrawal

[39]He was the author of the seven-volume *History of the Christian Church* (New York: Harper, 1858–1890) and coeditor of the multivolume *Select Library of the Nicene and Post-Nicene Fathers* (New York: The Christian Literature Co., 1886–1890).

[40]The reflection on this problem that followed the century of the Reformation and occupied Christian scholars of the seventeenth century is touched on in chapter 5 of this book.

[41]Indeed, Schaff's argument about the unrelenting "march" of the Christian faith has an uncanny (though coincidental) similarity to the view of Phyllis Tickle (see chap. 1), who believes that the Christian faith needs a rummage sale each five hundred years.

[42]G. R. Evans, *The Roots of the Reformation: Tradition, Emergence and Rupture*, 2nd ed. (Downers Grove, IL: InterVarsity Press, 2012). The first edition of Evans's work, released in earlier 2012, had been withdrawn because of inaccuracies. I have relied on the improved second edition.

of the Roman imperial government from the Italian peninsula in AD 476 to the end of the fifteenth century—was one in which a number of theological disagreements kept recurring without ever finding satisfactory resolution. A few examples will help us to grasp this in concrete terms.

The role of the papacy. The claims of the bishop of Rome to be not only "first among equals" (a tolerable idea to the bishops or patriarchs of other major cities of the Mediterranean world with which Christianity had been associated since apostolic times) but also supreme representative of Christ on earth had proved objectionable from the time they were first enunciated in the sixth century.[43] It is said of the Roman bishop Gregory the Great (who presided from AD 590 to 604) that while he was reluctant to refer to himself as supreme above the patriarchs of Alexandria, Jerusalem, Antioch, and Constantinople, he would not hear of any of these claiming that preeminence for himself. In time, unresolved tensions circling around claims to universal jurisdiction made by bishops of Rome were one of the major contributing causes to the Great Schism of AD 1054. In that year, both Constantinople and Rome pronounced anathemas against one another and broke off relationships until modern times.

The papacy asserted itself in 1077 against the monarchs of Europe in a controversy over which authority (papal or royal) could nominate bishops to their territorial dioceses. The papacy—which not long before had needed the help of monarchs to fend off its enemies—insisted that its spiritual authority trumped temporal authority, and it won that contest. Yet the time when the papacy could claim this precedence over earthly monarchs was checked both by the rise of Europe's nation-states in the fourteenth century (with England and France leading the way) and by division in the papacy in the same century. From 1378 to 1417 there were rival claimants to the office of pope, and the debacle produced by this papal schism was ended only by the assembling of representative councils composed of bishops and theologians who claimed to have power directly from Christ to resolve the impasses the church faced.[44]

[43]Ibid., 96.

[44]Ibid., 99-100. The claim that the power of councils was greater than that of the pope was enunciated at the Council of Constance in 1415. The bull (document) of Constance asserting this claim is named "Sacrosancta" and is printed in Henry Bettenson and Chris Maunder, eds., *Documents of the Christian Church*, 3rd ed. (Oxford: Oxford University Press, 1999), 149.

It should come as no surprise to us that early advocates of the reform of the church whose names have already appeared in this chapter were themselves among the aggrieved over this issue of the abuse of papal power. That John Wycliffe was posthumously condemned by the Council of Constance (1415) while John Hus was condemned to death by the same council (which overrode a promise of safe travel made to him) does not take away from the fact that there was unity of conviction on the underlying issue. And it should not surprise us either that Martin Luther, despairing of finding a sympathetic adjudication of his protests from Pope Leo, appealed from that pope's jurisdiction to a future general council.

General access to the Scriptures. The Latin Vulgate Bible that the Council of Trent (in the period from 1545 to 1563) decreed to be the official version of the church was, by that age, a Bible that only the learned could read. After all, Latin had by that era long ceased to be the spoken language of any substantial portion of the people of western Europe. It had been a very different situation when that Latin Vulgate had been revised by the fourth-century biblical scholar Jerome (345–419). Acting on the request of Pope Damasus, Jerome had taken up the task of standardizing the text and vocabulary of then existing Old Latin versions, which were already in circulation in handwritten form. To his great credit, Jerome checked the Old Latin versions against the best Greek and Hebrew manuscripts he could obtain, and this improved Latin Bible gradually commended itself to the congregations of the western Mediterranean.[45] In that era, those who could afford it were able to purchase hand-copied Scripture portions in the still-current Latin. All worshippers could, at any rate, hear the Scriptures read Sunday by Sunday in church in the language they spoke daily.

Yet it was the decline of Latin as the language of the common people that made it appear dangerous that this Latin Bible—now much harder to comprehend—would be allowed to circulate at large. Vernacular translations were needed for very obvious reasons yet frowned on because of the possibility that heresy would be generated by the unsupervised reading of them. This was the charge brought against the Lollards, loosely associated with John Wycliffe. Their vernacular translation of the Latin Vulgate into

[45]J. N. D. Kelly, *Jerome: His Life, Writings and Controversies* (New York: Harper & Row, 1998), chaps. 14 and 15.

fourteenth-century English was intended to address this very obvious need. Closer to the time of the Lutheran revolt, even Erasmus (who died a Catholic) aspired to have Scriptures in the hands of plowmen and milkmaids. Erasmus's contemporary, Lefèvre d'Étaples, who also died a Catholic, went further than only aspiring after this and actually produced a vernacular translation of the Psalms. It hardly needs to be stressed that when Martin Luther produced a German New Testament (employing in the process the Greek New Testament that had been produced by Erasmus at Basel in 1516) that he was keeping up solidarity with predecessors stretching back many centuries.

Understandings of the Lord's Supper. After the Fourth Lateran Council of 1215, one could be tried for heresy and burned for denying that the sacramental bread and wine had been changed into Christ's body and blood. Before 1215, there was open exchange and disagreement about the defensibility of such a belief, with some notable dissenting opinions represented and recorded for posterity. We have already seen how sixteenth-century Reformers such as John Jewel had worked to "mine" sacramental teaching older than the Fourth Lateran Council in support of the contrary opinion. He was in good company; English bishops of the previous generation, Nicholas Ridley (1500–1555) and Thomas Cranmer (1489–1556), had come to just such opinions in the 1540s by their readings of medieval theologians such as Ratramnus (d. 868). The early Swiss Reformer Johannes Oecolampadius (1482–1531) published an important book in 1530 that was read across Europe; it detailed by copious quotation from early and medieval Christian writers the alternate senses (compared to those stipulated in 1215) in which thoughtful Christians had understood the words of institution that Jesus spoke at the Last Supper.[46] There came more and more to the fore in the age of the Reformation a confidence that there had never been lacking writers and teachers who held that the key to the Lord's Supper lay less in the transformation of the two elements Jesus had ordained to be employed than in the appropriation by faith of Jesus' victory signified by them.

And so it went. A very high proportion of the doctrinal convictions enunciated by the Reformers of the sixteenth century had indeed been articulated

[46]Johannes Oecolampadius, *Quid de eucharistia veteres tum Graeci, tum Latini senserint* (Basel, 1530).

long before, and repeatedly, by earlier advocates of biblically rooted theology.[47] It seems that recognizing this continuity and recurrence of these convictions is the best way for us to see that the evangelical emphasis on Scripture, personal faith in Christ, and the importance of the pursuit of godliness was really a continuation of emphases that had always had advocates in the millennium following the death of the last apostle. And when we have granted this fact—that the Christian mainstream was often deficient and frequently mistaken in what it insisted on as non-negotiable, and in consequence provoked dissent and controversy that was generally suppressed—we have come to stare this conclusion in the face: the evangelical tendency has always been active within the church Jesus founded.

QUESTIONS FOR DISCUSSION

1. The author has maintained that if evangelical churches and movements merged with others (with different emphases) they would soon reemerge as identifiably different. Do you accept this idea that evangelical Christianity is perennial?
2. If evangelical Christianity is so perennial that it would recur, what is the superior explanation for this? Is it that an "ultra-supernaturalist" emphasis will always create a following (in whatever century)? Is it that evangelical Protestantism in effect represents a kind of advance within Christianity? Or is it best explained as a continuation of dissent against mainstream Christianity's approving of doctrines that are open to valid challenge from Scripture?
3. Could more than one of these explanations be true?
4. Could it be said that such explanations of the origin and persistence of evangelical Christianity produce what could be called "contrarian" thinking—that is, a determination to "hold out" in defense of a view beyond what is profitable?

[47]Chapter 14 of this book will explore the patristic and medieval antecedents of the Reformation understanding of justification by faith.

3

Needed for Appraising the Christian Past

A Principle of Authority

THUS FAR, WE HAVE TAKEN UP AND DEALT WITH *two* intertwined concerns. The first was that a considerable number of people are leaving evangelical Christianity because they have been led to suppose that this expression of the Christian faith is a latecomer and therefore lacking in legitimacy. The second concern was the supposition that evangelical Christianity is discontinuous with the teaching and standards of earlier Christianity. We can truthfully say that both as to their length of existence and constancy of teaching, evangelical movements have always been present in the Christian tradition.

Yet, to assert this last claim is one thing; to demonstrate it, another. Can it be cogently argued that central evangelical principles were in existence well in advance of the birth of Protestantism in Luther's day? This chapter is written in the confidence that this can indeed be shown, and shown regarding the cardinal conviction that unites evangelical believers across the centuries: the supreme authority of the Word of the Lord in all matters of faith and life.

Examining this issue is beset with difficulties that if not acknowledged early on will only lead to us spinning our wheels in futility. We need to admit at the outset that the affirmation of some kind of "Word" authority has been a hallmark of all major expressions of Christianity from the earliest times. So we begin by acknowledging that the central importance and authority of the Word of the Lord as recorded in the existing Old Testament and eventual New Testament was not, itself, a matter of contention in the early centuries among orthodox Christians. Yet there were *two* issues related to the central authority of the Word that were then and are now the subject of lively discussion.

First, how could the Christian movement have access to the authoritative Word of the Lord (considered as the message of Jesus, relayed by the eyewitnesses of his ministry) in advance of the composition and wide availability of the various writings that would eventually form our New Testament? And second, were there not also, of necessity because of this gradual coalescing of our New Testament, additional "guides" available in those early Christian centuries to help keep the young church firmly in the way of the Lord? If this second concern was to be answered in an unqualified way, the ripple effects would be very far reaching. We must take up these issues in turn.

QUESTION ONE

We will first consider how the words of Christ could function as authoritative in advance of the existence of a collection of New Testament writings. It is widely and properly acknowledged that the early Christian movement leaned heavily on the Old Testament Scriptures. Paul wrote to the Corinthians, "Christ died for our sins according to the Scriptures" (1 Cor 15:3). The apostle was referring to the Old Testament's anticipation of pivotal events in the earthly career of Jesus, and he expected his readers to acknowledge the authoritative role of those writings. Not only in the age of the apostles themselves but well into the second century, much Christian writing and preaching appealed to the Hebrew Scriptures in support of Christian claims. But this was never the whole story. The early Christian movement had, in addition to the Hebrew Scriptures, access to the sayings and deeds of Jesus as reported through the apostolic eyewitnesses who had "seen his glory."[1]

[1]John 1:14; 1 John 1:1-2. J. N. D. Kelly, *Early Christian Doctrine* (New York: Harper & Row, 1960), 32, speaks of the apostolic testimony as the "second doctrinal norm" of the earliest church, alongside the Old Testament. By the second half of the second century, the apostolic testimony came to occupy the position of "supreme authority" (35).

The propagation of the gospel and the training of new believers relied utterly on this oral communication about Jesus, his mission, and his message. One finds abundant references to the spread of the "word of the Lord" in the Acts of the Apostles (e.g., Acts 6:7; 12:24; 19:20).[2] Eventually, these authoritative sayings of Jesus, forwarded by the apostles, took written form in gathered collections. As Bruce Metzger puts it,

> At first Jesus' teachings circulated orally from hearer to hearer, becoming, so to speak, the nucleus of the new Christian canon. Then narratives were compiled recording the remembered words, along with recollections of his deeds of mercy and healing. Some documents of this kind underlie our Gospels and are referred to in the preface to the Third Gospel (Luke 1:1-4).[3]

These, then, were the materials out of which the eventual written Gospels would be composed.

Now, by generally acceptable estimates, the first portion of our New Testament to be composed was not any one of the four Gospels but Paul's letters to the Thessalonians and letter to the Galatians.[4] This piece of data alone should help us to grasp that it was not at first possible for first-century heralds of the gospel (whether apostles or others) to initially use the four Gospels as we know them (or any one of them, singly) in the spread of the Christian message. A time would come in the last third of the first century when copies of one or more of the three Synoptic Gospels could be had—and somewhat later the fourth Gospel. Thus, missionary and pastoral work needed to be carried on up to that time in reliance on something that adequately met the need for access to the Lord's words. The early Christian writer Papias (ca. 60–130) lived through this period and was the beneficiary of those who relayed to him definite sayings of Jesus. Living as he did at the transition time when the number of those who had personally heard Jesus was diminishing and the supply of the written Gospels was expanding, he was still fondest of the reports

---

[2]The *Handkonkordanz zum Grieschisen Neuen Testament*, ed. Alfred Schmoller (Stuttgart: Wurtembergishche Bibelanstalt, 1968), 315, lists thirty-two such usages of λόγος του θεού (word of God) and λόγος του κυρίου (word of the Lord) in Acts alone. Such phrases also find widespread use in the New Testament epistles. See also Colin Brown, ed., *Dictionary of New Testament Theology* (Grand Rapids: Zondervan, 1979) 1111, 1113, 1114.

[3]Bruce Metzger, *The Canon of the New Testament* (Oxford: Clarendon, 1987), 2-3.

[4]F. F. Bruce, *Paul: Apostle of the Heart Set Free* (Grand Rapids: Eerdmans, 1977), 475.

provided by the former.[5] Evidently, the gospel had traveled to a very considerable extent in his time on the basis of the words of Jesus, orally transmitted.

> I shall not hesitate to set down for you, along with my interpretations all the things which I learned from the elders with care and recorded with care, being well assured of their truth. For unlike most men, I had pleasure not in those who had most to say, but in those that teach the truth; not in those who recorded strange precepts, but in those who related such precepts as were given to the Faith by the Lord and are derived from the Truth itself. Besides, if any man ever came who had been a follower of the elders, I would enquire about the sayings of the elders; what Andrew said, or Peter, or Philip, or Thomas or James or John or Matthew or any other of the Lord's disciples; and what Aristion says and John the Elder, who are disciples of the Lord. For I did not consider that I got so much profit from the contents of books as from the utterances of a living and abiding voice.[6]

As the phase of early Christian history when oral transmission of the words of Jesus and the instructions of the apostles was giving way to another phase—that of written records—the same Papias was able to record,

> Mark, who had been Peter's interpreter, wrote down carefully, but not in order, all that he remembered of the Lord's sayings and doings. For he had not heard the Lord, or been one of his followers; but later, as I have said, one of Peter's. Peter used to adapt his teaching to the occasion, without making a systematic arrangement of the Lord's sayings. Mark was quite justified in writing down some things just as he remembered them. For he had one purpose only: to leave out nothing that he had heard and to make no misstatement about it. . . . Matthew compiled the *Sayings* in the Aramaic language, and everyone translated them as well as he could.[7]

Much farther to the west in Roman Gaul, the Christian bishop and theologian Irenaeus of Lyons (ca. 115–202) demonstrated a familiarity with all four of the Gospels familiar to us:

[5]F. F. Bruce, *The Canon of Scripture* (Downers Grove, IL: InterVarsity Press, 1988), 119.

[6]Papias, *Expositions of the Oracles of the Lord,* in Eusebius, *Historiae Ecclesiasticae*, trans. and ed. G. A. Williamson (New York: Dorset, 1984), 3.39.1. It is evident that in this place Papias is using as interchangeables the terms "elder" and "disciple" (in the sense of "original disciple"). The books to which he refers may either have been proto-Gospels (written collections of deeds and words of Jesus) or the Gospels themselves.

[7]Papias, *Exposition of the Oracles* 3.39.11.

> Matthew published his Gospel among the Hebrews in their own tongue, when Peter and Paul were preaching the Gospel in Rome and founding the church there. After their departure, Mark, the disciple and interpreter of Peter, himself handed down to us in writing the substance of Peter's preaching. Luke, the follower of Paul, set down in a book the gospel preached by his teacher. Then John, the disciple of the Lord, who also leaned on his breast, himself, produced his gospel while he was living at Ephesus in Asia.[8]

We are thus maintaining that a *kind* of supreme authority of the Word was operative, incrementally, well in advance of an eventual consensus regarding the ultimate boundaries of the New Testament, which we reckon to have been enunciated not later than the year 367.[9]

Further, second-century evidence of this organic and incremental growth of the authority of the Word is supplied by the existence of the *Diatessaron* of Tatian (ca. 110–172), a harmonization of the four Gospels in Syriac around the year 160. A recent writer has aptly said of this work, "It is the first document available to us that overtly recognizes the existence of the four Gospels."[10] Tatian's work therefore highlighted the earlier existence and circulation of the works he synthesized.

The discussion to date has focused almost exclusively on the apostles who functioned as eyewitnesses and the eventual recording of their remembrances of the career of Jesus in our Gospels. But we have noted at the same time that it was not the Gospel writers who first circulated their works, but Paul. These circulated in his lifetime (reckoned to have ended in AD 64) and were exchanged, at his instruction, between churches.[11] While it is not obvious that these epistles were widely regarded from the outset as constituting sacred Scripture, there was encouragement to do just this provided in statements such as 2 Peter 3:16, where the writer ranked the letters of Paul with "other Scriptures." By the early second century, Paul's letters were beginning

[8]Irenaeus, *Adversus Haereses* 3.1, in Eusebius, *Historiae Ecclesia*, vol. 8, as quoted in Henry Bettenson and Chris Maunder, eds., *Documents of the Christian Church*, 3rd ed. (Oxford: Oxford University Press, 1999), 30.

[9]Athanasius, "Festal Letter 39," in *Select Writings and Letters of Athanasius*, in *Nicene and Post-Nicene Fathers*, second series, ed. Archibald Robertson (New York: Christian Literature Co., 1890), 4:1290.

[10]Craig D. Allert, "The State of the New Testament Canon in the Second Century: Putting Tatian's *Diatessaron* in Perspective," *Bulletin for Biblical Research* 9 (1999): 17.

[11]Metzger, *Canon*, 4.

to circulate as a collection.[12] Thus, in the generations that followed that of the apostles,

> the expression "the Lord and the apostles" represented the standard of appeal to which reference was made in all matters of faith and practice. At first, a local church would have copies of only a few apostolic Epistles, and perhaps one or two Gospels. In the collections that were gradually formed, a place was found besides the Gospels and Epistles for two other kinds of books—the Acts of the Apostles and the Apocalypse of John.[13]

Thus, by mid-second century, in church services one would hear readings from one or more of the Gospels, from the Epistles, and Old Testament writings.[14] The eventual collection of New Testament writings may not yet have been fully defined and collated, but a working New Testament was coalescing. This is also the range of writings that we find reflected in the mid-second-century works of the apologist Justin Martyr (ca. 100–165); he knew and drew on all four Gospels as well as the Apocalypse of John.[15] Irenaeus of Lyons (whom we have mentioned) not only knew all four Gospels but insisted that none beyond these four were to be given credence; his writings reflect familiarity with twenty-two of our New Testament writings.[16] Hippolytus of Rome (d. ca. 235) similarly knew the four Gospels, thirteen epistles of Paul, Acts, 1 Peter, and 1 and 2 John.[17]

The consideration of these Christian leaders in the latter half of the second century leads us naturally to consider the important document now known as the *Muratorian Canon*.[18] This document, traditionally dated to the late second century but more recently alleged to have originated in the fourth century,[19] reflects the expanse of the collection of New Testament

---

[12]Bruce, *Canon*, 130.

[13]Metzger, *Canon*, 6.

[14]Bruce, *Canon*, 127.

[15]Metzger, *Canon*, 148; and Peter Balla, "Evidence for an Early Christian Canon (Second and Third Centuries)," in *The Canon Debate*, ed. Lee Martin MacDonald and James Sanders (Peabody, MA: Hendrickson, 2002), 377-78.

[16]Metzger, *Canon*, 155.

[17]Ibid., 150.

[18]This ancient document was first brought to light by its publication at Rome in 1740. I have utilized the text as set out in Bettenson and Maunder, *Documents*, 30-31.

[19]Metzger, following Everett Ferguson in his article "Canon Muratori: Date and Provenance," *Studia Patristica* 18 (1982): 677-83, maintains the traditional dating. As recently as 2002, the argument for the fourth-century dating was being reiterated by Geoffrey Hahneman in an essay,

writings known to one unnamed author, probably living in the vicinity of Rome. For our purposes, it is important simply to observe that in this document (as with the second-century authors just named) there are certain things that are unambiguous because they were accepted universally in the provenance of the writer. He names

> four Gospels, Acts, thirteen Epistles of Paul, Jude, two (perhaps three) Epistles of John, the Wisdom of Solomon and the Johannine Apocalypse. Secondly there is one disputed book, the *Apocalypse of Peter*, which some refused to have read in church. Thirdly there is one book, the Shepherd of Hermas, which, though rejected still ought to be read privately. Fourthly, several heretical books are mentioned as totally rejected.[20]

We have traveled only so far as the early third century. We have certainly seen that from an earliest reliance for doctrinal norms on the Old Testament Scriptures combined with reports (first oral, then written) passed down by those who were eyewitnesses of Jesus' career, the young church moved to an increasing familiarity with four written Gospels, many (if not all) New Testament epistles, the Acts of the Apostles, and the Revelation to John as its norms. The eventual full canon of the New Testament was not yet in place, but it was so substantially in place that it could serve as the plumb line for proclamation and teaching. It was perfectly natural that the writings produced by the apostolic eyewitnesses and those known to have been closely associated with them would find the most rapid acceptance.

It is true that a kind of closure on discussions of New Testament canon was eventually reflected by the year 367—the year in which Athanasius wrote his *Thirty-Ninth Paschal Letter*. Athanasius, in writing as he did in that year, was certainly not taking it on himself to define the boundaries of what constituted our New Testament Scriptures; he was only reflecting a common assessment of things current in his time. After stressing that the Old Testament Scriptures had been taken over by the Christian church, he added,

> It is not tedious to speak of the [books] of the New Testament. These are, the four Gospels, according to Matthew, Mark, Luke, and John. Afterwards, the

"The Muratorian Fragment and the Origins of the New Testament Canon," in MacDonald and Sanders, *Canon Debate*, 405-15. See also Bruce, *Canon*, 158.

[20]Metzger, *Canon*, 199.

> Acts of the Apostles and Epistles (called Catholic), seven, viz. of James, one; of Peter, two; of John, three; after these, one of Jude. In addition, there are fourteen Epistles of Paul, written in this order. The first, to the Romans; then two to the Corinthians; after these, to the Galatians; next, to the Ephesians; then to the Philippians; then to the Colossians; after these, two to the Thessalonians, and that to the Hebrews; and again, two to Timothy; one to Titus; and lastly, that to Philemon. And besides, the Revelation of John.[21]

But leaving aside, for the time, this document of 367, it should be clear that already almost two centuries earlier the young church was substantially in possession of the writings of the New Testament as we know it and that far earlier it had had recourse to the words of the Lord—both in oral and documentary form—as its rule.

In maintaining this, we do not need to insist that the young churches of the Mediterranean world had—in these writings—been furnished with nothing other than the *ipsissima verba* (the exact language) of Christ. The Gospels do not claim to be mere transcriptions. The comparisons we can undertake between parallel accounts in the Synoptic Gospels (for instance) indicate that the writers both undertook personal investigations regarding the Gospel events and enjoyed reasonable liberty in their compositions. The narrative, epistolary, and apocalyptic portions of the New Testament—because they make only periodic references to the words of Christ—generally depend for their authority on the known apostleship or a close relationship to the circle of the apostolic eyewitnesses. We only maintain that, by this kind of pedigree, the collection of New Testament writings were received as having the Lord's authority.

QUESTION TWO

The second question to consider is this: did not this only gradual coalescing of our New Testament writings into a collection require that additional "guides" were meanwhile available to Christians? During that era, demand for access to the words of Jesus would have outstripped their actual availability in writing. This reality has forced some thoughtful Christian writers to explore the question of what *additional* "norms" would have been utilized

[21]Athanasius, "Festal Letter 39," in *Nicene and Post-Nicene Fathers*, second series, 4:1290.

to help keep the early Christians firmly on the road. One modern writer in particular, William J. Abraham, has theorized that the young church relied on a range of additional resources for this purpose. Abraham specified (1) a "rule of faith" (or of truth), (2) creeds (such as the Nicene), (3) rites such as baptism and the Lord's Supper, (4) liturgical traditions, (5) icons, (6) ecclesiastical regulations, and (7) saintly leaders or thinkers. All of these, on his reckoning, could also be termed canonical.[22]

That there were authoritative guides or helps in addition to the Old Testament Scriptures, the words of Jesus orally transmitted, and the emergent collection of New Testament writings is hardly in doubt. What is debatable, however, is the sense in which more than half of the items specified by Abraham ever constituted a canon in the sense of a "rule" that encapsulates salient features.[23] In my judgment, we can properly have this confidence in only two of the items named: the rule of faith (accessible in the early creeds) and the rites instituted by Christ for his church (which found their basis in Jesus' own commands).

Already, in some of the earliest of the writings that would later be aggregated in our New Testament, we find paragraphs and extended statements that, even at the time of writing, had the purpose of summarizing salient aspects of the Christian faith. None is more obvious than Paul's compact summary of the gospel provided in 1 Corinthians 15:3-4, which is followed immediately by a list of the main persons privileged to see the resurrected Jesus Christ: "For what I received I passed on to you as of first importance: that Christ died for our sins according to the Scriptures, that he was buried, that he was raised on the third day according to the Scriptures, and that he appeared to Peter, and then to the Twelve."

We can locate similar brief summaries of important tenets of the faith in such places as Romans 10:9, Philippians 2:5-11, and 2 Timothy 2:8. It is not hard to conceptualize how a Christian believer who will have owned no New Testament writings (on account of the expense of scribal copies) could be assisted for a life of devotion and understanding armed with these summary statements. Bryan Litfin has defined a rule of faith as "a confessional formula (fixed neither in wording nor in content, yet following the same general

---

[22]William J. Abraham, *Canon and Criterion in Christian Theology* (New York: Oxford University Press, 1998), 35-38. Abraham's enumeration varies slightly from what is used above.

[23]Gerald Bray, *Creeds, Christ and Controversy* (Downers Grove, IL: InterVarsity Press, 1984), chap. 4.

pattern) that summarized orthodox beliefs about the actions of God and Christ in the world."[24]

If such rules or condensations of the faith were in use even in apostolic times, it should not surprise us that they continued in use in the second and third centuries as the Christian faith spread more rapidly than hand-copied Scriptures could be disseminated. So, for instance, in the early second century, Ignatius of Antioch (ca. 110) provided the following *rule* or summary of the faith:

> Be deaf, therefore, when any would speak to you apart from (at variance with) Jesus Christ [the Son of God], who was descended from the family of David, born of Mary, who truly was born [both of God and of the Virgin truly took a body; for the Word became flesh and dwelt among us without sin . . .], ate and drank [truly], truly suffered persecution under Pontius Pilate, was truly [and not in appearance] crucified and died . . . who was also truly raised from the dead [and rose after three days], his Father raising him up, [and after having spent forty days with the Apostles, was received up to the Father, and sits on his right hand, waiting till his enemies are put under his feet].[25]

Here in an unembellished way there is set out, assertion by assertion, major components of the Christian message—each of which has been excerpted from the gospel narrative.

The practice of framing these rules was long-lived and continued well into the third century. In general terms, they grew somewhat more extensive as is evident in a second example, that of Irenaeus:

> The Church, though scattered through the whole world to the ends of the earth has received from the Apostles and their disciples the faith in one God, the Father Almighty, who made the heaven and the earth, and the seas, and all that in them is, and in one Christ Jesus, the Son of God, who became flesh for our salvation, and in the Holy Ghost, who through the prophets preached

[24]Bryan Litfin, "Learning from Patristic Use of the Rule of Faith," in *The Contemporary Church and the Early Church*, ed. Paul A. Hartog (Eugene, OR: Pickwick, 2010), 79. Litfin cites thirteen examples of such rules in the second and third century yet takes the view that it is really only with Irenaeus (ca. 180) that such rules take on a "complete" (i.e., comprehensive) character. On this subject, one can also consult the essay of D. Jeffrey Bingham, "Evangelicals and the Rule of Faith: Irenaeus on Rome and Reading Christianly," in *Evangelicals and the Early Church*, ed. George Kalantzis and Andrew Tooley (Eugene, OR: Cascade, 2012), 159-86.

[25]Excerpted from Ignatius of Antioch, "Epistle to the Trallians," chap. 9 in Philip Schaff, *Creeds of Christendom* (New York: Harper & Row, 1919), 2:11. Schaff provides numerous other "rules of faith" from writings of the second and third century.

> the dispensations and the advent, and the birth from the Virgin and the passion and the resurrection from the dead, and the bodily assumption into heaven of the beloved Christ Jesus our Lord, and his appearing from heaven in the glory of the Father to comprehend all things under one head and to raise up all flesh of mankind.[26]

In summary, this chapter has attempted to show that a dominant characteristic of evangelical Christianity—its being strongly oriented to the Lord's words—is a characteristic evident in the earliest Christian centuries. Prior to the composition and first circulation of our New Testament writings, the words and message of Jesus were being relayed in oral form by the missionary apostles and others. As the New Testament writings were cumulatively composed, there was a transitional period—no doubt decades long—in which oral reports of Jesus' words and deeds and written reports (Gospels and Epistles) coexisted. We know that by mid-second century (at the latest) four Gospels and a growing collection of letters were being read in the churches. A functioning collection of New Testament writings—growing in similarity to that which we find in our Bibles of today—had found acceptance by AD 200. In such ways, the Lord and his apostles were heard in the churches. And since personal ownership of New Testament writings was still considered a luxury for the ordinary believer, thoughtful Christian teachers were regularly providing to them summaries of the major events of the saving life of Christ, which, when committed to memory, would help to establish them in the faith. Thus, the central authority of the Word of the Lord was enshrined from the earliest times.

QUESTIONS FOR DISCUSSION

1. Must one be in possession of a copy of the Scriptures in order to recognize scriptural authority in matters of faith and life? If one did not possess Scripture, how could Scripture be recognized in this way?
2. Has it ever occurred to you, in reading a Scripture such as 1 Corinthians 15:3-4 or Philippians 2:5-11, that you could in fact have been reading an early summary of important points in our faith?
3. Why would such short summaries (called "rules of faith") have performed an important role on public occasions such as baptisms?

[26]Irenaeus, "Contra Heresies," book I, chap. 10, in Schaff, *Creeds of Christendom*, 2:13-14.

4

Needed for Appraising the Christian Past

A Concept of Development in Doctrine

When one reads accounts composed by those who have left the evangelical movement to find a new home in the Church of Rome or one of the Eastern churches, one of the major reasons provided for their doing so is that these communions are understood to offer greater stability in worship practices and doctrinal belief. The claims of these churches to both continue in and to represent the teaching and practice of the apostles of Jesus (a claim incidentally made by most Christian churches) is itself not actually quite as straightforward as these converts make it out to be. But what concerns us here is the perception of stability within Roman Catholicism and the Orthodox churches in contrast to a perceived impermanence and fluctuation within evangelical Protestantism.

According to Tom Howard,

> Where we (non-Catholics) were pleased to live with a muddle, and even with stark contradictions (Luther vs. Zwingli, for example, on the Lord's Supper),

> the Church of antiquity was united. No one needed to remain in doubt forever as to what the Church might be, or where she might be found.[1]

Similarly, convert to Antiochian Orthodoxy Wilbur Ellsworth could write of how, having been welcomed into Orthodoxy with a circle of followers, they were relieved to observe

> the Holy Tradition of the Church consists of receiving, maintaining, and passing on the apostolic faith. There was no other determining factor to the church's worship . . . we were welcomed to "come and see" and become a part of this great stable tradition. This was most attractive to all of us.[2]

The question of where stability and permanence is to be found is a knotty issue, and thus we will need to untangle some subsidiary threads and deal with each separately. One person's perceptions of change, on the one hand, and one person's perceptions of permanence, on the other, are *not* necessarily accurate barometers of the real state of things.

ALL FORMS OF THE CHRISTIAN FAITH HAVE BEEN MODIFIED IN EXTERNALS

Evangelical Christianity is, admittedly, known for adaptation in externals. Yet, to assert this also about all expressions of Christianity may seem like a shocking statement, inasmuch as it is customarily evangelical expressions of Christianity that are faulted for their readiness to chase trends, ride cultural bandwagons, and the like. Especially in the twentieth century, evangelical Christianity's commendable missionary instinct spurred it forward to simplify the complex (think of Campus Crusade's *Four Spiritual Laws*), to provide Bible translations that are always more readable (the popular NIV Bible was originally aimed at seventh-grade reading levels), to make services of worship more accessible to the seeking, and to guarantee that youth ministry programming would be the opposite of dull. Evangelicalism's determination to avoid complacency and to embrace accessibility has driven a good

[1]Tom Howard, *Lead Kindly Light: My Journey to Rome* (1994; repr., San Francisco: Ignatius, 2004), 47. Howard, who will be discussed in fuller detail in chapter 15, left the Episcopal Church, USA, for the Roman Catholic Church in 1985.

[2]Wilbur Ellsworth, "A Journey to Eastern Orthodoxy," in *Journeys of Faith*, ed. Robert L. Plummer (Grand Rapids: Zondervan, 2012), 41. Ellsworth and a circle of Christians had earlier found their Baptist congregation at Wheaton destabilized by the intake of a pragmatic "seeker-sensitive" church-growth strategy.

number of thoughtful persons to distraction.[3] But it is a mistake to think that adaptation is a malady unique to forms of evangelical Christianity. For in different centuries, each expression of Christianity has made changes when strong circumstances have been in play.

Adaptation in externals in early Mediterranean Christianity. The early church of the Mediterranean world adapted when it became subject to imperial persecution. The explanation usually offered for the growing amount of time between conversion and baptism in post-apostolic Christianity is that the more extensive catechetical training (of up to two years) given during that extended period was needed to ensure that converts did not apostatize in the face of persecution.[4] Then, in AD 313, imperial persecution came to an end by the decree of Emperors Constantine and Licinius. Suddenly, confiscated religious objects as well as land and buildings were returned; imperial funds became available for large-scale church construction projects. Churches now began to be built on the "basilica" pattern, modeled after Roman governmental buildings, while ministerial dress began to resemble the togas of Roman senators. It rapidly became fashionable for the public to attend religious services, and the churches soon introduced more elaborate services opened by processions of robed officials preceded by censers of burning incense. Terms such as "diocese" were appropriated directly from Roman government usage to the Western church. Some speak of the adaptations undergone at this time as significant enough to warrant the term "imperial church."[5]

The removal of the seat of empire from Rome to Constantinople in AD 330 brought on further adaptations. From this time onward, the bishop of Rome—formerly working in the shadow of a resident emperor—became the leading dignitary in what was henceforth only the western capital of the empire. From the eastern capital, the emperor decreed in AD 380 that heretical forms of Christianity would no longer be tolerated. He required conformity to the form of Christianity maintained by the bishops of Rome and Alexandria. Meanwhile, by the time of the barbarian invasions from

[3]Ibid., 23-30.

[4]Everett Ferguson, "Baptism," in *Encyclopedia of Early Christianity*, ed. Everett Ferguson (New York: Garland, 1990), 132.

[5]Justo Gonzáles, *The Story of Christianity*, 2nd ed. (New York: HarperCollins, 2010), 1:142-47.

the north that commenced in 410, the bishop of Rome had begun to assume emperor-like importance in his region. By 452, it was left to the current bishop of Rome, Leo I, to negotiate with Attila the Hun and convince him to stay north of the Italian peninsula. When the marauding Vandals, led by Genseric, invaded the city in 455, Leo negotiated with them and helped to prevent the burning of Rome.[6] Out of such precedents, there began to be constructed a notion that the bishop of Rome was a temporal as well as spiritual leader.

In light of the above, it cannot be maintained that the early Western church was unaffected by the changes in the fortunes of the empire that had first persecuted, then tolerated, then endorsed, and finally left to their own defenses the churches of the west Mediterranean.

As for the churches in the East, the relocation of the central seat of empire from Rome to the new capital Constantinople in AD 330 brought significant changes. The patriarch (archbishop) of Constantinople now had to learn to be deferential to the resident emperor, just as his counterpart at Rome had needed to do in the past. The emperor now appointed such church patriarchs within his eastern territories and made it his business to trouble as many of his eastern subjects as the church identified as heretical. This kind of overreaching imperial policy toward the church—which goes by the name *caesaropapism*—was in time directly eroded, however, by the advances of the armies of Islam that swallowed up eastern Roman territory after AD 632: Jerusalem in 636, Antioch in 638, and Alexandria by 641.[7]

The stage had been set for an eastern Christianity lived out under unfriendly overlords, whose dominion over Christian territories would expand westward across North Africa and north into Spain until the year 733.[8] By 1453, even the eastern Roman capital at Constantinople fell subject to Islamic control. When one reflects on it, Eastern Christianity no less than Western, or even evangelical Protestantism, has adapted itself—in externals—to new and emerging circumstances. We are under no obligation

[6]Ibid., 243.

[7]Everett Ferguson, *Church History: From Christ to the Pre-Reformation* (Grand Rapids: Zondervan, 2013), 237-40.

[8]In that year, the armies of Islam—having conquered Spain—advanced to do battle at what is variously called the Battle of Tours, or Poitiers. In this battle the armies of Islam were defeated. See ibid., 333-34.

to accept that every adaptation was for the good, but the imprint of these adaptations has been lasting.[9]

IF WE MAY SPEAK OF ADAPTATION IN EXTERNALS, MAY WE ALSO SPEAK OF DEVELOPMENT WITHIN THE FAITH ITSELF?

Historically, this has proved to be a very prickly question. All expressions of Christianity wish to maintain that the Christian faith, as originally given in the age of Christ and the apostles, was complete in the sense that these representatives of Jesus proclaimed and explained what he had entrusted to them. With their commission to do this accomplished, what place might there be for development in teaching? Yet on closer examination we can see that there is more to the question of development than first meets the eye. Let us take first a moral-ethical example and then a doctrinal example.

Moral-ethical example: Jesus' teaching on divorce and remarriage. The saying of Jesus on this matter, recorded in Matthew 19:9, supports an understanding that divorce is permissible only where marital unfaithfulness has occurred. Jesus' saying contains no explicit provision for remarriage after divorce but only a caution that the one who remarries after an unwarranted divorce will commit adultery by so doing.[10] Gradually, the church came to the understanding that the warning against remarriage after wrongful divorce contained within it an *implicit* provision for remarriage (where sufficient grounds had existed for the dissolution of the first marriage). Further, the statement of the apostle Paul in 1 Corinthians 7:15 in which he advises a believing spouse that upon abandonment by an unbelieving spouse "a believing man or woman is not bound in such circumstances" (NIV 1984) was taken by Christian leaders to mean that a *second* substantive ground for divorce (and potential remarriage) had been provided: desertion.

Of course, it took time for Christian minds to work out the implications of the sayings of Jesus and Paul on this subject. But even when we admit to

[9]The consideration of adaptations undergone by the Eastern churches in the twentieth century under the jurisdiction of communist regimes would further reinforce this contention about obligatory adaptation.

[10]A parallel to the Matthew 19:9 statement is found in Mark 10:10, where while the *exceptive clause* found in Matthew 19 is omitted, an expansion of the caution against remarriage is given to warn females as well as males from proceeding wrongly.

this, we are allowing only that what was originally taught stood in need of being reflected on and gradually appropriated. Over time, there was an advance in Christian understanding of the scriptural provisions it already possessed for remarriage. There was, at the very least, development in Christian understanding of the legitimate implications that might be drawn from agreed-on Scriptures.[11]

Now what will result when, instead of selecting a moral-ethical example of development of Christian understanding, we select a doctrinal example for consideration?

Doctrinal example: the advance of the concept of God as three-in-one. Any Christian discussion of the tri-unity of God will very soon direct attention to New Testament Scriptures long-reckoned to provide support for this central conviction. There is the account of Jesus' baptism in which the Father is recorded as speaking from heaven in endorsement of his Son, and the Spirit is recorded as descending in the form of a dove to rest on him (Mt 3:16-17). There is the command of Jesus to his disciples to go throughout the world preaching, teaching, and baptizing in the name of the three persons (Mt 28:19-20). There is Jesus' claim to have come from the Father and to be returning to the Father (Jn 16:28; 13:1), which, taken in combination with his pledge that he will send the Spirit (Jn 16:7), enables us to perceive that within the one God, there are three. Outside the Gospels themselves, we have the threefold benediction of Paul (2 Cor 13:14) and the salutation of Peter, which lays stress on the role of three in the salvation of the believer (1 Pet 1:2-5).

But even with such scriptural statements in hand, early Christian thinkers had to "stretch" to find a way of articulating two principles that are admittedly difficult to combine. On the one hand, Christians affirm that God is solitary and unique. He is not a member of a "genus" called "deity," within which there are comparable beings. There is but one God (1 Tim 2:5; Rom 3:30). And yet, within God, there are three. Early Christian thinkers had to

---

[11]By the sixteenth century, thinkers such as the Protestant Reformer Martin Bucer argued for additional grounds for divorce in his *De Regno Christi*, drawing on early Christian writers such as Origen, Ambrose, and Jerome. The poet John Milton used Bucer's arguments in a series of pamphlets published in the 1640s urging that divorce ought to be granted for additional reasons. No translation of these portions of *De Regno Christi* is accessible other than those translated by Milton in a tract titled *The Judgment of Martin Bucer Concerning Divorce* (1644). I have consulted an online version, accessed September 10, 2013, available at archive.org/stream/doctrinediscipl i00miltrich#page/16/mode/2up.

discard inadequate ways of relating these two principles—ways such as "dynamic monarchianism," which conceived of the Father as supreme within the community of three. This conception could not properly accommodate the equality of three persons. The young church had also, eventually, to discard "modalistic monarchianism," which conceived of the relation of the Father to the Son and Spirit as one of successive and recurring manifestations of the one God under different names and in different roles. This conception, while it maintained the equality of the three, could not articulate the stability of their persons. Yet meanwhile, the sayings of Jesus (alluded to above) and the statements of the New Testament epistles furnished a common *pool* that lent support to all early Christian deliberation over this deep mystery.

We are told that the North African church father Tertullian (ca. 160–215) was the first to introduce the language of "trinity" and "the three."[12] Yet even as he did so, the inadequate formulations of the relations of the Father, Son, and Spirit were still making the rounds. Simple formulations, such as the baptismal creed we now designate the Apostles' Creed, assume the existence and operation of three persons in God but stop short of describing their mutual relations.[13] The fuller resolution of the question of how best to think and speak of the three persons in God awaited developments in the fifth century associated with the Council of Chalcedon (AD 451).[14]

In a very real and true sense, we are entitled to say that the church of Jesus Christ has always instinctively affirmed that in the one God, there are three. From earliest Christian time, recourse has been made to the sayings of Jesus and the writings of the apostles that support such an understanding. Yet, the adequate articulation of what was all along supportable out of the Scriptures of the church was very slow in coming.

---

[12]J. N. D. Kelly, *Early Christian Doctrine*, 2nd ed. (New York: Harper & Row, 1960), 113; and J. F. Bethune-Baker, *An Introduction to the Early History of Christian Doctrine*, 8th ed. (London: Methuen, 1949), 139.

[13]Henry Bettenson and Chris Maunder, *Documents of the Christian Church*, 3rd ed. (Oxford: Oxford University Press, 1999), 25, suggest a provenance of AD 340 for this creed, rooted in earlier baptismal practice.

[14]In connection with the Council of Chalcedon, there was articulated the revised version of the Nicene Creed sometimes known as the Niceno-Constantinopolitan Creed, which enshrined more satisfactorily the mutual relations of the three-in-one. The text is provided in Bettenson and Maunder, *Documents*, 28-29.

We find, therefore, in *this* case—as in the previous instance of a moral-ethical question—that over time, Christian understanding has matured and that there has been gradual clarification of what was held implicitly all along. There has evidently been doctrinal development in the sense that the church has moved from lesser to greater clarity in its way of affirming the great Christian realities reflected in the Christian Scriptures and highlighted in the early Christian rules of faith.

Yet the question begs to be asked: is this the *only* development of doctrine we may speak of? What we have observed thus far could hardly be made the basis of a contest between the various expressions of Christianity we are discussing.

DOCTRINAL DEVELOPMENT: THE HISTORY OF A CONTESTED CONCEPT

Early Mediterranean Christianity. The western Mediterranean theological tradition's thinking about the question of legitimate doctrinal development was deeply influenced by the writings of the early monastic writer Vincent of Lérins (d. ca. 450). A contemporary of Jerome and Augustine of Hippo, Vincent wrote a work called *The Commonitory* (the "Reminder" or "Remembrancer"), which was preoccupied with the question of what propelled theological errors such as Arianism that had troubled the life of the whole Mediterranean church in the fourth century.[15] His answer to his own question was that theological error was rooted *not* in the bald neglect of the Scriptures (which he readily confessed to be the supreme standard) but in idiosyncratic appeals to Scripture that did not accord with the church's own received understanding of them. Thus, when Arians appealed to Matthew 24:36 (in which place, the "day or hour" of the resurrection and judgment are said to be known to "only the Father") or to Colossians 1:15 (where Jesus Christ is described as "firstborn over all creation") as evidences of a subordinate and even creaturely status for Jesus Christ, Vincent meant to confront them with the charge of idiosyncratic interpretation.

[15]The description of Vincent and his *Commonitorium* provided here is indebted to the modern treatment of Vincent provided in Thomas G. Guarino, *Vincent of Lérins and the Development of Christian Doctrine* (Grand Rapids: Baker Academic, 2013), chap. 1. Also, see the discussion of Vincent in Jaroslav Pelikan, *The Christian Tradition*, vol. 1, *The Emergence of the Catholic Tradition (100–600)* (Chicago University of Chicago Press, 1975), 333-38.

The mainstream or "catholic" church of the Mediterranean world was quite aware of the existence and relevance of the Scriptures cited by the Arians, but it had come to an understanding of them that was consistent with firm belief in the co-eternality and co-equality of the Son with the Father. So the heretics erred (in Vincent's view) by departing from the church's commonly received understanding of a major Scripture's bearing on a central Christian reality:

> In the catholic church itself especial care must be taken that we hold to that which has been believed everywhere, always, and by all men. For that is truly and rightly "catholic," as the very etymology of the word shows, which includes almost all universally. This result will be reached if we follow ecumenicity, antiquity, consensus.[16]

When read carefully, Vincent's important argument can be seen to carry with it three provisions that go some distance to answering objections which might be legitimately posed to such a formula. First, Vincent specified that he saw the primary application of this *rule* to "those subjects of inquiry on which the foundations of the whole catholic doctrine rest."[17] In other words, he did not pretend that there was a "received position" about the proper statement of *every* Christian doctrine imaginable, such that no free-ranging discussion might take place. He intended that his rule serve to safeguard what we would call pillars of our faith. The divine status of Jesus Christ is hardly a peripheral matter to Christianity.

Second, and consistent with the first, Vincent addressed very directly the question of whether—in light of the deference to received interpretation that he was pleading for—there was any room left for further doctrinal progress or refinement.[18] Critical to Vincent's position was a distinction he drew between progress and alteration.

> Perhaps someone will say "Shall the church of Christ make no progress in religion?" Yes indeed, it should, as great as possible. Who is there so ungenerous

[16]Vincent of Lérins, *The Commonitory*, in *Early Medieval Theology*, ed. and trans. George McCracken and Alan Cabaniss (London: SCM, 1957), 2:3.

[17]Vincent of Lérins, *Commonitory*, 29:41, 82.

[18]Guarino, *Vincent of Lérins*, xii, is able to show that even within the Roman Catholic theological world, Vincent's addressing of this question has sometimes been misrepresented as tending to "mummify" doctrinal statement.

> toward men, so full of hatred towards God, that he would try to forbid it? Let it be, however, progress, not alteration of the faith. Involved in the idea of progress, of course, is the principle that the subject itself be increased; but in the idea of alteration, the principle is that something be changed from one form to another.[19]

Vincent envisioned theological progress of an organic kind accommodating developments that would constitute clear elaborations or extensions of what had been previously affirmed and were consistent with Scripture, the supreme standard.

Third, Vincent had given a very large place to the importance of securing consensus in doctrinal matters. It was his belief that affirmations that were adequately supported in Scripture would find hearty endorsement across the church. This is not to say that second opinions would never be offered on doctrinal matters but that there would eventually be convergence in the church regarding what was affirmed by the clear majority.

Now this "ideal" of doctrinal stability and doctrinal continuity articulated by Vincent was very widely appropriated in the first Christian millennium and beyond. Theological work proceeded on the basis of twin assumptions that what was affirmed in the church of the west Mediterranean *was* continuous with Christian antiquity, and—if constituting any kind of development—was certainly only an extension of things previously affirmed. These assumptions would not be forcefully challenged until the next millennium.

The influence of Vincent for the churches of the west Mediterranean was not strictly identical in the east. Yet as Vincent had been familiar with the theology and theologians of the whole region as he wrote his *Commonitory*,[20] his approach to these questions had some appeal beyond Latin-speaking areas. In the East the conception arose that the original epoch of crucial doctrinal elaboration extended through the career of the important theologian John of Damascus (ca. 675–749); the latter summarized theological deliberations up through his own time in *An Exact Exposition of the Orthodox Faith*.[21] While it is popularly believed that Orthodox theological formulation

---

[19]Vincent of Lérins, *Commonitory*, 23:28, 69.

[20]Vincent's examples of errant theologians who had been unwarrantably novel in their emphases and in their uses of Scripture had included Photinus, Apollinarius, Nestorius, and Origen (all from the East) as well as Tertullian.

[21]George C. Berthold, "John of Damascus," in Ferguson, *Encyclopedia of Early Christianity*, 498-99.

really ended with that era, thoughtful commentators resist this interpretation and insist that creative Orthodox theological reflection is ongoing.[22]

In the Protestant tradition. The Protestant Christian movement has origins hardly distinguishable from the western European Renaissance and the recovery of the resources of classical antiquity. This ambition to recover the resources of classical antiquity (in this case, of classical *Christian* antiquity) gave to the sixteenth-century Christian humanists a familiarity with early Christian writers of the first centuries that far exceeded the familiarity enjoyed by immediately preceding generations.[23] The advent of mechanical printing in the career of Johannes Gutenberg (d. 1468) soon enabled many editions of the works of ancient writers (Christian and otherwise) to be circulated.

Among these were the writings of Vincent of Lérins. His *Commonitory* was printed in thirty-five editions in the sixteenth century and served as the catalyst for lively discussions about how faithfully Christian doctrine had been transmitted across the preceding millennium.[24] We have already noted how one early Protestant apologist, John Jewel (1522–1571), who was informed by the scholarship of the Christian humanists, was ready to contend that the doctrines of the sixteenth-century Church of Rome did *not* closely correspond to the faith of the early church.[25] Jewel's contemporary, John Calvin (1509–1564), introduced his *Institutes of the Christian Religion* (1536) with the claim that it was the young Protestant movement (rather than the Church of Rome) that best upheld early Christian doctrine. "If the contest were to be determined by patristic authority, the tide of victory would turn to our side," claimed the young Calvin.[26]

Among the examples that Protestant Reformers cited as proof of Rome's doctrinal innovation (compared to the expressed faith of the church of the first five centuries) were:

[22]Timothy Ware, *The Orthodox Church* (Harmondsworth, UK: Penguin, 1964), 206.

[23]Alister McGrath, *The Genesis of Doctrine: A Study in the Foundation of Doctrinal Criticism* (Grand Rapids: Eerdmans, 1997), 104-11.

[24]Guarino, *Vincent of Lérins*, xi. Owen Chadwick, *From Bossuet to Newman: The Idea of Doctrinal Development* (Cambridge: Cambridge University Press, 1957), 16, reports that there were twenty-three editions within France alone in the seventeenth century.

[25]See chapter 2 above.

[26]John Calvin, *Institutes of the Christian Religion* (1536 edition), trans. Ford Lewis Battles (Grand Rapids: Eerdmans, 1975), Epistle Dedicatory, head 4, p. 6.

1. Rome's readiness since the ninth century to define the nature of Christ's presence in the Lord's Supper as corporeal, and since the thirteenth century as entailing the transformation of the elements of bread and wine into the body and blood of Christ.[27] In light of this believed transformation, the elements were deemed worthy of worship.
2. The related assertion that this Communion, or Mass, constituted a sacrifice offered to God for the living and the dead.
3. The endorsement, since at least the time of Gregory the Great, of the notion of postmortem purgatory—a state in which imperfectly sanctified believers were prepared for eventual entrance to the heavenly world.
4. The invocation of departed saints (including Mary, mother of the Lord) resident in the heavenly world, as if they possessed intercessory powers before the throne of God.
5. The veneration of early Christian relics and of religious statuary as a meritorious practice, when this veneration seemed to border on the idolatrous.

All this to say that early Protestantism chose to present itself as embodying a return to the less encumbered doctrinal allegiances of the earliest centuries of the church.[28]

Roman Catholic controversialists did not stand passively by. They contended both that Roman Catholic teaching in fact conformed to Vincent's canon of "always, everywhere, and by all" and that Protestants had themselves introduced doctrinal innovations never before countenanced.[29] This kind of Protestant charge and Roman Catholic countercharge went on for at least three subsequent centuries.

---

[27]The ninth-century development in sacramental theology featured strongly opposed treatises from Paschasius Radbertus of Corbie (who championed the idea of a corporeal presence of Christ) and Ratramnus of Corbie (who championed the idea that Christ's presence accompanying the sacrament was enjoyed within the believer). See their treatises in McCracken and Cabaniss, *Early Medieval Theology*. At the Fourth Lateran Council of 1215, the first opinion was endorsed as church dogma.

[28]We have shown above (chapter 2) that Protestant Reformers, because they were more fully informed by the scholarship of Renaissance Christian humanism, had an initial advantage in marshaling patristic authors in support of their contentions.

[29]No aspect of Protestantism was subjected to more polemical attack than the doctrine of justification by faith. The question of whether there were legitimate patristic antecedents for the Protestant view is explored below in chapter 13.

At the very least, we can say that during that era Protestants were not taken off guard (as they often are in our own time) by the adroit quotation of the Vincentian canon in print or in spoken debate. If anything, Protestant writers were *more likely* to make polemical usage of Vincent's dictum than were their Roman Catholic opposites.[30] They did not readily abandon their charge that on the kind of key doctrines identified above the change in Roman Catholic teaching was so obvious that that communion's claim to doctrinal constancy appeared to be a kind of fig leaf. Meanwhile, Protestant theology itself articulated no particular understanding of doctrinal development other than that it was evident that doctrinal teaching could so develop—negatively—from an earlier purity as to need the kind of recovery that the Reformation had provided.

Doctrinal development in and after J. H. Newman's* Essay on Development *(1846). John Henry Newman (1801–1890) had himself, while an Anglican minister in Oxford and a fellow in the university's Oriel College, used Vincent's canon in written argument aimed at demonstrating the Roman church's departure from ancient doctrinal fidelity.[31] However, a dozen years later and simultaneous with his departure from the Church of England, he published a most controversial book, *An Essay on the Development of Christian Doctrine,* in which he reversed this earlier argumentation. In a way countenanced by neither the Protestant nor Roman Catholic theology of that day, Newman argued for the "fact" of real doctrinal development and for the legitimacy of it on one ground in particular. Here, he was relying on Vincent.

Vincent had himself allowed that there *could* be progress in theology, provided that it constituted a true organic extension of what had previously been believed.[32] Newman built on this idea and (reversing himself markedly over things he had urged in the preceding decade) now argued that many of

[30]The use of Vincent in the post-Reformation period is helpfully described by Chadwick, *From Bossuet to Newman*, chap. 1.

[31]Guarino, *Vincent of Lérins*, 45-46, demonstrates that from 1834 onward, John Henry Newman was appealing to Vincent's canon as part of an argument that Rome's insistence on conformity with its teaching was, in effect, an illegitimate insistence on the acceptance of beliefs not countenanced in early Christianity.

[32]In making this allowance, Vincent had not put forward any concrete examples of what he considered to be legitimate doctrinal developments. He may be forgiven this failure, given the early stage of Christian doctrinal formulation in which he worked out his ideas.

the very practices which Protestant theology had long singled out as representing unwarranted doctrinal development (for example, the opinion that the presence of Christ in the Communion is a bodily presence) were in fact legitimate developments. Using the analogy of the growth of the human body, he argued that as surely as the mature man is the outgrowth of the child, so the elaboration of a corporeal presence of Christ in the Communion is the natural outgrowth of the earlier, less-specific general belief that Christ was truly present in the Communion in an unknown manner.[33] Again, the much-contested Catholic teaching about purgatory was, according to Newman's novel approach to development, reckoned to be a necessary outworking of the much older Catholic teaching about post-baptismal sin requiring penance.

Because this argumentation was revolutionary in its thrust, the Catholic authorities whose role it was to officially receive him into the Roman communion had to make explicitly clear that Newman's 1846 ideas about development of doctrine were not congruent with Roman Catholic teaching as it then existed. The theological authorities at Rome who subsequently interviewed him found his ideas on this subject a matter of deep concern.[34] Until the second half of the twentieth century, Roman Catholic theology had little use for the theory of Newman; in the nineteenth century it preferred instead to uphold the notion that there had never really been substantive change in Catholic theological conviction.[35]

Protestant thinkers, however, took immediate notice of Newman's theories—which, if left unchallenged, would have deprived them of their now-traditional argument that Roman teaching was considerably removed from the faith of the early church. One of Newman's most telling critics was his near contemporary and a former student at Oriel College, James B. Mozley (1813–1878). Mozley cautioned that while there was, no doubt, a principle of development at work in the advance of Christian theology, this development could as easily proceed by way of corruption or of exaggeration as in a positive organic fashion. Mozley held that there were Roman tenets, on behalf

---

[33]John Henry Newman, *Essay on the Development of Christian Doctrine* (1846; repr., Westminster, MD: Christian Classics, 1968).

[34]Avery Dulles, *Newman* (London: Continuum, 2002), 8; and Peter Toon, *The Development of Doctrine in the Church* (Grand Rapids: Eerdmans, 1979), 15.

[35]Chadwick, *From Bossuet to Newman*.

of which Newman pleaded that they were the mere extensions of an organic process, which were instead unsavory and unwarranted.[36] Mozley held that the dominant Catholic conceptions regarding purgatory, the adoration of Mary and the saints, and the infallibility of the pope represented just such unwarranted and extravagant developments. Newman's reasoning about these matters seemed to Mozley to contain a strong element of presumption of an always correct development and no sufficient safeguard against the danger of theological "drift."

Two Scots theological writers of that era, like Mozley, granted the clear possibility of theological development while requiring that any such developments would provide a clearer elucidation of what was already found in Scripture. Robert Rainy (1826–1906) devoted an entire series of lectures to this theme, published in 1874 under the title *The Delivery and Development of Doctrine*.[37] Whereas Newman had been very willing to suppose that doctrinal developments were almost inevitably warranted and divinely approved, Rainy saw that some developments had been sound and true, while others had been wrong-footed. He viewed the Protestant Reformation as an instance of doctrinal development in the positive sense; he saw it as successful both in clearing away superstitions and in providing an advance in the understanding of how the grace of God in the gospel is brought home to individuals.[38]

The viewpoint of Rainy, that there had been actual doctrinal advance at the Reformation, represented a development over earlier Protestant views on the idea of theological progress. Up to and including the Newman era, the dominant Protestant outlook had been that medieval theology had departed from apostolic and patristic clarity; such development as there had been was therefore primarily by way of decline and departure. Rainy, followed by a second Scot, James Orr (1844–1913), embraced the concept of positive theological development.

Orr, in his *The Progress of Dogma* (1901), embraced the concept that the definitive articulation of the great doctrines of the Christian faith has

[36]I have relied on the exposition of Mozley's views contained in *The Theory of Development* (1878) given by Peter Toon in his *Development of Doctrine*, 19-20.
[37]Robert Rainy, *The Delivery and Development of Christian Doctrine* (Edinburgh: T&T Clark, 1874).
[38]Toon, *Development of Doctrine*, 49-50.

proceeded by epoch.[39] Not only (as with Rainy) did the Protestant Reformation represent an advance in the understanding of the application of redemption to individuals, but Orr maintained that the much earlier conflict over Arianism had led to a definitive statement of the full divinity of the Son and to a definitive statement of the interrelationship of the three persons within God. The controversy between Augustine and Pelagius in the early fifth century over sin, grace, and predestination had marked another epoch of advance, as had the controversies of the eleventh century over the atonement secured by Christ.

Striking in Orr's treatment was his taking full note of Newman's argument (from a half century earlier) and his utilization of the language of evolution to describe the progressive articulation of the main themes of Christian doctrine.

TO SUM UP

We began this chapter by acknowledging that a growing number of persons leaving evangelical Protestantism profess to have found stability in doctrine and in worship by their entering the world of Roman Catholicism or Eastern Orthodoxy. We must acknowledge that the reality is far more complicated than the claim. It appears that far from this being the case, Roman Catholicism—while it has spent more than a millennium of its life denying that such a thing as theological development has ever occurred—has gradually acclimatized itself (since J. H. Newman) to the admission that such theological development has undeniably taken place. Later Roman Catholicism does indeed hold to articles of belief that are—though they may in fact be called outgrowths of things maintained earlier (for example, purgatory as an alleged development of an earlier belief in post-baptismal penance)—dubious and extravagant developments. Ready examples would include belief in the immaculate conception of the Virgin Mary (ratified in 1854) and the infallibility of the pope (ratified in 1870).

Conversely, Protestantism, which until Newman was overwhelmingly of the opinion that the only kind of theological development since the apostles and the patristic period was of a negative and degenerating type, has come to accept—through the services of Rainy and Orr—that there have been

[39]James Orr, *The Progress of Dogma* (1901; repr., London: James Clarke, 1966).

actual leaps forward in Christian theological understanding. Fuller comprehension of the two natures of Christ, of grace and predestination, and of the atonement of Christ have indeed come about sequentially with progressive understanding that moves forward by epochs. The difference between these two altered conceptions is that while Roman Catholicism has come to accept that theological advance has gone forward beyond what may be *directly* supported from the Scriptures, evangelical Protestantism has accepted only that theological advance encompasses a fuller and more sensitive interpretation of what the Scriptures in fact support.

The dictum of Vincent of Lérins—"always, everywhere, and by all"—recognized a difference between primary and secondary doctrines. It also recognized the supreme authority of the Scriptures. Fair-minded Christians will see that his approach is not intended to secure a kind of doctrinal inertia in which everything of importance was fixed with finality long ago. Rather, it is an approach to Christian doctrine that looks for stability, Scriptural accountability, and consensus.

QUESTIONS FOR DISCUSSION

1. Why, at bottom, do most Christians instinctively have objections to the idea that Christian beliefs or doctrines might be subject to change?
2. Why does it *not* necessarily follow from this (the idea that Christian beliefs should be stable) that the Christian understanding of various doctrines should be identical in all centuries?
3. What example might you give of a Christian belief or doctrine that came, over time, to be better understood than it was at an earlier period?
4. How can a Christian gauge whether what is proposed as a superior understanding of a Christian belief is in fact better than what came before?
5. Are you personally aware of any beliefs held by other Christians that fall short of the test you identified in answering question 4?

PART II

EVANGELICAL ENGAGEMENTS WITH ANCIENT CHRISTIANITY

Examples to Encourage Us

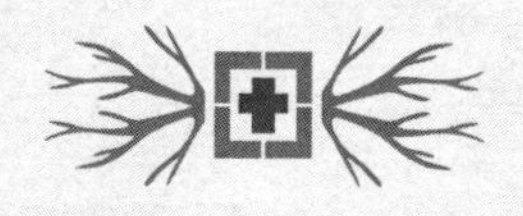

5

Five Hundred Years of Protestant Views of Pre-Reformation Christianity

To this point, we have attempted to probe the uncertainty felt by many believers about the longevity and stability of the evangelical expression of Christianity we have known. We have also come to terms with two concepts (scriptural supremacy and the advance of doctrinal understanding) that are necessary if we are going to think clearly about the sometimes competing claims of other expressions of Christianity. We can now turn to consider the fact that Protestant Christians (evangelicals among them) of ages earlier than our own showed great skill and confidence in tackling these questions.

It is now obvious that we are living in a time of resurgent interest in early Christianity. We hear reports of evangelical Protestant students visiting nearby Orthodox or Roman Catholic congregations. There are also reports of reaffiliations, sometimes of prominent names. We can recall that the late Yale historian of Christianity, Jaroslav Pelikan (1923–2006)—a lifelong Lutheran—was received into the Orthodox Church in the closing years of his life. And there are also the borrowings. More and more evangelical Protestant congregations, historically devoid of liturgical trappings, now experiment with Advent candles, sample practices associated with Lent, and mark Good Friday with a Tenebrae service.[1]

The question is, is this current fascination with the early church really something new for evangelical Christianity? The majority of voices commenting on this phenomenon fervently believe that it *is* something new; in their judgment, the swing of the pendulum toward the early church is a contemporary reaction against an endemic and systemic imbalance that has existed for nearly half a millennium. According to some of these observers, there have been rationalistic developments since the eighteenth century that have cut us off from the early Christian heritage mediated to us by more historic forms of Christianity.[2] According to others, it is the "semi-Manichaean" strain introduced into Christianity by the Reformers that has resulted in a retreat from aesthetic and physical aspects of the Christian faith and Christian worship.[3] Repeatedly, one finds the embrace of the principle that the guidance of the apostolic fathers of the second century is indispensable in the recovery of true New Testament Christianity—which is what evangelicals have professedly been seeking all along.[4]

We must be frank in admitting that such writers have reached their conclusions on the basis of perceptions gleaned from within the strands of evangelical Christianity in which they were nurtured. While this is of foundational importance (they *are*, after all, eyewitnesses of the movements of their lifetimes), it is also limiting. Their judgments have involved a readiness to extrapolate from the evangelical movement as they have personally experienced it to the whole of it. And such an approach contains a rather wide margin of error. Besides, evangelical Christianity sampled or experienced in one region cannot simply be equated with the global evangelical movement or even with evangelical movements elsewhere in the English-speaking world. It is possible, therefore, that the neglect of early Christianity that is complained against—for

[1]I am grateful to Dr. J. Ligon Duncan, Dr. Michael A. G. Haykin, and Dr. Ernest Manges, early church specialists, for commenting on an earlier version of this chapter.

[2]Robert Webber, *Common Roots: A Call to Evangelical Maturity* (Grand Rapids: Zondervan, 1976), 22; and Webber, *Evangelicals on the Canterbury Trail* (Waco, TX: Word, 1985), 24.

[3]Thomas Howard, *Evangelical Is Not Enough: Worship of God in Liturgy and Sacrament*, 2nd ed. (San Francisco: Ignatius, 1984), 35.

[4]See this especially in Peter E. Gillquist, *Becoming Orthodox: A Journey to the Ancient Christian Faith*, rev. ed. (Ben Lomond, CA: Conciliar Press, 1992), 34-40. See the same emphasis in Webber, *Canterbury Trail*, 61, and Howard, *Evangelical*, 107.

example, in North America—exists primarily there and primarily in the environs of fundamentalist or parachurch Protestantism.[5]

Now in fact there *is* evidence to suggest that fundamentalist or parachurch Protestant Christianity has not been the only variety of Christianity that has neglected the early church. Extremely liberal segments of Protestant Christianity in the early twentieth century—those that allowed to be called into question the virginal conception of Jesus, his physical resurrection three days after death, and his personal return at the end of this age—cannot be thought to have heeded the early ecumenical councils or the theological consensus of early Christianity. It is interesting that this is the exact complaint raised by the former evangelical Anglican (and later Antiochian Orthodox priest) Michael Harper (1931–2010) his former communion, the Church of England.[6] He witnessed what he believed to be the erosion of foundational doctrines in that communion and, looking for a safer harbor, claimed to find it in the Antiochian expression of Orthodoxy. I suggest, therefore, that the charge of early Christianity's neglect is a more complex phenomenon than this popular literature (which is chiefly of American origin) admits. The examples of the Harpers and the Pelikans of the Christian world should keep us from attributing all the driving force in the contemporary trend under discussion to the "blind spots" of evangelical Protestantism. The complexity of our contemporary upsurge of interest in early Christianity therefore requires a different line of explanation than what has been offered.

I propose that this line of explanation ought to be that the current resurgence of interest in early Christianity is *not* a swing of the pendulum toward something neglected for the five centuries of Protestantism's existence. It is, in fact, a return to emphases regularly present in historic Protestantism.

[5]This was the contention of the respected evangelical church historian Geoffrey W. Bromiley in an essay, "The Promise of Patristic Theology," in *Towards a Theology for the Future*, ed. David F. Wells and Clark H. Pinnock (Carol Stream, IL: Creation House, 1971), 125.

[6]Michael Harper's *The True Light: An Evangelical's Journey to Orthodoxy* (London: Hodder & Stoughton, 1997) is a fascinating account. Certain parallels suggest themselves in relation to the story of Pelikan (above). It is stimulating to consider, when reading these books in combination, that the theologically broad Anglicanism which Harper *fled* in search of historic Christianity is the very nexus in which Webber claimed to find it. In Howard's case, theologically broad Anglicanism was only a stopping-off point on his journey from a fundamentalist upbringing on the way to an eventual embracing of Roman Catholicism.

Those propounding the view that Protestantism has systematically neglected the early church have relied on observations drawn from within their lifespans. In what follows, we will depend on a series of vignettes drawn from the past five centuries; we must be selective because there is an embarrassment of riches in illustrative material. The contrast between our own times and past eras can be seen most clearly if we move backward in increments until, finally, we reach the era of Protestant origins.

THE TWENTIETH CENTURY

Among the welcomed emphases of the "new evangelicalism" of the 1940s and 50s was a rebirth of interest in the theology of early Christianity. Thus, a collection of Evangelical Theological Society essays, published in 1957 as *Inspiration and Interpretation*, featured writings on Irenaeus and Augustine; another collection, published in 1971 and titled *Towards a Theology for the Future*, featured an essay titled "The Promise of Patristic Theology."[7] Both were encouraging developments, given what had preceded for several decades. Beyond evangelical Protestantism, was not the joint issuing of the *Library of Christian Classics* series from Westminster Press / SCM Press in 1956 (including nine volumes representing the early church) itself a manifestation of the same renaissance of interest? Thomas Torrance's *The Doctrine of Grace in the Apostolic Fathers* (1948), H. E. W. Turner's *The Patristic Doctrine of Redemption* (1952), and J. N. D. Kelly's *Early Christian Doctrines* (1958) were, at their first publication, a part of this same mid-century revival of interest. Yet all of these welcome developments came after a nearly thirty-year hiatus in patristic interest. The reasons for this hiatus cannot be explored here, but it is sufficient to note that to whatever extent conservative

[7]John F. Walvoord, ed., *Inspiration and Interpretation* (Grand Rapids: Eerdmans, 1957); and Wells and Pinnock, *Towards a Theology*. Noteworthy also in the 1950s era was the translation by Gleason Archer of *Jerome's Commentary on Daniel* (Grand Rapids: Baker, 1958). The important expatriate British church historian Geoffrey W. Bromiley (1915–2009) did as much as any other resident North American evangelical leader to encourage this reorientation to patristic studies. In addition to his contribution to the Wells and Pinnock volume, he also contributed an important essay, "The Church Fathers and Holy Scripture," in *Scripture and Truth*, ed. D. A. Carson and John D. Woodbridge (Grand Rapids: Zondervan, 1983), 199-224. I am indebted to Dr. Ernest Manges for the Gleason Archer reference. In recognizing Bromiley's role, it is only proper to also mention two evangelical scholars who have furthered this reorientation as patristics specialists: the late D. F. Wright (1937–2008) of Edinburgh University and Everett Ferguson of Abilene (Texas) Christian University have properly enjoyed a reputation extending beyond Evangelicalism.

Protestants were guilty of neglecting patristic Christianity during these decades, they were far from alone in this neglect.

Yet even while this temporary suspension of interest in early Christianity was in effect, there was an exception within evangelical Protestantism. Should we be surprised to discover that early twentieth-century Pentecostal statesman Donald Gee (1891–1966) already in 1928 was probing second-century Montanism to determine its relationship to early Christian orthodoxy?[8]

THE NINETEENTH CENTURY

From the distance of a century, our supposition might easily be that the late Victorians had reasons to neglect the early church, living as they did in the age of a newly assertive papacy and the catholicizing tendencies of the Oxford movement, which continued its influence in Protestantism long after the actual 1845 reaffiliation to Rome of one its premier leaders, John Henry Newman.[9]

But such a hypothesis is not supported by the data. In just such a setting emerged the standard volume by J. F. Bethune-Baker, *Early History of Christian Doctrine* (1903);[10] this volume had a half century of influence until the publication of the J. N. D. Kelly volume in 1958. Two major histories of early Christianity were produced by Anglican authors in this same dawn of the century period—that of H. M. Gwatkin (1909) and B. J. Kidd (1922)—and an important study of the early Christian error of Apollinarism was published by C. E. Raven in 1923.[11] An Anglican author better

[8]Donald Gee, "Montanism," *Redemption Tidings*, December 1928, 5-6. I am indebted to the website www.earlychurch.org.uk for providing this article in a PDF file. It may well be that the writings of Stanley Burgess and of Ronald Kydd later in the twentieth century are only the continuation of this early twentieth-century Pentecostal curiosity. The former has provided volumes on the Holy Spirit in *Ancient Christian Tradition* (Peabody, MA: Hendrickson, 1984) and *Eastern Christian Traditions* (Peabody, MA: Hendrickson, 1989), while Ronald Kydd authored *Charismatic Gifts in the Early Church* (1984; rev. ed., Peabody, MA: Hendrickson, 1994).

[9]Late Victorian Protestantism recoiled especially at the Decree on Papal Infallibility, which was presented in the Vatican Council of 1870. See the text in Henry Bettenson and Chris Maunder, *Documents of the Christian Church*, 3rd ed. (Oxford: Oxford University Press, 1999), 288.

[10]Bethune-Baker was subsequently professor of Divinity at Cambridge from 1911 to 1935.

[11]These authors are mentioned simply on the basis of their Protestantism: B. J. Kidd, *History of the Church to 461* (Oxford: Oxford University Press, 1922); H. M. Gwatkin, *Early Church History to 313* (London: Macmillan, 1909); and Charles E. Raven, *Apollinarianism: A Study on the Christology of the Early Church* (Cambridge: Cambridge University Press, 1923).

known and more widely consulted by evangelical Protestants, H. B. Swete, provided the volumes *Patristic Study* (1902) and *The Holy Spirit in the Ancient Church* (1912). Also of note in this period was an important volume, *Persecution in the Early Church*, by the Methodist scholar H. B. Workman (1906).

Four pre–Great War Presbyterian theologians, B. B. Warfield, T. M. Lindsay, James Orr, and Robert Rainy, provided volumes reflecting their own researches into the theology of the early church. Many have at least handled Warfield's compiled essays titled *Studies in Tertullian and Augustine.*[12] T. M. Lindsay delivered as Cunningham lectures in the Scottish university faculties of divinity material that became *The Church and Ministry in Early Centuries* (1902).[13] James Orr was one of two Scots Presbyterians who wrestled with questions regarding the development of doctrine from early Christian times; Orr's volume (an intentional rejoinder to the massive work of Adolf von Harnack) was the still valuable *The Progress of Dogma* (1902). Similarly, Robert Rainy, principal of New College, Edinburgh, in addition to authoring the useful *Delivery and Development of Christian Doctrine* (1874)—a rejoinder to the John Henry Newman volume *Essay on the Development of Christian Doctrine* (1845)—also left a very creditable volume, *The Ancient Catholic Church* (1902), which was remarkable for its readiness to evaluate theological developments in the first four centuries of the Christian faith. Many of these volumes served as school texts for Protestant students in divinity.

Lest it be thought that this interest in Christian antiquity had primarily to do with historical or theological questions, it deserves to be acknowledged that the great history of preaching produced as the nineteenth century gave way to the twentieth displayed the same attention. In his two-volume work of 1905, E. C. Dargan of the Baptist Seminary at Louisville,

---

[12]The volume of gathered essays appeared in *Works of B. B. Warfield*, 10 vols., ed. Ethelbert D. Warfield (New York: Oxford University Press, 1927–1932). The Orr volumes referred to are *Neglected Factors in the Study of the Progress of Early Christianity* (New York: Armstrong, 1899) and *The Early Church: Its History and Literature* (New York: Armstrong, 1901). Though concerned with more than the patristic period, Union Seminary theologian W. G. T. Shedd's *History of Doctrine*, 2 vols. (New York: Scribner, 1864) and his historian colleague Philip Schaff's *History of the Christian Church*, 12 vols. (New York: Scribner, 1883–1893) show considerable skill in treating the patristic period.

[13]T. M. Lindsay, *The Church and Ministry in Early Centuries* (New York and London: Armstrong, 1902).

Kentucky, devoted extensive portions of his opening volume to preaching in the period to AD 430.[14]

In the same "fin-de-siècle" era appeared the four-volume series, coedited by the Anglican evangelical Henry Wace (1836–1924), *The Dictionary of Christian Biography and Literature to the End of the Sixth Century* (1911). Wace, at one time professor of ecclesiastical history in the University of London, showed the breadth of his interests by on the one hand helping to edit the series *Shorter Writings of Luther,* and on the other, to coedit (with Philip Schaff of Union Seminary, New York) the series *Nicene and Post-Nicene Church Fathers* (1887–1900)—still in such widespread use in the English-speaking world. That series had consciously augmented another, the *Ante-Nicene Fathers*, originating with the Edinburgh publisher T&T Clark. In this instance, we know that part of the impetus for the launching of this Edinburgh series under the coeditorship of Alexander Donaldson and James Robertson in 1860 was the concern that the Oxford movement (which gave rise to the defections of Newman and others to Rome) was creating the misperception that Christianity prior to the Council of Nicaea in AD 325 was *necessarily* in favor of Catholic expressions of the faith. It is noteworthy that this major publishing undertaking proceeded on a very different assumption: that the early church prior to the Nicene era was not the exclusive property of any particular branch of the church and was therefore awaiting the inspection of all modern Christians.[15] There was a clear confidence that wider familiarity with pre-Nicene Christianity would promote open-minded thinking about such questions.[16] We cannot survey this period

---

[14]Edward Charles Dargan, *A History of Preaching*, 2 vols. (New York: A. C. Armstrong, 1905). Dargan's first two epochs surveyed were titled "Preaching During the First Three Centuries" and "The Culmination of Preaching in the Fourth Century to 430 A.D."

[15]The intriguing story of the launch of the T&T Clark Ante-Nicene Fathers series in 1860, its financial backing from sugar refiner Robert Macphie (also a major backer of the launch of the Evangelical Alliance in 1846), and its eventual strained relationship with the American publishers of the enlarged American series edited by A. Cleveland Coxe is expertly told by David F. Wright, "'From a Quarter So Unexpected': Translation of the Early Church Fathers in Victorian Scotland," *Records of the Scottish Church History Society* 30 (2000): 124-69. Wright acknowledged his own debt to Richard W. Pfaff, "Anglo-American Patristic Translations, 1866–1900," *Journal of Ecclesiastical History* 28, no. 1 (1997): 39-55.

[16]Representative of this heightened curiosity in early Christianity in mid-nineteenth-century western Europe is the volume of the Ulster Presbyterian church historian W. D. Killen (1806–1902), *The Ancient Church: Its History, Doctrine and Worship Traced for the First Three Hundred Years* (New York: Scribner, 1859). The French evangelical Protestant Edmond de Pressensé had

without acknowledging the impact made by J. B. Lightfoot's edition and translation of the *Apostolic Fathers* (1869, 1885) or the freedom with which the popular Anglican commentator J. C. Ryle (1816–1900), later first bishop of Liverpool, drew on various patristic commentators in his seven-volume series *Expository Thoughts on the Gospels.*[17]

The *Ante-Nicene Library* series was not, after all, the first Protestant effort at translating the early church fathers in the nineteenth century. This honor belongs to the series *The Library of the Fathers*, edited by the Oxford professor of Hebrew E. B. Pusey (1800–1882). The fact that John Henry Newman had been associated with the launch of this series in 1838 and that his reaffiliation with Rome in 1845 meant an end to his involvement in the project ought not obscure the fact that the motivation behind this series of patristic translations was not the advancing of any particular Roman agenda but the containing of an incipient Protestant liberalism that was raising its head in early Victorian Oxford. The latter unfolded in connection with the liberal theological influence there of Professor Renn Dickson Hampden (1793–1868), whom the early Tractarian leaders had come to view with great alarm.[18]

THE EIGHTEENTH CENTURY

In the previous century, there was also high interest in the early church—though the materials of the church fathers had yet to be made available to the wide readership they would gain through the various nineteenth-century translation projects. A major milestone came at century's end with the gradual release of Joseph Milner's multivolume *History of the Church of Christ* (1794–1797).[19] Milner aimed to overcome the shortcomings of another church history; it was widely perceived that the German church

---

in the same period composed a four-volume series, *The Early Years of Christianity* (1859; repr., English trans., London: Hodder & Stoughton, 1870–1871).

[17]It is especially instructive to note concerning Ryle, so often associated with opposition to the Tractarian legacy of the Oxford movement that was spreading in late nineteenth-century Anglicanism, that his use of such patristic commentators as Origen, Cyril of Alexandria, Chrysostom, Augustine, Theophylact, and Euthymius is widespread in his *Expository Thoughts*. There was evidently no "odium by association." See, for example, his *Expository Thoughts on John* (London: William Hunt, 1879), 1:xi.

[18]Richard W. Pfaff, "The Library of the Fathers: The Tractarians as Patristic Translators," *Studies in Philology* 70, no. 3 (1973): 329-44.

[19]I have consulted the five-volume edition of 1827, brought to completion by Isaac Milner, brother to Joseph.

history so widely available in translation in the eighteenth century, J. L von Mosheim's *Institutes of Church History* (1755, English trans. 1768), spent too many pages detailing various early heresies. Milner, an Anglican evangelical, wished to demonstrate the tenacious survival of the doctrine of justification by faith from the earliest centuries. He must have made the story interesting for early nineteenth-century readers, for one such—John Henry Newman—recalled while writing his memoir, the *Apologia Pro Vita Sua* (1864), that it was Milner who had "nothing short of enamoured him with long extracts" from the church fathers.[20] Milner's more comprehensive effort had been anticipated, in degree, by the earlier efforts of fellow Anglican evangelicals John Newton and Thomas Haweis.[21]

In that eighteenth century, some teaching of the early church was being put to polemical usage. Early in the century, liberal (or as they were then called, "latitudinarian") Anglican theologians were becoming aware, by their reliance on seventeenth-century Remonstrant theologians—notably Gerard Jan Voss (1577–1649) and Philipp van Limborch (1633–1712)—that there were certain non-Augustinian church fathers whose views of human depravity and of the redemption wrought by Christ tended to undermine the emphases of the eighteenth-century evangelicals.[22] This polemic, articulated by a series of liberal Anglicans commencing with Daniel Whitby (1638–1726) and extending through George Tomline, bishop of Winchester (1750–1827),[23] required that a whole range of evangelical writers would need to meet such criticisms, informed by the writings of the early church fathers, on their own ground. The principle the evangelicals upheld was that the early church formed an important but not utterly determinative witness on

[20]The reference by Newman is to his reading material at age fifteen! See *Newman's Apologia Pro Vita Sua: The Two Versions of 1864 & 1865*, ed. Wilfrid Ward (London: Oxford University Press, 1911), 110.

[21]The story surrounding the production of Milner's work is effectively told by John Walsh in "Joseph Milner's Evangelical Church History," *Journal of Ecclesiastical History* 10, no. 2 (1959): 174-87. A. Skevington Wood provides a similar sketch of the work of John Newton in "John Newton's Church History," *Evangelical Quarterly* 23 (1951): 51-70.

[22]These seventeenth-century developments so heavily impacting eighteenth-century Christianity are well described in Norman Sykes, *From Sheldon to Secker: Aspects of English Church History, 1660–1768* (Cambridge: Cambridge University Press, 1959), chap. 5.

[23]This theological criticism of the evangelical Protestant position, informed by patristics, is illustrated, for example, in Daniel Whitby, *A Discourse Concerning the True Import of the Words "Election" and "Reprobation"* (London, 1710), 96-109; and George Tomline, *A Refutation of Calvinism* (London, 1811), chap. 5. Tomline openly quotes Whitby from the preceding century.

theological questions. Evangelical theological writers such as John Edwards (1637–1716), Thomas Haweis (1734–1820), and Thomas Scott (1747–1821) upheld their essentially Augustinian position by maintaining a stance that, while it welcomed patristic authorities, declined to be bound by them. Then, as now, the apostolic fathers of the second century were being utilized to insist that the evangelical claim to represent the original Christianity of the New Testament era was tendentious. Thomas Scott, knowing this, argued:

> Can the language of Justin Martyr regarding baptismal regeneration be paralleled from any record of baptism in the New Testament? . . . If Justin corrupted Christianity by philosophy, are we bound to bow to him as an oracle or copy him as an example, merely because he lived in the second century?[24]

Nonconformity seems not to have been at a disadvantage, as regards patristic learning, if the *Body of Divinity* (1767) of the London Baptist minister John Gill (1697–1771) is taken as a sample. Particularly in his treatment of the divine attributes, Gill demonstrated a very wide classical as well as patristic learning. Given his loyalty to high Calvinism, it is not surprising to find numerous quotations from Augustine of Hippo; yet in addition we find Justin Martyr, Tertullian, Irenaeus, Jerome, Gregory of Nazianzus, and Cyril of Jerusalem.[25]

But while this readiness to test the teaching of early Christianity by Scripture (a habit of mind transmitted forward from the Reformation of the sixteenth century) was so characteristic of eighteenth-century evangelicals, there unfolded alongside this a most refreshing readiness to borrow from early Christianity a range of ideas and practices deemed useful for the age. Ludwig von Zinzendorf (1700–1760) recovered many interesting ideas from the early church, a number of which, such as end-of-year watch night services and love feasts, were passed on to Methodism. Moreover, Zinzendorf, leader of the Moravians, further demonstrated his familiarity with the early church when he drew on episodes in the life of the early missionary Martin of Tours (335–400) while preaching about the "wounds of Christ" (a Moravian hallmark). Just as Martin had been ready to dismiss as hellish a

---

[24]Thomas Scott, *Reply to Bishop Tomline's "A Refutation of Calvinism"* (London: Macintosh, 1817), 276, 690.

[25]John Gill, *A Complete Body of Practical and Doctrinal Divinity*, 2 vols. (London, 1767; repr., Grand Rapids: Baker Books, 1978), 1:109, 154, 183, 225-27.

vision of an unscarred Christ who promised to show to him *alone* a sight of his own glory (prompting in Martin the question "But where are your wounds?"), so, argued Zinzendorf, the gospel is brought to nothing without the message of a crucified savior.[26]

John Wesley (1703–1791) was himself a student of the early church. The self-imposed austerities he endured while a member of the Holy Club at Oxford were largely austerities pursued in search of a "Primitive Christianity" associated with the ancient "Apostolic Constitutions."[27] Later in his career, while not allowing that singleness should be made a condition of ministry in the church, he regularly urged the single life on his band of young preachers (even after he took the plunge and married). He maintained fasts twice per week and encouraged other Methodists to do the same.[28] Wesley drew on the literary resources of the early church when compiling his fifty-volume *Christian Library*; he commenced the series in 1750 with a volume providing various letters of the apostolic fathers and the sayings of Macarius, a fourth-century bishop of Jerusalem.[29] Volumes two through four provided an abridged martyrology commencing with early Christian times, courtesy of the Elizabethan chronicler John Foxe (1516–1587).[30]

THE SEVENTEENTH CENTURY

In the seventeenth century, the challenge faced by the heirs of the Reformation tradition was the emergence of stronger evidence of the diversity of Christian teaching after the death of the apostles than had ever been observed since the introduction of the printing press. Beginning in the 1630s, attention had come to be focused on the writings of the apostolic fathers.

---

[26]Ludwig von Zinzendorf, "Concerning the Proper Purpose of Preaching the Gospel," reprinted in *Classics of Christian Missions*, ed. Francis M. DuBose (Nashville: Broadman, 1979), 294.

[27]Henry Rack, *Reasonable Enthusiast: John Wesley and the Rise of Methodism* (London: Trinity Press, 1989), 90; and Jeffrey Barbeau, "John Wesley and the Early Church: History, Antiquity, and the Spirit of God," in *Evangelicals and the Early Church*, ed. George Kalantzis and Andrew Tooley (Eugene, OR: Cascade, 2012), 52-76.

[28]David Butler, *Methodists and Papists: John Wesley and the Catholic Church in the Eighteenth Century* (London: Darton, Longman and Todd, 1995), 71-72.

[29]Butler, *Methodists and Papists*, 74, with full details of the contents of the *Christian Library* available from the Wesley Archive maintained online by Northwest Nazarene University, Nampa, ID, available at wesley.nnu.edu/john-wesley/a-christian-library.

[30]On Foxe, see more below under the heading "The Sixteenth Century."

The epistles of Clement were published at Oxford in 1633; a debate about the authenticity of the epistles of Ignatius raged until 1644. The study of second-century Christianity was at this time largely a novelty. Some post-Reformation Protestants, on reading this literature of the second century, found reasons to consider whether an Episcopal church order was not of greater antiquity than earlier assumed; many learned to look behind and beyond Augustine, their erstwhile authority of choice in Christianity's early centuries.[31] The undermining or qualifying of Augustine's hitherto dominant theological role was also a major subtext in that challenge to high Calvinism that has subsequently been called Arminianism.[32]

Yet this is only half the story, and the half—we may say—upon hearing that our modern ears most prick up. The other half is that Protestantism both in Europe and Britain set to work in this century in an honest attempt to grapple with the church fathers taken as a whole. It was the seventeenth century, rather than the preceding century of Reformation, that got down to work to prepare volumes of patrology—that is, volumes seeking to interpret the theological diversity and development of the earliest Christian centuries. The earliest attempts—such as those by the Heidelberg Protestants Abraham Scultetus (1566–1624) in 1598[33] and Daniel Tossanus (1541–1602) in 1603,[34] the English writer (and Oxford librarian) Thomas James (1573–1629) in 1611,[35] and French Protestants André Rivet (1572–1651) in 1619[36] and Jean Daillé (1594–1670) in 1632[37]—though of quite mixed quality, were one and all attempts to move beyond the somewhat atomistic quotation of patristic writers that had too much characterized both Catholic and Protestant polemical appeals to this material in the sixteenth century.[38] In these

---

[31]Henry Chadwick, *The Reformation* (Grand Rapids: Eerdmans, 1964), 218.

[32]Ibid., 220.

[33]Scultetus had released the contents of the eventual, posthumously published volume *Medulla Theologiae Patrum Syntagma* (Frankfurt, 1634) in installments commencing in 1598.

[34]Whose *Synopsis de Patribus* (Heidelberg, 1603) appeared in English translation in 1637 as *Synopsis of the Fathers.*

[35]This was *Treatise of the Corruption of Scripture, Councils and Fathers by Prelates, Pastors and Pillars of the Church of Rome for the Maintenance of Popery and Irreligion.*

[36]*Critici Sacri Specimen: hoc est censure doctoram* (Dordrecht, 1619).

[37]*Traité de l'employ des saints pères*. An English translation was published in London in 1675 as *Treatise Concerning the Right Use of the Fathers*. This volume was reprinted at London in 1841.

[38]I am indebted to the masterful survey of this seventeenth-century literature provided by Irena Backus, "The Fathers and Calvinist Orthodoxy: Patristic Scholarship," in *The Reception of the Church Fathers in the West: From the Carolingians to the Maurists*, ed. Irena Backus, vol. 2 (Leiden:

literary attempts, there emerged a trend toward modern critical study of the Fathers. While some of the volumes attempt to "sort" the Fathers (by indicating which of them most helpfully or soundly articulates a particular topic or doctrine), there is a progression toward understanding the development of thought, over time, in the writings of particular patristic authors and toward the discerning use of the whole body of literature.[39]

Yet to emphasize only this about the seventeenth century would be to leave the false impression that patristic study was something considerably removed from the week-in, week-out practice of pastoral ministry and proclamation. In fact, proclamation in this period seems to have shown a remarkable readiness to allude to the church fathers for sermon illustration or for a suitable bon mot. In his sermonic expositions of the Westminster Shorter Catechism, the Puritan preacher Thomas Watson (d. 1686) called on the services of Tertullian, Cyprian, Augustine, Chrysostom, and Bernard to assist him in making plain what it is "to glorify God and enjoy him forever" and to take the Scriptures as the rule toward the pursuit of this.[40]

THE SIXTEENTH CENTURY

The century of the Reformation is full of paradoxes as we pursue this question: what was the orientation of Protestantism toward the church fathers? On the one hand it may be said comprehensively that the various forms of Protestantism took late-medieval Catholicism off guard with their facility in calling on the church fathers. This happened because early Protestantism was more leavened by the then-contemporary humanist orientation toward Christian and classical antiquity than was current Catholicism. Then-contemporary Catholicism had fewer fundamental quarrels with medieval theology and philosophy and, consequently, had not taken as much

E. J. Brill, 1997), 839-65. See also the companion essay by Jean-Louis Quantin, "The Fathers in 17th Century Anglican Theology," in Backus, *Reception of the Church Fathers*, 987-1008.

[39]Backus, *Reception of the Church Fathers*, 858, 859. It is the contention of D. H. Williams, "Scripture, Tradition and the Church: Reformation and Post-Reformation," in *The Free Church and the Early Church*, ed. D. H. Williams (Grand Rapids: Eerdmans, 2002), 105, 118-23, that whatever enhancements in patristic study may have been achieved in the seventeenth century, it was not accompanied by the respect for authoritative tradition characteristic of the early Reformation period. The Reformed theologians Wollebius and Turretin and the Lutheran theologian Chemnitz are said to represent this development.

[40]Thomas Watson, *A Body of Divinity* (1692; repr., London: Banner of Truth, 1965), chap. 1.

interest in the in-vogue Renaissance appeal to antiquity. As regards this epoch, the Catholic scholar Ralph Keen has written:

> The rediscovery of Christian antiquity and its appropriation by the reformers forced Roman Catholicism to reclaim a heritage of which it had not consciously been the custodian. The need to prove a positive relationship between the catholic church and the patristic tradition was thus as difficult as it was urgent.[41]

Protestant Reformers such as Ulrich Zwingli (1484–1531) and John Calvin (1509–1564), just because they were part of the Christian humanist movement of the Renaissance era prior to their acceptance of the message of the Reformation, were already highly conversant with patristic literature. By the year 1516, Zwingli owned the printed works of Ambrose, Athanasius, Augustine, Basil of Caesarea, John Chrysostom, Cyprian, Cyril of Alexandria, John of Damascus, Gregory of Nazianzus, Gregory of Nyssa, Jerome, Lactantius, Origen, and Tertullian.[42] Oecolampadius of Basel (1482–1531) caught the attention of serious scholars across Europe in 1530 when he published a study calling into question medieval Catholic transubstantiation doctrine in light of many writings from the early church.[43]

John Calvin's first-ever literary production had been a translation of a treatise by the Roman jurist Seneca;[44] the preface to the first edition of his *Institutes* (1536) enunciated the claim that "the doctrines of Rome are contrary to the teaching of the early Church and . . . that the teaching of the Reformers is in fact very close to that of the 'ancient writers of a better age of the Church.'"[45] Witnessing a public theological debate at Lausanne in 1536, Calvin—who had planned only to observe—was stung into action by the Catholic claim that the Protestants lacked patristic support.

[41]Ralph Keen, "The Fathers in Counter-Reformation Theology in the Pre-Tridentine Period," in Backus, *Reception of the Church Fathers*, 2:702.

[42]Irena Backus, "Ulrich Zwingli, Martin Bucer and the Church Fathers," in Backus, *Reception of the Church Fathers*, 2:628-39.

[43]Oecolampadius's treatise, *Quid de eucharistia veteres tum Graeci, tum Latini senserint, Dialogus* (Basel, 1529), was highly significant, especially in England where it was read by persons as diverse as John Fisher, Catholic bishop of Rochester; the future Henrician martyr John Frith; and eventually Reformation bishops Cranmer and Ridley.

[44]Johannes Van Oort, "John Calvin and the Church Fathers," in Backus, *Reception of the Church Fathers*, 2:663. On the whole question of Calvin and the patristic age, see also A. N. S. Lane, *John Calvin: Student of the Church Fathers* (Grand Rapids: Baker, 1999).

[45]Backus, *Reception of the Church Fathers*, 665. Van Oort here quotes the 1536 *Institutes*.

From memory, he quoted copiously from the Fathers and reversed the direction of the debate.[46]

It was this humanist predisposition to prefer the teaching of Christian antiquity rather than the teaching of the church in more recent history (the onset of which coincided roughly speaking with the sack of Rome in 410 or, at very least, the papacy of Gregory the Great circa 590–604) that separated such early Protestants from current Catholic theology, which viewed Christian theology as an unbroken continuum from antiquity to the present. Such a Protestant stance had been "served up whole" by the humanistic studies of the day.[47]

Yet on the other hand, there were prominent Protestant leaders who came to their appreciation of Christian antiquity after having traveled a distinctly different road. For Martin Luther (1483–1546) and Martin Bucer (1491–1551), their own theological training had oriented them toward late-medieval Catholic theology—*rather than* the church fathers—and it was only gradually that they learned to use the early church as a tool for critiquing the contemporary church. Further, while the Protestant Reformers learned to use the early church to critique the contemporary church, they did so selectively—for they rapidly learned to admit that the early church was not univocal. Catholic theology might have preferred the notion that there was an unbroken continuum of teaching from the second century through to the sixteenth (a view extremely difficult to demonstrate), but the sixteenth-century Protestants, preferring the early church, needed to gauge the church fathers critically. At a fairly early stage in the age of Reform, Martin Bucer could claim on a title page, "Here, Christian reader, you will see that we have admitted nothing in the doctrine or rites of our churches which is not in fine harmony with the writings of the Fathers and the observances of the Catholic church."[48]

But with the passage of time, each such Reformation leader knew that the early church provided authorities on both sides of many questions. Calvin

---

[46]Backus, *Reception of the Church Fathers*, 672.

[47]The Reformation (including the perspective of Anabaptists) attitude toward the church fathers is helpfully surveyed in D. H. Williams, *Retrieving the Tradition and Renewing Evangelicalism* (Grand Rapids: Eerdmans, 1999), chap. 6.

[48]The quotation, from the title page of the 1534 polemical title *Defensio adversus Axioma Catholicum*, is provided in Cornelis Augustijn, "Bucer's Theology in the Colloquies with the Catholics, 1540-41," in *Martin Bucer: Reforming Church and Community*, ed. David F. Wright (Cambridge: Cambridge University Press, 1994), 119.

found support for the Protestant doctrine of justification in Augustine, Ambrose, and Bernard—a very short list![49] Luther found in writing his *Galatians* commentary that Jerome's exposition of the critical second chapter (dealing with controversy between Paul and Peter at Antioch) was skewed by Jerome's precommitment to Petrine primacy, whereas Augustine was the saner interpreter.[50] It emerged, therefore, that the Protestants found in the early Christian theologians and commentators invaluable resources—yet all the same resources auxiliary to a Scripture to which they awarded supreme authority. It has been well said that the Reformers used the Fathers to test or evaluate the plausibility of their own convictions, but this is very far from admitting that they accepted them as a judge.

It would not be proper to speak of the sixteenth century and not mention its Protestant chroniclers such as the Lutheran Matthias Flacius Illyricus (1520–1575), who guided a composite project of thirteen volumes (one for each Christian century through the thirteenth) that we now call the *Magdeburg Centuries* (1559–1574); this demonstrated the ill fortunes of a Western Christendom that had been dominated by the Roman papacy. A second chronicler, the Anglican John Foxe (1516–1587), had helped correct the page proofs of these *Centuries* while a religious refugee at Basel in the reign of Queen Mary Tudor (1553–1558).[51] Even though we know his *Acts and Monuments* as an eight-volume colossus, for our present purpose it is important to grasp that whether in its Elizabethan bulk *or* in the digested Victorian single-volume versions, Foxe gave lengthy attention to early Christian martyrdoms up to AD 449.[52] In this way, he gradually helped to make the early Christian martyrs what we might call household names. Foxe in this lighter dress was a fixture on the bookshelves of many Protestant families well into the twentieth century; this by itself is a powerful indicator that the early

[49]See John Calvin, *Institutes of the Christian Religion* (1536 edition), trans. Ford Lewis Battles (Grand Rapids: Eerdmans, 1975), 3.11.23–12.3.

[50]Manfred Schulze, "Martin Luther and the Church Fathers," in Backus, *Reception of the Church Fathers*, 2:600-609.

[51]On both Illyricus and Foxe, see the helpful treatment of V. Norskov Olsen, *John Foxe and the Elizabethan Church* (Berkeley: University of California Press, 1973), 19-22.

[52]The first volume of eight in the reprint edition of *Acts and Monuments* edited by George Townsend (1843; repr., New York: AMS, 1985) is completely given over to patristic martyrology. Compact one-volume editions have traditionally devoted two chapters to this period to AD 449. I have verified this in the edition of 1886 (London: Nisbett) and 1926 (Chicago: Winston).

church was not utterly eclipsed in the ecclesiastical and theological divisions of the early twentieth century.

TO SUM UP

In summary, as one considers the prevalent fresh appropriation of early Christianity in our own time, one finds on closer inspection that the evangelical Protestant tradition, rather than exhibiting a history of neglect, has quite often been exemplary in investigating and appropriating early Christian theology and practice. The history of evangelical Chrstianity is in fact full of salutary lessons and models that can guide us as we make fresh appropriation from the early church today. Let us tease out some implications for the contemporary scene from this rapid survey.

First, the neglect of the early church and its teaching is a relatively modern phenomenon, afflicting both conservative and liberal Protestantism for a period of some three decades early in the twentieth century, and waning since the 1950s.

Second, one hardly finds any evidence in the five hundred years surveyed of an attitude that *cedes* the first centuries of Christianity to Roman Catholicism (or to Orthodoxy). This conception, which is alleged to be very widespread in evangelical Protestantism, is remarkably hard to locate in the literature available.

Third, at the dawn of the Reformation, the advocates of reform enjoyed (at least temporarily) the position of "frontrunner" in the appropriation of early Christian teaching and in the advancing of the notion that the early church, because not yet "fallen," could help to judge the later church. This idea had arisen in connection with the Renaissance preference for antiquity and was then commended by various Christian humanists such as Erasmus (1466–1536), not all of which joined Protestant movements.

Fourth, today's fascination with the Christianity of the second century—so powerful an influence on the number of evangelical Protestants who have decamped to Roman Catholicism or Orthodoxy—is an attitude very different from that displayed in both Roman Catholicism *and* Protestantism since the Renaissance. Among such persons, the Christianity of the second century has been explicitly reckoned to provide a kind of "lodestone" for highlighting the failings of twentieth-century Christianity—whether liberal, evangelical, or fundamentalist.[53] Instead, historic Protestantism has customarily used the first five centuries as a "control." Sadly, the pattern of today is that those who enthrone the second century as the test of genuine Christianity end up embracing the notion of an unbroken succession of church and Christian teaching that has been free from the possibility of any real decline from Christian truth. Having used the second century to critique the twentieth, they are left without possibility of further critique of what they have embraced by this process.

Fifth, it is urgent that the Protestantism of today recapture the principle, apparently obvious until the twentieth century, that the Reformation was *itself* a fresh appropriation of all the early Christianity deemed to be consistent with the supreme authority of Scripture. Today there is afoot a questionable rival attitude that sweeps aside this historic perspective and treats as suspect all aspects of the Reformation deemed not consistent with an early church naively judged to have contained no dross. This latter judgment, I would argue, is symptomatic of a diminished understanding of the classical world rather than an advance in understanding.

Sixth, Western Christianity's ability to draw on and to appraise patristic Christianity has customarily gone hand in hand with the cultivation and maintenance of a curriculum of classical studies of the ancient Mediterranean world, its cultures, and its languages. It is an open secret that this curriculum has fallen on very hard times at the university level since the middle of the twentieth century. It is a very great paradox that as fascination with early Christianity has revived in our times, the number of persons well equipped to study this era and its theological literature on its own terms has declined. Surely, the Christian community should be making its voice heard in favor of a restoration of classical studies at multiple levels.

QUESTIONS FOR DISCUSSION

1. Before you read this material, were you of the general opinion that Protestants hadn't really invested much time and energy in past centuries investigating early Christianity?

---

[53]Note this emphasis especially in Peter Gillquist, *Becoming Orthodox*, 34-40; Robert Webber, *Canterbury Trail*, 61; and Tom Howard, *Evangelical Is Not Enough*, 108.

2. If you were of that opinion, can you recall what the basis was of your holding that attitude? Was it that you had heard someone speak disparagingly about early Christianity? Can you think of any additional reason?
3. Did you ever see in a family library or church library John Foxe's *Book of Martyrs*? If you did, and opened it, did it leave any strong impressions?
4. Have you ever attended a watch night service on New Year's Eve? If so, was any explanation given as to how old this practice was?
5. If there is one thing you would really like to know about the Christians of the early centuries, what is that one thing?
6. What is something you would be prepared to do to become more familiar with early Christianity?

6

The Apostolic Fathers in the Hands of Protestants

1600–2000

WE HAVE SHOWN IN THE PRECEDING CHAPTER that though neglect of early Christianity may have characterized evangelical Protestantism in the middle decades of the twentieth century, this neglect was not at all representative of the intervening centuries since the sixteenth-century reforms. We can now proceed to consider how a specific type of early Christian literature, that of the second century, was especially made the subject of Protestant investigation in some of those same centuries.

OUR CURRENT CONTEXT

By the designation *apostolic fathers*, I refer to a body of late first- and early second-century Christian literature that includes the letters of Clement, of Ignatius, and of Polycarp, along with the Martyrdom of Polycarp, the Didache, and other literature.[1] Since about 1984, the evangelical Protestant

[1]I pass over, because of less significance for this chapter, the epistle of Barnabas and epistle to Diognetus, with the Shepherd of Hermas and Fragments of Papias included in modern editions of the apostolic fathers such as *The Apostolic Fathers*, 2nd ed., trans. J. B. Lightfoot and J. R. Harmer, ed. and rev. Michael W. Holmes (Grand Rapids: Baker, 1989).

world has been repeatedly roiled by claims made by writers departing from the evangelical movement after having been drastically reoriented through their reading of this second-century literature.

In 1984, Thomas Howard penned *Evangelical Is Not Enough*, in which he relates that reading the apostolic fathers was one of the factors that moved him beyond Episcopalianism to Roman Catholicism.[2] Within a year, similar appreciation for the apostolic fathers had been registered by the late Robert E. Webber, formerly a conservative Presbyterian but by then received into the Episcopal Church USA. In his *Evangelicals on the Canterbury Trail* (1985) Webber declared that he found in these second-century writers a "link with primitive Christianity" as it had been left to us by the apostles themselves.[3] In that same period, former Campus Crusade for Christ director Peter E. Gillquist wrote retrospectively of his quest (with close friends also formerly in the Crusade movement) to "find" New Testament Christianity—since it seemed to them to be so hard to locate within American evangelicalism. As reported in *Becoming Orthodox* (1989) Gillquist and friends had their "eureka moment" while reading the apostolic fathers. In Ignatius, in Clement, and in Justin Martyr they found the liturgy, the sacramental views, and primitive episcopacy that they took to be none other than that of the apostolic age itself.[4] Soon they were founding the Evangelical Orthodox Church (1979), the majority of which entered Antiochian Orthodoxy by 1987. And as if to show that such happenings were not confined to North America, the British Anglican Michael Harper described a similar road traveled as he left the Church of England for Antiochian Orthodoxy. In his *The True Light: An Evangelical's Journey to Orthodoxy* (1997), Harper recounted how influential the writings of Ignatius of Antioch were in his determination to reaffiliate.[5]

---

[2]Thomas Howard, *Evangelical Is Not Enough: Worship of God in Liturgy and Sacrament* (San Francisco: Ignatius, 1984), 107. In 1984, Howard noted the impact made on his thinking by the sacramental views of Ignatius of Antioch, one of those reckoned to be apostolic fathers.

[3]Robert E. Webber, *Evangelicals on the Canterbury Trail: Why Evangelicals Are Attracted to the Liturgical Church* (Waco, TX: Word, 1985), 61.

[4]Peter E. Gillquist, *Becoming Orthodox: A Journey to the Ancient Christian Faith* (Ben Lomond, CA: Conciliar Press, 1989), 34, 35. See the same indebtedness recorded in Charles Bell, *Discovering the Rich Heritage of Orthodoxy* (Minneapolis: Light and Life, 1994), 11.

[5]Michael Harper, *The True Light: An Evangelical's Journey to Orthodoxy* (London: Hodder & Stoughton, 1997), 63.

ORIGIN OF THE CONCEPTION OF APOSTOLIC FATHERS

Thus, my initial point is proven. There *has* been quite a stir over the apostolic fathers among evangelical Protestants in the past quarter century. With this established, it is worth pointing out that the terminology itself, apostolic fathers, is not of ancient origin. While Robert M. Grant claimed to find this terminology as early as the sixth century in the writings of Severus of Antioch,[6] in early modern Europe, the terminology is reported to have surfaced only in 1677 in a volume by the English clergyman and patristics scholar William Wake.[7] While in modern times we are accustomed to conceiving of these writings as a somewhat cohesive body of second-century literature, the unfolding history of the terminology reminds us that this is a collective conception which came into use rather late. Moreover, this was a body of literature augmented as recently as 1873 by the recovery of the Didache.[8] Thus, on several fronts, our modern perceptions of the apostolic fathers fail to do justice to the complex issues surrounding this late first- and second-century literature.

WRITINGS LOST IN OBSCURITY IN THE MEDIEVAL PERIOD, THEN RECOVERED

Now, what also deserves to be much better known is that for some four hundred years in the late medieval period, the writings that are today reckoned to form a collection, and to be so determinative, effectively dropped out of sight and consequently had no influence to speak of. This is partially to be explained by the decline in the ability of western Europeans to read Greek. This was a state of affairs that persisted until the migration of Greek scholars of Constantinople into Europe; the Greek scholar Manuel Chrysoloras (ca. 1349–1415) led this migration when he came to Florence in 1397. Only in light of this Greek revival was it possible for Europeans to

[6]Robert M. Grant, "The Apostolic Fathers: The First Thousand Years," *Church History* 31 (1962): 421.

[7]H. J. De Jonge, "On the Origin of the Term 'Apostolic Fathers,'" *Journal of Theological Studies* n.s. 29 (1978): 503-5. De Jonge alludes to long-circulated reports crediting the French seventeenth-century writer Cotelier with devising the terminology, but prefers the claim of Wake.

[8]Henry Chadwick, *The Church in Ancient Society: From Galilee to Gregory the Great* (Oxford: Oxford University Press, 2001), 84.

begin to study this early Christian literature in the language in which it had originally been composed.[9]

It is true that manuscripts and collections of the apostolic fathers did survive (albeit neglected) in western European libraries in Latin translation, and it was from such sources as these that the first fresh attention began to be given to them as part of the *ad fontes* pursuit of the Renaissance era. Yet, before we consider the developments by which they were recovered, it is important to acknowledge that for nearly a half millennium these writings had really played no role at all in the Western Church.

Yet rediscovered they were. In 1498 there reemerged portions of the eventual collection of apostolic fathers in a Latin edition by Jacques Lefèvre d'Étaples (1455–1536), the French Christian humanist and advocate of ecclesiastical reform. Lefèvre, a man who was seeking the purification of European Christianity, wished to draw attention to these early writers as exemplars of a more biblical earnestness and piety; he loved to contrast their fervor with the more labyrinthine sentiments of the medieval scholastics who were still so favored in the late-medieval theological schools.[10]

With the epistles of Ignatius and the Shepherd of Hermas once again in circulation, a debate soon broke out. There were strong differences expressed between Catholic scholastics and advocates of Catholic reform (such as Lefèvre) as to the rightness of appealing to these post-apostolic writings on current questions. Catholic scholastics intensely disliked the suggestion that these early writers, because they were representative of a more pristine age, could be used as a plumb line against which to measure later Catholic thought—and to show its decline. The contemporary of Lefèvre and dean of

[9]The obstacle posed for patristic study in the late medieval period by the dearth of Greek study in the West is helpfully described by S. L. Greenslade in *The English Reformers and the Fathers of the Church* (Oxford: Oxford University Press, 1960), 9-10. On Chrysoloras, s.v. "Chrysoloras, Manuel," in *Encyclopedia of the Renaissance*, ed. Paul F. Grendler (New York: Scribner's Sons, 1999), 1:448-50.

[10]Norman Sykes, *From Sheldon to Secker: Aspects of English Church History, 1660–1768* (Cambridge: Cambridge University Press, 1959), 108; Eugene F. Rice Jr., "The Humanist Idea of Christian Antiquity: Lefèvre d'Etaples and His Circle," in *French Humanism: 1470–1600*, ed. Werner L. Gundersheimer (London: MacMillan, 1969), 165-67; and William P. Haugaard, "Renaissance Patristic Scholarship and Theology in Sixteenth-Century England," *Sixteenth Century Journal* 10, no. 3 (1979): 39.

the faculty of theology at the Sorbonne—Noel Beda (ca. 1470–1537)—wrote that Lefèvre and his kind pretended

> to drink from rivers which flow close to the very source of divine wisdom and not from those rivulets which have degenerated because of their great distance from that source; that is to say, they always have in their hands Origen, Tertullian, Cyprian . . . and others like them, but never scholastics like Peter Lombard, Alexander Hales . . . and so on. Thus do the humanists boast in their own words.[11]

As these writings came once more into view, scholars of the Renaissance and Reformation period discerned that there were no standard texts of these writings and certainly no standard collections of texts. This textual uncertainty was the consequence of the overall neglect of these writings during the previous half millennium.[12] Those who wished to call fresh attention to the significance of these writers thus had very extensive textual criticism to engage in—and this whether the surviving manuscripts were Greek or were Latin translations derived from them. There were spurious writings needing to be set aside as well as genuine writings needing to be identified.

Textual questions of this kind were not sorted out by the pre-Reformation Christian humanists. When Lefèvre provided the epistles of Ignatius and the Shepherd of Hermas in Latin dress to European readers in 1498, he was passing on only what he had unearthed in his expeditions to various monastic libraries that had long held these writings in Latin translation. The age of the Reformation itself drew only minimally on these writers because they were not yet widely recirculated.[13] The sorting out of textual questions relating to them largely awaited the seventeenth century. What would then become of the apostolic fathers in the hands of Protestants?

---

[11]The quotation, from Beda's *Annotationes Natalis Bedae Doctoris Theologii Parisiensis in Jacobum Fabrum Stapulensem libri duo: et in Desiderium Erasmum Roterdamum liber unus* (Paris, 1526), preface, is provided in Rice, *Humanist Idea of Christian Antiquity*, 174.

[12]Grant, "Apostolic Fathers," 27, reports that after AD 1056 Ignatius is the only one of the second-century writers to receive any ongoing attention. Taken collectively, they were ignored. See also Greenslade, *English Reformers*, 9-10.

[13]A. N. S. Lane, *John Calvin*, 41. Henry Chadwick, *Church in Ancient Society*, 66, draws attention to Calvin's suspicion of the authenticity of the letters of Ignatius in the *Institutes of the Christian Religion* (1536 edition), trans. Ford Lewis Battles (Grand Rapids: Eerdmans, 1975), 1.13.29.

FROM LEFÈVRE D'ÉTAPLES TO JAMES USSHER

No name is so closely associated with breakthroughs in the study of the apostolic fathers in the post-Reformation era as that of James Ussher (1581–1656), the Irish Protestant clergyman who eventually became the archbishop of Armagh, Ireland. That his sizeable breakthrough in the study of the apostolic fathers occurred in Ireland and relatively late in the Reformation era was due to three factors, which need to be identified.

First, the extension of the Reformation to Ussher's native Ireland from Tudor England did not gain much momentum until late in the Elizabethan period. So entrenched was Irish Catholicism and so anti-English was Irish sentiment that there was precious little native desire to follow England's lead and embrace the Reformation. Second, the effort to extend Protestantism into Tudor Ireland was met by the concerted resistance of Roman Catholic clergy and controversialists who had not been removed or silenced as they had been in Elizabethan England; these began steady efforts to challenge the advancing Protestantism's claim to stand in any actual continuity with the church of the patristic era. Third, James Ussher—native born, a distinguished graduate of Trinity College, Dublin, and a promising patristics scholar—devoted himself to nineteen years of reading through all available church fathers, whether in Greek or Latin.[14] His motive in doing so was at least in part apologetic; he aimed to prepare himself to marshal the resources of the patristic period in support of the Protestant interest in then-inhospitable Ireland.[15] Some of Ussher's early efforts aimed to demonstrate that the emphases of the Protestant Reformation had been anticipated by a succession of leaders in earlier ages—extending backward to the age of the apostles.[16]

Ussher's scholarly attainments with the writings of some of the apostolic fathers were very considerable. By hard-slogging detective work that took him to various English university and cathedral libraries and involved extensive

---

[14]J. E. L. Oulton, "Ussher's Work as a Patristic Scholar and Church Historian," *Hermathena* 88 (1956): 5.

[15]The context of Ussher's patristic scholarship within Ireland's traditional Catholic setting is masterfully surveyed in Alan Ford's *James Ussher: Theology, History and Politics in Early Modern Ireland* (Oxford: Oxford University Press, 2007), chap. 1.

[16]This first work is identified in brief as *De Successione*. Its full title is *Gravissimae Qvaestionis, De Christianarvm Ecclesiarvm, In Occidentis praesertim partibus, Ab Apostolicis Temporibvs ad nostram usq; aetatem, continuâ successione & statu, Historica Explicatio* (Dublin, 1613).

correspondence with Continental patristics scholars, Ussher eventually resolved a sizeable mystery surrounding the epistles of Ignatius.

Ussher pursued these studies in a context that was highly complex. Not only were scholarly Catholics—both in Ireland and on the Continent—beginning by this time to appeal to writings of the post-apostolic period (as then known) so as to argue that Protestantism stood in a very weak relation to this formative era (arguments we are seeing more of in our own time), there was also an extended and increasingly shrill debate among Protestants as to whether episcopal forms of church government could still be maintained. What was to be made of the evidences of episcopacy found in this literature?

Certainly from the 1570s onward, many Protestants in the Reformed tradition had come to accept it as axiomatic that episcopacy—at least as handed down from the medieval church—was irreconcilable with a Reformed Church polity. The successor to Calvin (d. 1564), Theodore Beza, had occupied this ground; Andrew Melville, the major successor to Scotland's John Knox (d. 1572), had taken the same line.[17] And in England, such Geneva-leaning Protestants as Thomas Cartwright (1535–1603) and Walter Travers (1548–1635) had been taking this same line from the 1570s onward; their sentiments had not been forgotten a half century later.[18]

Ussher was far from being a professional controversialist. Yet he carried out his thorough researches with these contemporary questions very much in mind. As to the letters of Ignatius, he began to work with a Greek edition of twelve alleged Ignatian letters designated as the "Long Recension."[19] Yet, having compared the documents available to him in this Greek edition with a thirteenth-century Latin version that had been in the possession of the former bishop of Lincoln, Robert Grosseteste (1175–1253), Ussher was "set upon the track which ultimately led to the discovery of the genuine Ignatius."[20]

---

[17]Melville's role in the post-Knox era Church of Scotland is explored in both James Kirk, ed., *The Second Book of Discipline* (Edinburgh: Saint Andrew Press, 1980) and the same author's *Patterns of Reform: Continuity and Change in the Reformation Kirk* (Edinburgh: T&T Clark, 1989).

[18]A. F. S. Pearson, *Thomas Cartwright and Elizabethan Puritanism: 1535–1695* (Cambridge: Cambridge University Press, 1925); and S. J. Knox, *Walter Travers: Paragon of Elizabethan Puritanism* (London: Methuen, 1962).

[19]Greenslade, *English Reformers*, 13.

[20]Oulton, "Ussher's Work," 9. Oulton goes on to explain that the other remarkable breakthrough in patristic study attributable to Ussher was his work in settling the wording of the earliest version of the Old Roman Creed, which underlay what came to be known as the Apostles' Creed.

Of twelve alleged letters, Ussher determined that only seven were genuine; and for this work, published in Latin in 1644, he gained international recognition.[21] But with the corpus of Ignatius now defined and the possibility of appealing to spurious letters in support of strange doctrines curtailed, what would Ussher—in his heated context—*do* with his discoveries? Not what one might expect.

In the context of the 1640s in which the parliament of England (and its summoned Westminster Assembly of Divines) were now debating the potential elimination of the episcopal form of church government, Ussher put forward a proposal, drawn from these very second-century Ignatius researches, to the effect that episcopacy as practiced in England should be reduced or modified so as to make every bishop both elected by and accountable to the clergy under him. He wrote,

> Of the many elders, who in common thus ruled the church of Ephesus, there was one president, whom our Saviour in his epistle unto this church (i.e. in *The Revelation*, ed.) in a peculiar manner styleth "the angel of the Church of Ephesus" and (whom) Ignatius in another epistle, written about twelve years after unto the same church, calleth the bishop thereof. Betwixt the bishop and the presbyter of that church, what an harmonious consent there was in the ordering of the church government, Ignatius doth fully declare.[22]

This was not just some cobbled-together halfway measure intended to pacify both the pro-episcopal and anti-episcopal forces of the 1640s. Rather, it was a serious historical argument proposing that monarchial episcopacy such as this had come to exist in both Roman Catholic and early Anglican communions and had developed considerably *beyond* the dimensions of the office, as it could be shown to have existed in the post-apostolic age of Ignatius. Christian antiquity provided no direct sanction for episcopacy *as it had developed.*

Sadly, Ussher's views were not sufficiently compelling to restrain either those who were intent on the utter abolition of episcopacy in the 1640s or

---

[21]Ussher's second-century researches were published as *Polycarpi et Ignatii Epistolae* (Oxford, 1644). It is the judgment of Jean-Louis Quantin, in his "The Fathers in Seventeenth Century Anglican Theology," in *The Reception of the Church Fathers in the West: From the Carolingians to the Maurists*, ed. Irena Backus (Leiden: E. J. Brill, 1997), 2:996, that this work "may be regarded as the masterpiece of seventeenth century Anglican scholarship."

[22]*The Reduction of Episcopacy* (1641) as reprinted in R. Buick Knox, "Archbishop Ussher and English Presbyterianism," *Journal of the Presbyterian Historical Society of England* 13 (1964): 32-35.

those (subsequently) intent on the unmodified restoration of it as the Commonwealth period was ending in 1660. Circulated originally in manuscript form in 1641, *The Reduction of Episcopacy* was formally published in 1656 and reprinted seven times before the century ended.[23] But the fact remains that at this time, the foremost authority in Europe on Ignatius was a stalwart Protestant, and an archbishop of the Church in Ireland. Ussher firmly believed that this writer—rather than obliging seventeenth-century Protestants to hew more closely to a Roman position—showed Protestants something very different. Ignatius pointed the way for them to embrace a system of church leadership and government with far fewer accretions than had come to be hallowed over time. In this matter, Ussher's use of the apostolic fathers of the second century could be called part of a revisionist Protestant program.[24]

FROM USSHER TO LIGHTFOOT

Ussher was not the only Protestant scholar of the seventeenth century working with this literature. There had already been published the important cautionary work on the use of the patristic writers by the French scholar Jean Daillé (1594–1670), *On the Right Use of the Fathers.* Appearing first in the French language in 1631 and in English twenty years later, Daillé had cautioned his readers that to that point in time, the surviving manuscripts (as well as many of the early printed editions) of the church fathers (including those of the late first and early second century) were compounds of the genuine and the spurious and marred by so many interpolations that they could not yet be used to elucidate any particular Christian doctrine.[25] This

[23]Ford, *James Ussher*, 229-30, 298. In 1641, High Episcopal dissatisfaction with Ussher's proposal for a modification of episcopacy was represented in the writings of Henry Hammond (1605–1660). See G. V. Bennett, "Patristic Tradition in Anglican Thought, 1660–1900," *Oecumenica* (1971–1972), 65, 66.

[24]The text of *The Reduction of Episcopacy* is quite widely available. See it, for instance, in R. B. Knox, "Archbishop Ussher and English Presbyterianism," *Journal of the Presbyterian Historical Society of England* 13 (1964): 32-35. It may also be read online on the web pages of the church society: www.churchsociety.org/issues_new/history/ussher/iss_history_ussher_episcopacy.asp. In the larger picture of things, Ussher's approach meant a return to more modest Anglican conceptions of episcopacy such as were set out in the 1560s. See W. D. J. Cargill Thompson, "Anthony Marten and the Elizabethan Debate on Episcopacy," in *Essays in Modern English Church History in Memory of Norman Sykes*, ed. G. V. Bennett and J. D. Walsh (London: A&C Black, 1966), 44-75.

[25]I have consulted the American edition published by the Presbyterian Board of Publication (Philadelphia, 1842).

was the situation in which Ussher had set to work. There had already been published in 1633 the sole genuine epistle of Clement by Patrick Young. The Shepherd of Hermas was made available by 1645.[26] In 1646, the Dutch Protestant scholar Isaac Vossius published six of the seven Ignatian letters, in Greek, from a Florentine manuscript in the possession of the Medici family.[27] All this represented Protestant scholarship.

As the seventeenth century neared an end however, the recovered second-century writers began to fill a new role: that of a bulwark against theological drift in a new era of doctrinal latitudinarianism. As the claims of reason in matters of theology grew in that dawning age of the Enlightenment, there came about a division of opinion among Protestants about the worth of the patristic writings in general. Those influenced by Enlightenment thought, and who therefore rejected the supposition that the most ancient must be the more authoritative, tended to look on these writers as primitive and provincial. Why prefer these, from the hoary past? Under this approach, central doctrines of the faith, such as the doctrine of the Trinity, were not safe when patristic witnesses to the doctrine were discounted.[28] This was a far cry from the stance of Ussher, who had been confident in marshaling this literature as crucial historical evidence.

Now, in reaction to this concessive attitude, there arose a tendency of thought that exalted the writings of the church's post-apostolic period as well as other patristic writings as important anchors against the relativizing of major Christian doctrines. Yet, this emerging "High Church" party, exemplified by the patristic scholar and bishop George Bull (1634–1710), carried this preference for patristic theology to such lengths that they began to evaluate the creedal theology of their own Church of England (summarized in the Thirty-Nine Articles of Religion) by the consensus of the church fathers of the first three centuries.[29] According to such a view, the Anglican *Articles of Religion* could teach *no more than* and nothing *beyond* utterances of the early Fathers. The Protestant (and Anglican) doctrine of justification was seen to be undermined by this evaluative approach. This approach, so

---

[26]Quantin, "Fathers in Seventeenth Century Anglican Theology," 996; and Greenslade, *English Reformers*, 13.

[27]Chadwick, *Church in Ancient Society*, 66.

[28]Bennett, "Patristic Tradition in Anglican Thought," 73, 74; and Sykes, *From Sheldon to Secker*, 65.

[29]Bennett, "Patristic Tradition in Anglican Thought," 75.

largely concerned with the ancient historical precedents for Christian doctrine, lost its hold as the eighteenth century progressed. As the eighteenth century faded, interest in the church fathers was at a low ebb.[30]

The young John Henry Newman (1801–1890), initially exposed to the church fathers through reading the *History of the Church of Christ* (1797–1809) by Joseph Milner, was subsequently influenced by his reading of Ignatius and Justin Martyr.[31] Having done so, he was next caught up, for a time, with the High Church school of writers of the preceding century. Yet his transition from this variety of High Church Anglicanism to something else—which he and friends called *Apostolical*[32]—and finally to Roman Catholicism in 1845 marked, for him, an abandonment of the project of trying to establish that the Church of England most fully approximated the church of the patristic era. And just prior to his reception into the Church of Rome in 1845, Newman embraced a view—not then welcome in Roman eyes—that Christian doctrine had shown clear development over time.[33]

Yet it was not this nettlesome issue raised for Protestantism by Newman and his circle so much as another crisis that stimulated the definitive nineteenth-century Protestant work on the apostolic fathers—the impact of which is still being felt today. I refer to the five-volume critical edition of the apostolic fathers of J. B. Lightfoot (1828–1889), the publication of which extended from 1885 to 1890.[34] That "other" crisis was the emergence in the 1860s of serious skepticism regarding the historical value of the New Testament writings.

From two sources—both British and German—biblical scholarship after 1860 had to reckon with writers who cast doubt on the historical value of the New Testament writings as they have been passed down to us. Some of these wrote at a popular level: Lightfoot was especially aggravated by the production of an English merchant, retired after a career at Bombay. The year was 1874, and the writer W. R. Cassels anonymously published a work, *Supernatural Religion,* which attacked the Gospel miracles and went on to

---

[30]Ibid., 75-76.

[31]John Henry Newman, *Apologia Pro Vita Sua* (1864; repr., London: Longmans Green, 1934), 7, 26, 50.

[32]See the discussion of this terminology in Frank M. Turner, *John Henry Newman: The Challenge to Evangelical Religion* (New Haven, CT: Yale University Press, 2002), 84, 127, 164.

[33]The influence of Newman on Christian thinking about the development of Christian doctrine has been described in chapter 4 above.

[34]J. B. Lightfoot, ed., *The Apostolic Fathers* (New York: MacMillan, 1885–1890).

attack the composition of the biblical canon. He alleged that there was no adequate basis for affirming the Gospels' traditional first-century dates of composition. As a means of elaborating this proposal, the author had claimed that the early Christian historian Eusebius (263–339), had been ominously silent about these historical witnesses (the apostolic fathers), proximate to the alleged time of the writing of the gospels. Thus (argued Cassels) late first- and early second-century writers—granted no real existence in Eusebius's accounts of post-apostolic Christianity—could not be called on in any confirming capacity as to the time of origin of the Gospels. In this book, Cassels was only giving circulation in popular form to skeptical views emanating from German universities, most notably Tübingen.[35]

The strategy of Lightfoot, therefore, was to be that of establishing the status of Ignatius, of Justin Martyr, and Papias as credible early witnesses to the Gospels. This he did commendably. And what he had shown with regard to these early second-century writers he also amply showed with regard to Irenaeus (d. 202), the late second-century bishop of Lyons. Lightfoot was therefore advancing, in a most convincing manner, the use of attestation from external authorities in dating the New Testament documents—a procedure that we now accept as foundational.[36] Claims along these lines, earlier circulated by Lightfoot in a series of articles in the journal *The Contemporary Review*, commencing in 1867, appeared again in fuller form when Lightfoot eventually published his detailed investigations of the apostolic fathers themselves after 1885.

---

[35]I rely here on the excellent account of Geoffrey R. Treloar, *Lightfoot the Historian: The Nature and Role of History in the Life and Thought of J. B. Lightfoot (1828–1889) as Churchman and Scholar* (Tubingen: Mohr Siebeck, 1998), 340-46. Less specialized, but still helpful, is Mark A. Noll, *Between Faith and Criticism: Evangelicals, Scholarship and the Bible in America*, 2nd ed. (Grand Rapids: Baker, 1991), 67-71. The work of the Tubingen "school" is masterfully described in Horton Harris, *The Tübingen School* (Oxford: Oxford University Press, 1975), chaps. 10–12. Lightfoot's work on the apostolic fathers took place simultaneously with the publication of an edition of the apostolic fathers (as they were then known to exist) in the *Ante-Nicene Christian Library*, ed. James L. Donaldson and Alexander Robertson (Edinburgh: T&T Clark, 1867). The story of the production of the Ante-Nicene Library and its eventually being subsumed into the more comprehensive American series, the Ante-Nicene Fathers, edited by Cleveland Cox, is masterfully provided by David F. Wright in "'From a Quarter So Unexpected': Translation of the Early Church Fathers in Victorian Scotland," *Records of the Scottish Church History Society* 30 (2000): 124-69.

[36]Treloar, *Lightfoot the Historian*, 350-52. Intimations of the same approach in employing second-century witnesses can be seen also in B. F. Westcott's *A General Survey of the History of the Canon of the New Testament During the First Four Centuries* (London: Macmillan, 1855).

It was very clear to him that behind the popular skirmish agitated by Cassels stood the Tübingen School; they had worked to discredit the apostolic fathers as reliable witnesses to the time of origin of the Gospels.[37] The net effect for Gospel studies of Lightfoot's second-century researches had been to rehabilitate the apostolic fathers as important witnesses on this vital question.[38]

THE TWENTIETH CENTURY TO THE PRESENT

In a new century, there was continued evidence that the Protestant world was at the forefront of researches into the writings of the apostolic fathers. Kirsopp Lake (1872–1946), who had a distinguished academic career in Leiden and Harvard universities, was writing on the Didache as early as 1905. By 1912–1913, he had prepared for inclusion in the Loeb Classical Library series a still-consulted two-volume edition of the apostolic fathers.[39] By 1950, a new English translation had been prepared by the New Testament scholar E. J. Goodspeed of the University of Chicago.[40] Still further on in the twentieth century, Robert M. Grant of the same university produced a fresh translation of the apostolic fathers in six volumes.[41] Meanwhile, the nineteenth-century labors of Lightfoot have been kept before the Christian world by the scholarly and editorial work of Michael W. Holmes of Bethel University, St. Paul, Minnesota, whose various editions of the apostolic fathers have been appearing since 1989.[42]

DRAWING OUT SOME IMPLICATIONS

Today we live in a time when scholarly interest in the apostolic fathers is proliferating. Since the Second Vatican Council, Catholic scholars have

---

[37]L. W. Barnard, "Bishop Lightfoot and the Apostolic Fathers," *The Church Quarterly Review* 161 (1960): 424.

[38]The impact of this approach is still visible in such recent Protestant works as Charles Hill's *Who Chose the Gospels?* (Oxford: Oxford University Press, 2010), chap. 9.

[39]J. K. Elliot, s.v. "Kirsopp Lake," in *Dictionary of Major Bible Interpreters*, 2nd ed., ed. Donald McKim (Downers Grove, IL: InterVarsity Press, 2007), 636-40. That Lake identified himself with modernist expressions of Christianity is acknowledged. The Lake volumes in the Loeb Classical Library were eventually superseded by two volumes prepared by Bart Ehrman (2003, 2005).

[40]E. J. Goodspeed, ed. and trans., *The Apostolic Fathers* (Chicago: University of Chicago Press, 1950).

[41]Robert M. Grant, *The Apostolic Fathers*, 6 vols. (New York: Thomas Nelson, 1964-68).

[42]Holmes's various editions include *The Apostolic Fathers*, 2nd ed. (Grand Rapids: Baker, 1989); *The Apostolic Fathers: Greek Texts and English Translations* (Grand Rapids: Baker, 1992), further revised in 1999; and *The Apostolic Fathers in English*, 3rd ed. (Grand Rapids: Baker, 2006).

shown renewed interest in this second-century literature, reflected in numerous publications.[43] This heightened interest within Catholicism illustrates a striking reversal of the relative disinterest in the material shown in the Renaissance era in which Lefèvre d'Étaples did his spadework. Then, it was largely the advocates of reform, rather than Roman Catholic academia, which found this subject matter interesting. Today, there are very large areas of consensus in dating and interpreting this early Christian literature.

As for the treatment of this literature by Protestants in the post-Reformation era, it is important for us to see the emergence of a pattern especially in the period 1600 to 1960—that is, as Protestants immersed themselves intensively in early Christian studies (to the point of leading that inquiry) the church at large (Catholic as well as Protestant) was enriched and stabilized. It was not the case any more in 1644 (when Ussher published his second-century researches) than in 1885 (when Lightfoot began to publish his in book form) that this was a field on which Protestant players did not belong because the Roman or the Eastern Churches had exercised some preemptive claim to ownership.

Sadly, these are lessons that have largely eluded writers since the 1980s, to whom I referred in opening this chapter. As one reads the exaggerated claims of what a reading of the apostolic fathers provoked them to think and to do, one could be forgiven for supposing them to have believed that in consulting the apostolic fathers, they had stepped on a kind of terra incognita, where not only evangelical Protestants but Protestants of all kinds had never before dared to tread. The ironic aspect of this is that they were almost certainly dependent for their reading on the editions of the apostolic fathers prepared by Protestant scholars Lightfoot, Donaldson and Robertson, Lake, Grant, or Holmes in reaching their extravagant conclusion that in this literature they had found a kind of "holy grail."

At the same time, we should admit that their seeming intoxication with this early Christian literature, when first introduced to it, tells us something about the neglect of these ancient writers in the churches and classrooms of evangelical Protestantism in much of the twentieth century. It tells us equally something about the cast of mind of many late twentieth-century and early

---

[43]So, for example, Simon Tugwell, *Apostolic Fathers* (New York: Continuum, 1989) and Clayton N. Jeffords, *Reading the Apostolic Fathers: An Introduction* (Peabody, MA: Hendrickson, 1996).

twenty-first-century evangelicals: too many are of a romantic cast of mind that lends itself easily to the embracing of *imagined* pasts—imagined pasts that are somehow preferable to our own times and places. Our own age is certainly not the only age in which evangelical Christianity has been afflicted in this way. Does not this romanticism lie at the root of many of what we correctly call "Restorationist" movements? These are movements that have tried, in different centuries, to recapture the ethos of the Acts of the Apostles or the church before the church-state alliances that followed Constantine's reign, or the church of the Gothic cathedrals or the churches of the Reformation or Puritan age. The cure for overheated romanticism among evangelical Christians is not ignorance of the past but critical engagement with it, and that is what the likes of Ussher and Lightfoot model for us. In the hands of such pioneering Protestants, these early Christian writers speak to us in constructive voice.

QUESTIONS FOR DISCUSSION

1. In recent decades, a number of Christians have, upon reading the apostolic fathers of the second century, treated them like the long-lost "holy grail" and concluded that they had stumbled on material that was all but forgotten. What was wrongheaded about these assumptions?
2. What was one major factor that led to the writings of the apostolic fathers dropping out of sight for so many centuries of Christian history?
3. The pioneers in the recovery of the apostolic fathers, beginning just over five hundred years ago, had certain beneficial uses in mind as they released them to the reading public. What were some of those beneficial uses?
4. What important distinction is worth preserving between the apostles themselves and these leaders and writers of the generation that followed them?

7

Eighteenth-Century Evangelicals and the Frequency of the Lord's Supper

TWO PREVIOUS CHAPTERS HAVE demonstrated that—contrary to popular notions of today—Protestant Christians (evangelicals among them) were highly conversant with the literature of early Christianity. We can see this same principle illustrated yet again in this examination of the labors of two eighteenth-century Protestant pastors.

THE SITUATION SINCE 1930

Across the last century, a growing number of evangelical Protestants came to accept what they had not previously accepted: that the Lord's Supper is the central act of Christian worship.[1] Such an assertion entails more than an affirmation that the Lord's Supper should be frequently observed; it in fact holds this rite to be so indispensable that it must be central in the service. This conviction spread under a number of influences, the chief of which was the

[1]See evidence of the growth of this opinion, for instance, in Robert Rayburn, *O Come Let Us Worship* (Grand Rapids: Baker, 1980), 255, 256; and Leonard J. Vander Zee, *Christ, Baptism and the Lord's Supper: Recovering the Evangelical Sacraments for Evangelical Worship* (Downers Grove, IL: InterVarsity Press, 2004), 162, 163.

Oxford or Tractarian movement. This early nineteenth-century movement influenced first Anglicans, then Presbyterians, Methodists, and Baptists in the direction of heightened frequency of administration of the Supper and the recovery of pre-Reformation ideas about worship and ministry.[2]

Yet, two hundred years ago, even Anglicans—known today for their weekly observance of Holy Communion—would have maintained this rite between two or four times annually. David Bebbington has argued in his *Holiness in Nineteenth Century England* that the Oxford movement had a more pervasive influence in the English-speaking world in the reign of Queen Elizabeth II (of our time) than it did in the reign of Victoria.[3] The relaying of these impulses to wider Protestantism was accomplished nowhere as effectively as through the writings of W. D. Maxwell.[4]

It is important to grant that this renewed emphasis has also come in the wake of nineteenth-century Restorationist Christianity. Rooted in the small Glasite-Sandemanian movement of eighteenth-century Scotland and continuing into the Churches of Christ and the Plymouth Brethren movement, this stream also championed the idea that the Lord's Supper—if not the *central* act of Christian worship—was at least an essential part, such that it ought to be a weekly observance.[5]

---

[2]The young Oxford movement's plea for frequent Communion was the thrust of "Tract 26: Bishop Beveridge on the Necessity and Advantage of Frequent Communion," in *Tracts for the Times*, vol. 1, *1833–1834* (London: Rivingtons, 1834). The best short history of this movement is that of S. L. Ollard, *A Short History of the Oxford Movement* (1915; repr., London: Faith Press, 1963). For the repercussions of this movement beyond England, see, for example, the evidence of this in nineteenth-century Scotland in J. R. Fleming, *The Church in Scotland, 1843–1874* (Edinburgh: T&T Clark, 1927), 116-23; A. L. Drummond and James Bulloch, "Changing Worship," chap. 7 in *The Church in Victorian Scotland, 1843–1874* (Edinburgh: St. Andrew Press, 1975); and J. M. Barkley, "The Renaissance of Public Worship in the Church of Scotland 1865–1905," in *Renaissance and Renewal in Christian History*, ed. Derek Baker, vol. 14, *Studies in Church History* (Oxford: Blackwell, 1977), 339-50. The reach of this movement into the twentieth century is explored in Stewart J. Brown and Peter B. Nockles, eds., *The Oxford Movement: Europe and the Wider World* (Cambridge: Cambridge University Press, 2012).

[3]David Bebbington, *Holiness in Nineteenth-Century England* (Carlisle, UK: Paternoster, 2000), 28.

[4]W. D. Maxwell, *An Outline of Christian Worship* (Oxford: Oxford University Press, 1936); and Maxwell, *Concerning Worship* (Oxford: Oxford University Press, 1948). Maxwell (1901–1971), Canadian by birth, received his theological education in Scotland and served churches there before becoming a theological professor in South Africa. See D. H. Murray, "Maxwell, W. D.," in *Dictionary of Scottish Church History and Theology*, ed. Nigel M. de. S. Cameron (Downers Grove, IL: InterVarsity Press, 1993), 554-55.

[5]John Glas (1695–1773) was ordained as a Church of Scotland minister in 1719 and proceeded into Independency in 1730. While he had upheld a monthly practice of Communion as a Presbyterian (a high frequency given the "status quo" in that time), he introduced weekly Communion in the

The aim of this chapter is to show that responsible evangelical theologians of the eighteenth century had begun to review the question of the frequency of observance of the Lord's Supper quite in advance of these two stimuli, for quite distinct reasons, and that they reached distinct conclusions worthy of our current consideration.

AMBITIOUS EARLY REFORMATION PRACTICE GIVES WAY TO SEASONAL OBSERVANCE

In both Reformation Europe and Reformation Scotland, the expectation was that each believer would participate in the Lord's Supper between four and twelve times per year.[6] But this standard was hard to achieve both because of the initial shortage of pastors (only a fraction of pre-Reformation priests and monks had entered the ministry of the Reformed churches) and because of the low expectations regarding the holy meal that rank-and-file Protestants (all former Roman Catholics) brought with them in the first generation after the Reformation.[7] It was hard to explain to such novice Protestants that their minimalist expectation of participating only once annually in Communion (though Masses, which they mostly observed, had been celebrated at least weekly) suggested some lack of spiritual vitality on their part.[8]

1730s. Robert Sandeman (1718–1771) became Glas's son-in-law and transmitted his ideas into England and America. See entries for each in Cameron, *Dictionary of Scottish Church*. For the early roots of the Churches of Christ movement, see David M. Thompson, *Let Sects and Parties Fall* (London: Berean Press, 1980), chap. 1.

[6]James K. Cameron, ed., *The First Book of Discipline* (1560) (Edinburgh: St. Andrew Press, 1972), ninth head, 183. The book of service forms produced by John Knox, while still at Geneva (1556), and formally adopted by the Church of Scotland in 1564 assumed a cycle of monthly Lord's Suppers. See *The Liturgy of John Knox* (Glasgow: The University Press, 1886), 138. The wider practice of the European Reformed churches in mid-sixteenth century is admirably surveyed in W. D. Maxwell, ed., *John Knox's Genevan Service Book* (Edinburgh: Oliver and Boyd, 1931), appendix E.

[7]The acuteness of the ministerial shortage, lasting decades after 1560, is highlighted in George B. Burnet, *The Holy Communion in the Reformed Church of Scotland 1560–1960* (Edinburgh: Oliver and Boyd, 1960), 14. The ways in which seventeenth-century Presbyterians continued to fall short of the expectations of their Reformation regarding the Lord's Supper are helpfully detailed by Gordon Donaldson's chapter "From Covenant to Revolution," in *Studies in the History of Worship in Scotland*, ed. Duncan Forrester and Douglas Murray (Edinburgh: T&T Clark, 1984), 55, 59.

[8]A striking example of the laxity that confronted the Reformers in the matter of the Lord's Supper is supplied by the recent biography of John Knox by Jane Dawson. Dawson reports that as John Knox commenced his Edinburgh ministry, only about one in five adult citizens of the city participated in the Communion services. Jane Dawson, *John Knox* (New Haven, CT: Yale University Press, 2015), 223.

A further complication was that pre-Reformation Catholicism had often linked this prevailing infrequent participation in Communion with seasonal festivals and pageantry such as the feast of Corpus Christi and especially of Easter. These festivals had served to glamorize the rite by associating it with pageantry. The multigenerational project of working to uproot and displace a lingering Catholic mythology surrounding the administration of the Lord's Supper entailed seventeenth-century Presbyterians in Scotland and North Ireland taking over the Catholic practice of such seasonal Communion festivals and turning them into large-scale public events involving gospel preaching and administration of the Supper.[9] This interesting adaptation carried with it certain unforeseen ripple effects, among which were these:

- Communion festivals tied to particular seasons required multiple preachers drawn from a wide region for a long weekend. The staging of a Communion festival in one place thus meant that church services (and the availability of the Lord's Supper) in *other* places took a back seat. Peter was robbed to pay Paul, as we would say.
- Communion seasons promoted on this scale could not be staged even the four times yearly mandated in light of distances traveled, personnel required, and the expectation that communicants be free from a Thursday through a Monday.
- By the early 1700s, there was a growing sense of unease over the negative effects of these practices. While Communion festivals had "morphed" into evangelistic events, they had, for the two reasons just named, made the Lord's Supper less accessible as an ordinary means of grace. Communion festivals were, by definition, only periodic and seasonal. And against this, protests began in earnest. We read that already by 1708 at Glasgow, the regional synod (a regional aggregate of presbyteries) commended to its churches a somewhat more energetic practice of four times yearly Communion. This commendation was renewed in 1748.

---

[9]This adaptation of Reformation principle regarding the Supper to long-established Scottish Catholic custom is detailed by Leigh Eric Schmidt's *Holy Fairs: Scotland and the Making of American Revivalism*, 2nd ed. (Grand Rapids: Eerdmans, 2001), chap. 1. An important alteration introduced with these Protestant festivals was the change of season (usually summer or autumn) so that there would be clear differentiation between the old and the new festivals.

TWO WHO PROTESTED AGAINST THE PREVAILING INFREQUENCY

John Erskine (1721–1803). John Erskine was a well-born Edinburgh native who had been encouraged by his family to prepare for a career in law, a discipline of which his father was a professor at Edinburgh University. Nevertheless, young Erskine was redirected toward theological studies and the Christian ministry. After theological studies in Edinburgh University, where he had earlier pursued studies in law, Erskine entered the pastoral ministry in 1743 at Kirkintilloch, at that time some ten miles to the east of Glasgow. This placed him in the vicinity of the earliest Scottish venues in which George Whitefield had, in the year previous, preached in conjunction with outdoor Communion festivals. Erskine made it his business to defend the Anglican evangelist's reputation against some criticisms that were leveled.[10]

In that same decade, however, and in a manner unrelated to Whitefield's activity, there began to be a fresh attempt (just as in 1708) to encourage congregations of the Church of Scotland to celebrate more frequent Communions. Kirkintilloch was within the Synod of Glasgow and Ayr, and in 1748 that body went on record as urging its churches to aim at recovering the Reformation-era standard of Communion four times yearly, in the face of lackadaisical practice that had seen frequency decline to once or twice per year. Young Erskine went into print in 1749 to add such arguments as he could muster in support of this stance.

Especially of note is the fact that this treatise, *Dissertation on Frequent Communicating*, was composed in his twenty-seventh year, the fifth year of his pastoral ministry at Kirkintilloch, and at what was by the standards of that time an inconvenient distance from theological libraries at Glasgow or Edinburgh.[11] In the treatise of seventy pages are displayed the considerable theological skills that would eventually secure for him the doctor of divinity degree from Glasgow University in 1766.[12]

---

[10]Henry Moncreiff-Wellwood, *Account of the Life and Writings of John Erskine* (Edinburgh: Archibald Constable, 1818), 114; and Jonathan Yeager, *Enlightened Evangelicalism: The Life and Thought of John Erskine* (New York: Oxford University Press, 2011), 35-36.

[11]We cannot rule out that Erskine went, at intervals, to draw on the theological holdings of Glasgow or Edinburgh Universities.

[12]N. R. Needham, "John Erskine," in Cameron, *Scottish Dictionary of Church*, 300-301. The doctorate was conferred in the aftermath of the publication, in two volumes, of Erskine's *Theological Dissertations* (London: Edward and Charles Dilly, 1765) in the year preceding.

Erskine began by addressing two important preliminary issues related to the frequency of Communion. He insisted that (1) the motivation behind the determination to see Communion frequency increased to four times annually was wholesome and commendable, and (2) there was no denying that the means designated for securing more frequent observance (simpler, less-extended weekends, not requiring extra visiting preachers, and with all congregations observing on the same Sundays) were proper and unexceptionable.[13] With these fundamentals in place, he posed the searching question: "And are there any whose faith is so lively and vigorous, that they seldom need the help of this ordinance to strengthen and increase it?"[14]

But he knew better than to leave matters there, at the level of reckoning up of practical benefits; he understood that his case would be made or broken by his supplying biblical and theological reasoning in support of Communion frequency, and to that he turned next.

The New Testament evidence. Like a good number of evangelical Christians in the eighteenth century, Erskine took the view that the church in the apostolic and post-apostolic age had enjoyed the Lord's Supper at least weekly. He believed this to be supported by the "as often" language of 1 Corinthians 11:26 (ESV) and still more certainly by Acts 2:42, 46 (where he took the "breaking of bread" language to be an unambiguous reference to the Supper). While acknowledging that we have no apostolic command to uphold weekly observance, he reminded his readers that we have not either any command from the apostles regarding the alteration of our day of rest from the seventh to the first day.[15] He showed himself familiar with the rejoinder of those like Daniel Whitby (a standard commentator of that era) that the "breaking of bread" language of the New Testament has a much wider usage than references to the Lord's Supper;[16] however, he believed that the scope or context of the passages he cited required this

[13]John Erskine, "Dissertation on Frequent Communicating," in *Theological Dissertations*, 2:244.
[14]Ibid., 248.
[15]Ibid., 256-57, 265.
[16]Whitby's well-founded caution about the range of occurrences of NT "breaking of bread language" came in his commentary on Acts 2:42; mysteriously, he took the opposite view when treating the same phrase in his comment on Acts 20:7. His *Critical Commentary and Paraphrases on the New Testament* (1710) has been accessed through the expanded, multiauthor *Critical Commentary and Paraphrases on the Old and New Testaments and Apocrypha* (New York: Wiley and Putnam, 1845), 4:430, 487.

meaning. He also found strong New Testament support for weekly Communion in Acts 20:7, 11.[17]

From this New Testament material, he passed naturally to the period of the church fathers and showed by appeals to Ignatius, Justin Martyr, Tertullian, Cyprian, Jerome, and Augustine that frequent and even weekly Communion was widespread in the second- through fourth-century church.[18] In order to undergird this historical-theological point, he then showed how such Protestant authorities as Calvin, Buddaeus, and Waterland had cited these same Fathers in their own descriptions of the early church's practice of frequent Communion.

Seeds of decline. Yet, having done so, Erskine needed to deal with the evident fact that this frequency of observance in the early Christian centuries had disappeared.[19] Where did he affix the blame for this decline? Erskine proposed that it was the official toleration granted under Constantine (AD 313), which opened the way for the eventual adoption of Christianity as the religion of the Roman Empire:

> The most probable cause I can assign for this, is, that till then the religion of Christ being persecuted, few professed it who had not felt the power of it on their hearts. But soon after, Christianity became the established religion of the Roman empire, a greater number of hypocrites, from views of worldly interest, intermingled themselves with the true disciples of Christ. And in a century or two more, this little leaven leavened the whole lump. . . . Such nominal Christians could have no just sense of the use and benefits of the Lord's Supper and the obligation to frequent it. . . . Their example would soon be followed by lukewarm Christians who had fallen from their first love.[20]

Erskine is asserting more here than that the imperial toleration and eventual recognition of the early church contributed to a decline in frequency

[17]Appeals to this passage in favor of weekly observance suppose that the "breaking of bread" (which itself may indicate only a common meal) was a Lord's Supper and that this constituted the central purpose of this assembly. Given the range of usage of this terminology across the NT, it is not possible to be dogmatic in upholding the interpretation that Erskine favored. That second-century writers understood these passages in such a sense was evident to Erskine, and this may have colored his interpretation of this NT language.

[18]Erskine, "Dissertation on Frequent Communicating," 258. His access to these church fathers in Greek editions while a pastor in a country town implies either an impressive private library or regular visits to Glasgow University.

[19]Ibid., 266.

[20]Ibid., 267.

of Communion; it is that this toleration and eventual recognition contributed to a decay of piety, and the decay of piety showed itself in indifference to the Holy Meal. He cited conciliar decisions from Elibris (Spain) in AD 324 that forbade monetary contributions to the church from those who declined to participate in the Supper. Another council, held at Antioch in 341, agreed that those who came to services only to hear the Scripture read and then departed before the administration of the Supper were to be "cast out of the church, till such time as they gave public proof of their repentance." He noted that this problem only intensified over time; by late fourth century Chrysostom had lamented that at the administration of the Holy Meal "we stand in vain at the altar and none care to receive." The Council of Toledo in 400 had needed to depose clergy who absented themselves from "daily prayers and communion."[21]

Thus far, Erskine had sketched a trajectory depicting a weekly administration of the Lord's Supper from apostolic times to the year 450, yet with a steadily diminishing regular participation of the bulk of professed Christians. In reliance on the early Christian historian Socrates (b. AD 380), he took the view that the first church to abandon this weekly standard was Rome, followed by Alexandria. By the year 506, he found that in the West the stated expectation for a professed Christian's participation in the Lord's Supper had been lowered to three times per year. For a further two centuries the principle of weekly Communion was upheld in the churches of the East. The process of decline had gone on, almost unchecked, so that by the time of the Council of Trent (1545–1563), the Church of Rome had stipulated that once-annual participation in the Supper was sufficient.[22]

Reformation seeds of recovery. Erskine took special pains in demonstrating that the Reformers and Puritans, while determined to distance themselves from the errors of the Roman Mass, were united in zeal to far surpass the actual frequency of participation insisted on by Rome. Rome, despite its many Eucharistic services (offered even on behalf of the dead) still in Erskine's day upheld the minimalist expectation that once-annual participation was sufficient.

---

[21]Ibid., 268. Such a policy indicates the existence of a widely divergent dual policy, with expectations on the clergy very lofty in comparison with those laid on ordinary believers.

[22]Ibid., 271.

Situated in the west of Scotland, Erskine lamented that he did not have at his fingertips all the information about Europe's Protestant churches that he desired. He had entered into correspondence with European pastors to try to fill gaps in his understanding. On this basis, he could tell his readers that the Bohemian Brethren and the French Reformed churches were insisting on four celebrations of the Supper per year and the Church of England three. Lutherans he understood to be still maintaining a weekly Lord's Supper. Erskine knew of Puritans in Old and New England upholding the practice of the Lord's Supper on the first Sunday of each month, or eight times per year.[23] It was his understanding that Calvin, who personally had preferred the early church practice of weekly Communion, had settled for a monthly administration, as had the English congregation at Geneva led by John Knox during the persecuting reign of Queen Mary Tudor.[24]

Now having reached the career and example of Knox, Erskine had his opportunity to detail the expectations regarding administration of the Supper, set out at the parliamentary legal enactment of the Scottish Reformation in 1560. The *First Book of Discipline* (1560) had set out the expectation that each congregation would celebrate the Supper four times annually.[25] This policy had been modified only slightly, two years later. Given the shortage of ministers it was agreed that rural congregations might have the Supper twice annually and that those in towns would be expected to maintain quarterly administration.[26] But the combination of shortage of ministers, political turmoil pitting the young King James VI against the General Assembly, and the long-established medieval pattern of neglect of regular participation meant that these Reformation expectations were as often honored in the breach as in the observance. The whole question needed to be revisited in 1638 and 1641.[27]

As to why, even in the second half of that century, the problem of infrequent Communion seemed so intractable, Erskine pinpointed issues already mentioned in passing. First was political and religious turmoil with the Stuart monarchy that, both before and after the Commonwealth period

[23]Ibid., 273-74.
[24]*Liturgy of John Knox*, 138.
[25]Cameron, *First Book of Discipline*, 183.
[26]Erskine, "Dissertation on Frequent Communicating," 278.
[27]Ibid., 280.

(when there was no monarch), meddled too much in the government and liturgy of the Scottish Church and that polarized churches and ministers by these efforts.[28] Second was the practice (alluded to in our introduction above) adopted by pastors who sought to capitalize on the evangelistic possibilities of regional Communion festivals, stretching from a Thursday through a Monday and involving as many as ten preachers. Whatever these festivals achieved in exposing vast crowds to the preaching of the gospel and admitting many hundreds in attendance to participation in the Lord's Supper came at the expense of other nearby congregations that lost their preachers and people to these mass rallies. Whatever these Communion festivals were, they were not an effective method of instilling stated, frequent congregational Communions, community by community. Erskine noted that the General Assembly of 1701, surveying the ongoing popularity of these festivals, recommended that congregations and pastors give higher priority to the administration of the Supper "in their bounds."[29] He concluded his historical survey by pressing the question:

> Are our times better than the Reformation and covenanting periods, when our church approached much nearer to the primitive simplicity in dispensing the Supper of the Lord? Has our church gained anything, has practical religion been increased by the change of the old for our present way? Does it not deserve inquiry, if our neglect of frequently communicating be not one cause why "the love of many has waxed cold"?[30]

Answers to objections. Yet Erskine could not leave his subject without dealing with objections that his support for more frequent Communion would have provoked. One objection, which will strike us as rather from the blue, insisted that Christian believers in primitive times had lived at a higher plane and could benefit from frequent participation in the Supper without the more extensive preparations that had grown customary of late. Erskine turned this aside by insisting that this argument failed to reckon with how more-frequent Communion could elevate rank-and-file Christians of modern times.[31]

---

[28]Ibid., 282.
[29]Ibid., 284. This stance was reiterated in 1712 and 1724.
[30]Ibid., 287.
[31]Ibid.

A second argued that as the Jewish Passover was observed but once a year, the Lord's Supper might be administered appropriately on that same plan. In reply, Erskine (relying on the late Puritan Stephen Charnock) maintained that Passover did not stand so solitarily as this objection maintained, inasmuch as the Jewish sacrificial system was ongoing—weekly, monthly, and annually—and thus, the Passover as an offering of sacrifice was not utterly solitary in the cycle of the Jewish calendar.[32]

A third argument insisted that too-frequent participation in the Supper lessened its solemnity, whereas participation at long intervals preserved this. Erskine responded by warning against trying to be wiser than God: if it was God's will that we participate frequently, then the question of hypothetical ill effects was his to deal with. Other means of grace such as prayer and hearing the Word did not suffer from frequent use; why suggest this of the Supper?[33]

Fourth, Erskine needed to respond to the insistence that more-frequent Communion—even if it be quarterly—represented a clear innovation. This he turned aside with the reminder that the eighteenth-century practice fell below that recommended at the Reformation, and before it in the primitive church.[34]

Fifth, he needed to address the insistence that the Christian population of Scotland did not favor the recommended frequency. This objection, which may have been very well founded, he turned aside with a proper insistence that the church is to decide such matters on biblical grounds, not on the basis of popular sentiment. And that great Christian pastors and writers in previous days had argued for frequent participation in the Supper, he demonstrated by providing details regarding the biblical arguments of John Calvin, Richard Baxter, and his contemporaries John Willison and Jonathan Edwards.[35]

There was, last of all, the veiled threat that the General Assembly's policy of proposing not less than quarterly Communions might drive people out of the Church of Scotland and into the breakaway Secession movement

[32]Ibid., 288.

[33]Ibid., 291-92.

[34]Ibid., 295.

[35]Ibid., 296-301. John Willison (1680–1750), long the minister of Brechin and Dundee South, had himself been an advocate of more frequent Communion in his *Sacramental Directory* (1716) and *Sacramental Companion* (1720). His significance has been highlighted in very recent times by Kimberly Bracken Long, *The Eucharistic Theology of the American Holy Fairs* (Louisville, KY: Westminster John Knox, 2011), chap. 6.

(begun in 1733), where the administration of the Supper was also still following the festival pattern. To this, Erskine calmly replied that as the reason for the Secession two decades earlier had nothing to do with Communion practice, and as its leaders were very reasonable people who could not find fault with the Church of Scotland's determination to address this problem, this threat was exaggerated.[36]

John Mitchell Mason (1770–1829). Our second eighteenth-century evangelical to press the case for more frequent Communion was a full generation younger than our first, and clearly in his debt. John Mitchell Mason was born in New York City and was the son of a prominent immigrant Presbyterian minister (also named John Mason). Educated in his native city's Columbia College (now University) as well as Edinburgh University, he was from 1793 successor to his father as pastor of the city's Associate Reformed Presbyterian congregation.[37] It is clear from correspondence between father and son, conducted while young John matriculated at Edinburgh, that John Erskine, by then a minister of Old Greyfriars Church, very near the university, was familiar to them.[38]

Though John M. Mason (like his late father) served a congregation of the Associate Reformed Presbyterian Church (the American denomination descended from a division in the Scottish Church in 1733), it is evident that in the matter of the administration of the Lord's Supper, there was little or no distinction between the mother church and the congregations that had stood apart from her since 1733. The frequency of Communion was, in neither, in excess of once or twice annually. And the crossing of the Atlantic by the various branches of the Scottish Presbyterian family had, if anything, exacerbated this infrequency due to the ongoing shortage of ministers. It was in his first decade of pastoral ministry at New York and while he was not yet thirty years old that Mason took up his pen to write *Letters on Frequent Communion*.[39]

---

[36]Erskine, "Dissertation on Frequent Communicating," 302.

[37]The outlines of Mason's *Life* are provided in Philip W. Butin, "John Mitchell Mason," in *Dictionary of the Presbyterian and Reformed Tradition in America*, ed. D. G. Hart (1999; repr., Phillipsburg, NJ: P&R, 2005), 150; Jacob Van Vechten, *Memoirs of John M. Mason* (New York: Carter, 1856); and Cornelius van Santvoord, "John Mitchell Mason," *The Presbyterian Review* 3, no. 10 (1882): 264-77.

[38]Van Vechten, *Memoirs of John M. Mason*, 47-48.

[39]The publication of 1798 was issued by T. & J. Swords, Pearl Street, New York. An Edinburgh

Mason's approach to the question of Communion frequency could be described as pastoral and practical. He maintained that Holy Communion as practiced (especially) in the Associate Reformed Presbyterian Churches was embraced by the people with neither "that frequency nor simplicity which were the delight and ornament of the primitive churches." He described a current Communion practice of "once in twelve months or once in six"; moreover, this practice was also "loaded with encumbrances which lack scriptural warrant."[40] He was focusing, in late eighteenth-century New York, on the identical practices that had motivated Erskine to write almost half a century before. Mason would take the two issues in turn.

The New Testament evidence. Mason was very quick to admit that Jesus himself had left no explicit indication in the Gospels of the frequency with which he intended his followers to remember him in the Lord's Supper. "Something is, no doubt, to be left to Christian prudence."[41] This restraint on Jesus' part he took to be the basis for a reasonable flexibility on the church's part. "Incidental hindrances" could, in this way, be honestly accommodated.

Yet with this admission in place, Mason went on to lament the fact that the Presbyterian churches of his time—far from simply dealing with the question of frequency in light of Jesus' reserve—had fallen into carelessness. He attributed to many an attitude that supposed "whether we communicate twice in a year, or once; or only every other year is . . . indifferent." At root, this casual attitude toward the frequency of the Supper sidestepped the expectation of *frequent* Communion services. The apostle Paul had instructed "as often" as you eat and drink (1 Cor 11:26 ESV).[42] Pressing the issue further, he asked, "And does not the tenor of this command teach thee, that the *frequency* of thy sacramental commemorations of him will be in proportion to the ardor of thy love? Alas, brethren, if this is a criterion of love to our Lord, the pretentions of most of us are low indeed."[43]

edition, published by J. Ritchie, was issued in the same year. I have consulted the work as it is printed in Ebenezer Mason, ed., *Complete Works of John M. Mason, D.D.*, vol. 1 (New York: Baker and Scribner, 1849).

[40]Mason, *Letters on Frequent Communion*, in *Complete Works*, 1:377.

[41]Ibid., 379.

[42]Ibid., 380.

[43]Ibid., 383.

Objections needing answers. Having acknowledged, initially, the fact that Jesus himself left us with no firm policy on frequency of Communion and then personally advocated a heightened frequency of administration as an expression of love to him, Mason first faced an objection that represents his proposal as an unwarranted innovation. In response, he will only allow that if innovation is found in his argument, it is of a kind that challenges *recent* rather than *ancient* custom. In sum, Mason argues that the infant church practiced a frequent Communion that was lost only because of the advance of the carnality that installed itself in the church after Rome's decree of toleration of Christianity in AD 313.[44]

He found evidence of this frequency of observance in New Testament Scriptures now familiar to us. They are proofs, still being cited: Acts 20:7, 11, where "breaking bread" is named as a purpose of the gathered assembly in which Paul preached until nearly midnight. He found similar support in 1 Corinthians 11:20; there also he claimed to find that participation in the Communion meal was central to the assembling of the believers of that city.[45] Explicitly following earlier author Erskine, he went on to claim that the weekly Communion associated with Paul and his churches continued on as the practice of the early churches for "above two centuries" and as universal practice.[46] Declension from this uniformity was observable "towards the close of the fourth century." By AD 506 he found that the expectation of the early church had been lowered; believers were by then expected to participate in the Lord's Supper at "Christmas, Easter, and Whitsunday." By the time of the Fourth Lateran Council of AD 1215, this expectation had been lowered to a mere once-annual participation in the Supper.[47]

It was this shrunken conception of participation in the Lord's Supper that had confronted the Reformers of the sixteenth century. John Calvin had

---

[44]Ibid., 389.

[45]Ibid., 400, 402. This interpretation of the signification of the verb "*sunerchomai*," still remarkably widespread in the Christian world, does not properly take into account that even in 1 Corinthians 11–14, the verb and its cognates need imply no more than an assembling for religious purposes. Thus, for example, at 1 Corinthians 14:26 the verb is used to introduce the idea of a highly participatory church service that will include numerous elements. There is no mention of the Lord's Supper occurring in the church service Paul describes there.

[46]Ibid., 403.

[47]Ibid., 405-6.

denounced such a practice as "a contrivance of the devil."[48] Mason was aware that Calvin's own preference would have been to institute a weekly observance of the Supper; he also found that Calvin's contemporary, the Lutheran theologian Martin Chemnitz, was of the same mind.[49] He reported that the Belgic Confession of the Reformed churches of the Netherlands had stipulated a six-times-yearly cycle for the Supper, while the Reformed churches of France had set a minimum number of observances at four. Scotland's own Reformed Church had set a similar standard at the enactment of her Reformation in 1560.[50] As for the seventeenth century, he reported that a monthly Communion had been the practice of many of the ministers who participated in the sessions of the Westminster Assembly (1643–1649).[51] With all this in place, Mason could confidently plead that "the facts will convince every honest inquirer that frequent communion is not an innovation. . . . Let us return to the old way in which the first confessors of the cross have walked before us."[52]

Mason knew that he must also deal with the protest that the consequence of very frequent participation in the Lord's Supper would "deaden affection, destroy solemnity, banish reverence and thus be injurious." He was utterly unimpressed by such an objection inasmuch as he judged it to be the sentiment *not* of the person who was truly seeking to advance reverence for God but "of the formalist, who goes to the communion table only once or twice a year to save appearances, or to quiet conscience. . . . That such (an opinion) should ever be proposed by a living Christian is truly astonishing."[53]

To this seemingly perennial line of reasoning, Mason countered with another question: "Do *other* duties grow contemptible by their frequency? Is the Sabbath vile because of its weekly return? The Divine Scriptures, family religion, secret prayer?" No. Believers, entrusted with the Lord's Supper for their spiritual nourishment, "should not refuse, and justify their refusal by

---

[48]John Calvin, *Institutes of the Christian Religion* (1536 edition), trans. Ford Lewis Battles (Grand Rapids: Eerdmans, 1975), 4.17.46, quoted in Mason, *Letters on Frequent Communion*, 407.

[49]Mason, *Letters on Frequent Communion*, 408.

[50]Ibid., 410. Mason here cites the Scottish church's First Book of Discipline, art. 13. I have searched in vain for any reference to frequency of Communion in the Belgic Confession, art. 35, which pertains to the Holy Meal.

[51]Mason, *Letters on Frequent Communion*, 412.

[52]Ibid.

[53]Ibid., 413.

pleading that it would (if frequent) diminish their reverence." Could it really be possible that "the seldomer we communicate the better"?[54]

Both in Scotland and early America, annual or semiannual Presbyterian Communion festivals had incorporated into their extended weekend formats a preliminary day of fasting and a concluding day of thanksgiving. Mason could well anticipate that the proposal for more frequent Communion would encounter a serious objection that more frequent Communions would threaten these now-hallowed days that were like prelude and postlude to the main event. It would do so by making unsustainable (through a quarterly or still more frequent Communion schedule) that extended Thursday through Monday program that had come to be considered inseparable from the Communion itself. People could simply not be away from their daily toil (Thursday through Monday) *multiple* times during the yearly round. And any argument for frequency of Communion (such as made by Mason) thus threatened to strip away these now-revered practices associated with the ordinance.

To this considerable objection, Mason abruptly emphasized, "They have no warrant in the book of God." Neither Jesus nor the apostles had done anything to encumber the Lord's Supper with these additional practices. To this he added, "They are contrary to the judgment of almost the whole Christian church." However venerated these fasts and thanksgivings had come to be regarded among seventeenth- and eighteenth-century Protestants, they were no part of the practice of the church of the ages.

He went on to add that though days of fasting and of thanksgiving are innocent enough in and of themselves, "the question is whether (these) are divine ordinances *with* the holy supper."[55] By extending the number of days necessary to be spent in attending the established Communion festivals, these fasts and thanksgivings in effect served as barriers to the frequent observance of the Supper provided for by Jesus and the apostles. The multiplying of services in which sermons needed to be preached necessitated the calling away from their congregations of additional ministers who, by their assisting in Communion festivals away from home, deprived whole congregations of their regular diet of the preached Word on given Lord's Days.[56]

---

[54]Ibid., 415-20.

[55]Ibid., 430.

[56]Mason's treatise, though written in North America, was read on both sides of the Atlantic. A

ANALYSIS

Though both treatises were written by young pastor-theologians not yet thirty years of age, and in overwhelming agreement, it is not difficult, at the same time, to draw distinctions between them. The treatises differed as to setting, depth of investigation, and form of argument. Erskine had written in open support of his denomination's repeated appeals for greater frequency of administration. Mason dealt with the same practical realities yet had no existing denominational initiative to strengthen by his writing. The treatise of Mason deserves to be seen as the less-original work when compared with the writing of Erskine on this subject; Mason showed a clear literary dependency on that work of 1749 (as recirculated in Erskine's *Theological Dissertations* of 1765).[57] Erskine was one of the two near-contemporary theological writers on whom Mason leaned most heavily. Thus, when Mason referred to patristic writers, he seems only to have cited these opinions to the extent that they were provided in the named authors.[58] Yet while the laurels for depth of research would fall to Erskine, it can honestly be said that it was Mason who took the fruits of the researches of others and set them out in the compelling way that was more likely to be consulted by laymen and by church officers. His answers to potential objections came earlier in his treatise and were more extensive than comparable material offered by the earlier writer.

If the two treatises on frequency of Communion can be contrasted in these ways, they may also be viewed aggregately (since constituting largely overlapping sentiments). The following commonalities can be observed:

- Each writer granted, from the outset, that neither Jesus nor his apostles left to the church any actual pronouncement on the subject of frequency of Communion. At best, there are inferences that may be drawn from the New Testament.

reply was composed by a Glasgow minister of his denomination, John Thomson, titled *Letters Addressed to the Rev. John Mason M.A. of New York*. Of this, an American edition was prepared at Troy, New York, in 1801.

[57]Note that Erskine's treatise is explicitly cited at Mason, *Complete Works*, 1:404, 406, 412.

[58]The other authority was that of Joseph Bingham (1668–1723), *Origines Ecclesiasticae* (Halle, 1738). Intriguingly, both the Bingham and the Erskine volumes are among the holdings of the Burke Theological Library associated with today's Columbia University, New York. John Mitchell Mason was founding professor of theology in the first American theological seminary of his denomination, begun at New York in 1805 and enduring until 1821.

- Each agreed that a primitive high frequency of Communion in the first Christian centuries had gradually given way in medieval Catholicism to a minimalist expectation of once-annual participation.
- Each accepted that the now-hallowed Presbyterian practice of annual or semiannual Communion festivals represented an innovation of the early seventeenth century and as such represented a departure from the original Reformation expectation of an at least quarterly administration.
- The annual or semiannual Communion festival—whatever might be said about its evangelistic potentialities for preaching the gospel to the mixed multitudes that gathered—was inadequate to the spiritual needs of ordinary Christians and provided insufficient opportunities for communing with their Lord.
- The annual or semiannual Communion festival was not only inadequate to the needs of the ordinary Christian believer, it was also injurious to the health of neighboring congregations that—forfeiting their preachers who went to assist in these weekend-long events—had no Sunday preaching services of any kind.
- While each writer was personally convinced that the primitive church had enjoyed the Lord's Supper weekly and knew that the restoration of that primitive frequency had been the desire of John Calvin, they also accepted that from the time of Constantine the church had declined from its original purity and cohesiveness. The mixed nature of the church from Constantine forward rendered it less capable of delighting in the frequency of practice enjoyed in earlier times. Sadly, that mixed character continued to their own day, two and a half centuries after the Reformation.
- The common position of Erskine and Mason, therefore, was that evangelical churches and believers needed to resort to the Lord's Supper more frequently than the Communion-festival practice had allowed—while *not* attempting to recover precisely the practices they believed were characteristic of apostolic times. A quarterly, six-times-yearly, or monthly Communion all represented a giant step in the desired direction, and they asked for no more at that time.

No one will suggest that our ecclesiastical situation is identical to that faced by Erskine and Mason. The case for weekly administration of the Supper has since their times been forcefully made *twice* by the dawning of nineteenth-century Restorationist initiatives such as the Plymouth Brethren and the Stone-Campbell movements and by the percolation into evangelical Protestantism of ideas whose genesis lay in the nineteenth-century Oxford movement.[59] Now, in our own time, one also regularly hears appeal being made to the preference of John Calvin for weekly Communion.

To me, the literary efforts of Erskine and Mason are salutary in three respects. First, we should note that both men were renowned for their evangelical zeal and pan-denominational interests. No one could charge either with a love of ritual or liturgical embroidery at the expense of gospel proclamation.[60] Let those who want to contend for heightened frequency of administration of the Supper in our time demonstrate the same double zeal, lest heightened sacramental observance be brought in at the expense of the proclamation of the gospel that is so necessary for encouraging the pious hunger and aspiration that the Lord's Supper presupposes to exist.

Second, they show themselves to be vitally concerned that evangelical practice surrounding the Lord's Supper be at least *informed* by early church practice. That is not the same thing as to say that evangelical practice must be *only* that of the early church. Our evangelical Protestant tradition is being faulted in our day for having shown itself to be so utterly unconcerned with conformity to the early church as to be threadbare. Erskine and Mason stand as important examples of how ancient Christian practice *was* consulted with

[59]The contemporary influence of these two nineteenth-century movements has been alluded to in the introduction to this book.

[60]The biographers of Erskine, Moncreiff-Wellwood, and Yeager make it plain that Erskine was the forthright leader of the rising "popular" or evangelical party in the Church of Scotland in the period up to his death as well an evangelical leader of transatlantic significance. He had been the means of the publication of most of the works of Jonathan Edwards in Edinburgh and was the benefactor of numerous American college libraries. Similarly, Mason was a minister and seminary professor in New York City; president of Dickinson College, Carlisle, Pennsylvania; and was known for his pan-evangelical sympathies and efforts at collaboration with Presbyterian bodies beyond his own. He had been a founding member of the New York Missionary Society (1790) and the American Bible Society (1816). Even more influential than his *Letters on Frequent Communion* (1798) was his written advocacy of inter-Communion between various Presbyterian bodies, which to that point would neither open their pulpits or Communion tables to ministers and members of the other denominations. This was his *A Plea for Holy Communion on Catholic Principles* (1816), also published in Mason's *Works*, vol. 2.

care in the very period when our evangelical movement is thought to have grown doctrinally superficial. Yet their consultation of Christian antiquity did not lead them to endorse any wooden conformity to it.

Third, Erskine and Mason are important examples of how the study of early Christian practice by Christians in a later age must involve more than simple imitation of the practices of an earlier time. They illustrate an understanding that the early church's Communion practices had been seriously compromised by the transformation of the church begun in Constantine's time. By this transformation, which cost the fourth-century church much of its zeal and purity, the existing high frequency of administration of the Supper came to be perceived as burdensome and intrusive. It followed (for Erskine and Mason) that unless this loss of zeal and purity was addressed, an increase of frequency of the Supper (in and of itself) would face opposition all over again for similar reasons. They sensed a reciprocal relationship between two factors that modern Christians are perhaps more likely to take separately. A survey of various denominations' current practices of administering the Lord's Supper will illustrate that weekly administration does not *itself* engender health and zeal. The Supper presupposes at least a measure of spiritual hunger and some desire to grow in grace in those who partake. Where these spiritual appetites are present, good can result from a more frequent resort to the Supper, but where they are lacking, it is not so much these symbols of Christ that are needed but Christ himself—available to us now through the Word preached and applied. The infrequent Communion festivals that both Erskine and Mason sought to curtail had at least upheld this important priority: the gospel itself was first preached to gathered multitudes and the Supper subsequently administered to that portion of hearers who demonstrated the requisite faith and zeal.

QUESTIONS FOR DISCUSSION

1. With what frequency is the Holy Communion or Lord's Supper administered in the church you attend? Do you know how long that pattern of frequency of administration has existed?
2. From your perspective, what are the pros and cons of the frequency of administration you are accustomed to in the church you call

home? Against what standard will you measure your congregation's present practice?

3. Were you aware, prior to reading this chapter, that outside Protestantism there is a major difference between the frequency of administration of the Holy Communion and the actual frequency with which professed believers participate? Does this discrepancy exist also in evangelical Protestant churches?
4. Were you aware, prior to reading this chapter, that in Protestant history there was a struggle to overcome the legacy of the above-named practice: high frequency of administration / low frequency of participation?
5. What is a preparatory service relative to Holy Communion? Have you ever attended such a service?

8

Early Church Baptism in the Hands of Evangelical Protestants

In the preceding chapter, we were able to observe two thoughtful evangelical Christians examining the practice of the early Christian church for answers to a pressing pastoral issue of the eighteenth century. In this chapter, we will try to observe the work of two other scholars who made use of early Christian resources in reexamining a pressing pastoral issue of our own time.

A General Principle: Primary Doctrines Should Not Be Open to Contradiction by Historical Inquiry

Christians of orthodox faith are in general agreement that, as to what are considered as "primary" doctrines of our faith, we ought not to hold as theologically true what can be shown to be historically doubtful. When the apostle Paul summarized elements of the early Christian "kerygma" in 1 Corinthians 15:3-7, the thrust of his argument was that these elements of our faith (Christ's death for our sins, his burial, and resurrection on the third day)—because faithfully witnessed—are necessary parts of our Christian confession. The same emphasis on corroboration by eyewitnesses is maintained elsewhere in the New Testament (Acts 26:26; 2 Pet 1:16; 1 Jn 1:1-2).

Now it is at the same time true that orthodox Christians hold *some* major truths that are not so obviously commended to us on this basis of trustworthy witnesses. The existence of God (subsisting in three equal persons) is not established for us as true in a way identical to those gospel events that Paul recites. We hold God to exist (in three persons) on the combined basis of the divine revelation conveyed to us by Jesus Christ, in the Holy Scriptures, and of some inferences drawn from the world around us. Note that even here we do not knowingly contravene the principle that we may not hold as theologically true what can be shown to be historically doubtful. The difference between the gospel truths that Paul names in 1 Corinthians 15 and a major doctrine like that of God's existence in Trinity is that historical corroboration is not available to us in the same manner or to the same degree in both cases.

SECONDARY DOCTRINES OUGHT, AT LEAST, TO FIND SOLID HISTORICAL PRECEDENTS

Now the situation is admittedly more complicated when we come to consider what may be termed "second-order" doctrines of our faith. That the Christian day of rest and worship should be the first day of the week rather than the last, or that the Lord's Supper employs bread and wine in a way that is chiefly representational or undergoes transformation—these are questions about which different sincere convictions are held by persons and parties who find some antecedent for their preferred view in New Testament writings and early Christian witnesses. In even these secondary convictions, we seek to uphold the principle that we should not hold as theologically true what may be shown to be historically doubtful. Even when we acknowledge that the post-biblical historical evidence is diverse, we are seeking the existence of historical precedents in and after the apostolic age. We look for doctrinal continuity between the current preferred view or practice and the earliest known formulations regarding that subject.

APPLYING THIS STANDARD TO THE QUESTION OF BAPTIZING THE INFANTS OF CHRISTIAN PARENTS

It is the achievement of two broadly evangelical patristic authorities—the late David F. Wright (1937–2008), formerly of New College, Edinburgh, and

Everett F. Ferguson, emeritus professor of Abilene Christian University (Texas)—that they have demonstrated, on a massive scale, the historical difficulties associated with upholding the practice of infant baptism. Their arguments have centered especially on the paucity of evidence for the practice in the apostolic age and second century. We return to the question: *may we hold a Christian belief as theologically true, even if historical validation is doubtful?* We must tread carefully here!

The two authors named, Wright and Ferguson, have not stood on strictly identical ground. Wright had made Christian baptism a topic of research for a quarter century. Beyond academic life, he was an active elder in a local congregation and denomination (in both of which infant baptism was predominant). A long series of research articles on baptism in both the patristic and Reformation periods came together at career's end in both a distilled form, the popular-length treatment *What Has Infant Baptism Done to Baptism?*,[1] and in an anthology volume that reproduced articles written over a quarter century, *Infant Baptism in Historical Perspective*.[2] It may be fairly said that Wright wrote as one motivated *not* to see the baptism of infants uprooted and removed but reformed and practiced on a principled basis in a setting in which indiscriminant infant baptism was and is rife.[3]

By contrast, Ferguson has long been associated with the Christian Churches, one distinctive tenet of which is that forgiveness of sins and the gift of the Holy Spirit is tied to the administration of baptism—that is, baptism upon profession. His massive volume, *Baptism in the Early Church*, represents the consolidated results of published researches into early Christian baptism extending back three decades.[4] While Ferguson taught

---

[1]David F. Wright, *What Has Infant Baptism Done to Baptism?* (Carlisle, UK: Paternoster, 2005). The volume of 116 pages began life as a series of lectures at the Nazarene Theological College, Didsbury, Manchester, UK, in 2003. The present author reviewed this volume in *Presbyterion* 36, no. 2 (2006): 122-25.

[2]David F. Wright, *Infant Baptism in Historical Perspective* (Carlisle, UK: Paternoster, 2007). This volume may very well have been the last material sent into print by Wright, who passed away the following year.

[3]These are certainly the sentiments expressed by Wright in the special issue of the *Evangelical Quarterly* given over to an analysis of his 2005 volume, *What Has Infant Baptism Done to Baptism?* See the *Evangelical Quarterly* 78, no. 2 (2006): 163. In his response, "Christian Baptism: Where Do We Go from Here?," to those interacting with his book, Wright speaks of himself as "one who still endorses the acceptability of infant baptism (but with an enthusiasm considerably more muted than a generation ago)."

[4]Everett Ferguson, *Baptism in the Early Church* (Grand Rapids: Eerdmans, 2009).

the whole sweep of the history of Christianity, his researches on baptism focused primarily on the early centuries. I think it is only fair to say that Ferguson's massive volume is driven, at least in part, by a desire to burnish the distinctive baptismal theology of his own communion.[5]

With these individuals' distinctive emphases noted, we may mention that Ferguson and Wright had earlier collaborated in such projects as the *Encyclopedia of Early Christianity.*[6] Ferguson provided a cover endorsement for and contributed to the 2006 comprehensive review of Wright's *What Has Infant Baptism Done to Baptism?*[7] He also honored Wright as one of three external readers who evaluated his massive 2009 volume.[8] Wright's two books show a good awareness of Ferguson's research and a strong element of concurrence with Ferguson's view that conversion-faith-baptism should ideally form an indivisible unit.[9]

THE AGGREGATE WRIGHT-FERGUSON FINDINGS REGARDING INFANT BAPTISM

Of course, the two authors did not parrot one another. But we may fairly speak of a convergence in their researches. Their conclusions precipitate something like this:

- The baptism of Jesus rather than baptism as administered in the apostolic ministries recorded in Acts was reckoned by early Christianity as the pattern or paradigm of Christian baptism.[10]
- Jesus neither commanded nor explicitly provided for the baptism of infants. As for his blessing of children (recorded in Mk 10:13-16), this was not used as a support for infant baptism until the seventh or eighth century.[11]
- The household baptisms of Acts 16 and 1 Corinthians 1 will not bear the weight assigned to them by advocates of infant baptism. We can be no

[5]I have drawn attention to this *apologetic* emphasis in *Baptism in the Early Church* in a review in *Themelios* 35, no. 1 (April 2010): 107-9.

[6]Everett Ferguson, ed., *Encyclopedia of Early Christianity*, 2nd ed. (1999; repr., New York: Garland, 2009). In this reference work, Ferguson did write on infant baptism, while Wright did not.

[7]Wright, *Evangelical Quarterly* 78, no. 2 (2006).

[8]Ferguson, *Baptism in the Early Church*, xx.

[9]Wright, *Infant Baptism*, xxiv.

[10]Ferguson, *Baptism in the Early Church*, chap. 7.

[11]Wright, *What Has Infant Baptism Done*, 72; and *Infant Baptism*, chap. 11.

more than agnostic about the ages of any children included in such baptisms. Evidently, those baptized had also believed.[12]

- There is no support to be found for infant baptism in the Didache or in the writings of those second-century leaders known as the apostolic fathers.[13]
- No church father before Cyprian (d. 258) proposed that the Old Testament circumcision of infant males found its fulfillment in the baptism of the infant children of Christians. Augustine later developed this idea further.[14]
- No major early Christian writer substantially addresses the question of the baptism of children before Tertullian (ca. AD 220), soon followed by Origen. Tertullian's preference that children not be baptized until they can answer for themselves is an indication that infant baptism was on the scene with sufficient frequency for him to want to register his dissenting opinion.[15]
- Infants suffering from life-threatening conditions probably provided the occasion that made baptism seem appropriate for the very young.[16] (However, implicit in this practice was a notion that most Protestant Christians do not endorse: the absolute necessity of the reception of this sacrament for salvation.)
- There is no biography of a church father in the opening centuries making plain that the individual (even if raised in a Christian family) received baptism in infancy.[17]
- Early Christian architectural remains indicate that pools or baths, supplied with moving water, were the normal venue for baptisms, which were administered by immersion or pouring; this pattern was departed from only in the fifth century (reflecting the universalizing of infant baptism), except in the East, in which immersion has remained the norm.[18]
- Under all normal circumstances, early Christian baptism followed extensive catechetical training ensuring that the baptismal questions were

[12]Wright, *What Has Infant Baptism Done*, 36; and Ferguson, *Baptism in the Early Church*, 178-79.
[13]Wright, *Infant Baptism*, chap. 3; and Ferguson, *Baptism in the Early Church*, chaps. 12, 14.
[14]Wright, *What Has Infant Baptism Done*, 18, 19; and Wright, *Infant Baptism*, chap. 6.
[15]Tertullian, *On Baptism*, chap. 18 in *Ante-Nicene Fathers*, ed. Alexander Roberts and James Donaldson, vol. 3, *Latin Christianity: Its Founder, Tertullian* (Grand Rapids: Eerdmans, 1963), 677-78.
[16]Ferguson, *Baptism in the Early Church*, 355-57; and Wright, *Infant Baptism*, chap. 1.
[17]Wright, *What Has Infant Baptism Done*, 6.
[18]Ferguson, *Baptism in the Early Church*, chaps. 53-54, 849-52.

answered by instructed persons. As it was practiced and spread, infant baptism employed the same questions as previously, yet directed these questions to parents or sponsors of the infants.[19]

- The theological writings of Augustine against Pelagius, by their exposition of the doctrine of original or birth sin, provided a plausible theological basis for the necessity of the baptism of the young. This theological necessity had not been so apparent earlier to writers like Tertullian.[20]

Because it is unlikely that other writers will soon investigate again the terrain as assiduously as Wright and Ferguson have done, it is fair to stand back and to now assess the size of the "impact crater" that their historical researches have made on the position maintained by Protestant defenders of infant baptism.

SUPPORTS CUSTOMARILY CITED FOR INFANT BAPTISM BY ITS PROTESTANT DEFENDERS

It is thought-provoking to observe the relatively small recognition given to the paucity of apostolic and second-century historical evidence by very recent advocates of infant baptism. There may be more than one reason for this. Yet, I ask the question again: *may we hold to be theologically true what can be shown to be historically doubtful?*

In surveying standard Protestant treatments since 1830 that advocate infant baptism, we find reliance on the following themes.

Biblical-theological themes.

- A readiness to believe that Jesus' blessing of children provides a kind of corroboration for the inclusion of believers' children in baptism.[21]
- A readiness to suppose that not only the Abrahamic covenant continues but that its sign and seal (circumcision) continues under baptism—now available to children of either gender. Peter did tell the repentant thousands

---

[19]Wright, *What Has Infant Baptism Done*, chap. 2.
[20]Ibid., 25.
[21]John Murray, *Christian Baptism* (Philadelphia: Orthodox Presbyterian Church, 1952), 62; and Geoffrey W. Bromiley, *Children of Promise: The Case for Baptizing Infants* (Eugene, OR: Wipf & Stock, 1998), 5.

at Pentecost that the gospel promise was "for you and your children" (Acts 2:39).[22]

- A readiness to argue from the standpoint of imaginary Christian-Jewish parents who, in the aftermath of Pentecost, receive a child into this world and wish to know what provision the young church makes for signing and sealing such infants with the sign of the covenant.[23]
- A readiness to suppose that the families named in the *oikia* passages (the household baptisms) recorded in Acts 16:15, 33 and 1 Corinthians 1:16 were, in accepting family baptism, motivated by a kind of proto-covenant theology. (Here, at least, we are dealing with historical occurrences that likely included children.)[24]

Post-apostolic themes.

- A readiness to accept the reports of persons such as Polycarp that he had been a Christian eighty-six years (almost certainly reckoned from the year of his birth, likely the year of his baptism).[25]
- A readiness to accept that a mention of the baptism of infants in the *Apostolic Tradition* thought to be associated with Hippolytus (ca. AD 220 but which in fact contains elements as old as AD 150) indicates the existence of this practice at Rome.[26]
- A readiness to accept that the delay of baptism for infants urged by Tertullian in his treatise *Of Baptism* (ca. AD 220) is that writer's attempt to modify a baptism of infants already current in North Africa.[27]

---

[22]Samuel Miller, *Infant Baptism Both Scriptural and Reasonable* (Philadelphia: Joseph Wetham, 1835), 22; Murray, *Christian Baptism*, 48-49; and Bryan Chapell, *Why Do We Baptize Infants?* (Phillipsburg, NJ: P&R, 2006), 6-13.

[23]Miller, *Infant Baptism*, 25; and Murray, *Christian Baptism*, 71.

[24]Miller, *Infant Baptism*, 23; Murray, *Christian Baptism*, 68, 69; Bromiley, *Children of Promise*, 2; and Chapell, *Why Do We Baptize Infants?*, 18-19.

[25]"Martyrdom of Polycarp," as reprinted in Henry Bettenson and Chris Maunder, *Documents of the Christian Church*, 3rd ed. (Oxford: Oxford University Press, 1999), 11; and Sinclair Ferguson, "Infant Baptism View," in *Baptism: Three Views*, ed. David F. Wright (Downers Grove, IL: InterVarsity Press, 2009), 80.

[26]Alistair Stewart-Sykes, ed. and trans., *On the Apostolic Tradition: Hippolytus* (Crestwood, NY: St. Vladimir's Seminary Press, 2001). The reference to the baptism of infants comes at paragraph 21 (p. 110). See also Ferguson, "Infant Baptism View," 81.

[27]Tertullian, *On Baptism*, 677-78; and Ferguson, "Infant Baptism View," 78, 80.

RESPONSE

What must be grasped straightaway is that—in the judgment of Wright and Ferguson—it is only when we come to consider the *final* two items listed (Hippolytus and forward) that we are dealing with historical material, and historical material that implies infant baptism's *actual emergence.*[28] I feel the force of the Wright-Ferguson challenge very keenly, having a sense of chagrin that standard authors writing to advocate infant baptism have found so little to discourage them in the meagerness of such historical materials. In light of this, what ought to be done? There seem to be three possibilities.

Disregard the problem of patchy historical evidence.[29] To date, this seems to be the prevailing (though not exclusive) response from the conservative Protestant community that still upholds infant baptism. During past centuries, the argument for infant baptism has depended far more on inferences about the degree of continuity between the testaments than it has on apostolic and post-apostolic precedents. Yet it is worth bearing in mind that the percolation rate by which new ideas and assessments are diffused throughout any culture is quite slow—whether the field of study is theology or physics. A decade or fifteen years hence, we can more assuredly expect that this shift in historical assessment will be factored into the writing of new textbooks on the subject of infant baptism.

One significant reason why we should hope that this shift in historical perspective will be noted more thoroughly in the future than it is now is that global ecumenical theological discussion of baptism has *already* coalesced around the position that the missionary baptism of converts making profession was the

---

[28]This view is, in effect, a reiteration of the view of A. Harnack, set out in 1906 in *The Mission and Expansion of Christianity in the First Three Centuries*, trans. James Moffat, 2nd ed. (English trans., London: Williams & Norgate, 1908), 1:388-89. Harnack, doubting that the practice of infant baptism could be traced earlier than mid-second century, supposed that it had been inaugurated at that time. So doubtful is Wright that any earlier existence of infant baptism can be demonstrated that he advises current advocates of this doctrine to relent from efforts to demonstrate its earlier existence and to concentrate on demonstrating its biblical-theological grounds. See *Evangelical Quarterly* 78, no. 2 (2006): 163.

[29]"Frustratingly patchy" is the characterization given to the early evidence for infant baptism by Sinclair Ferguson in his fine essay, "Infant Baptism View," 79. Having said this, Ferguson's essay offers the most judicious handling of the various evidence available. The recent work of John V. Fesko, *Word, Water, and Spirit: A Reformed Perspective on Baptism* (Grand Rapids: Reformation Heritage, 2010) is sadly deficient in this respect. Having acknowledged that Tertullian took a dim view of infant baptism, he moves promptly to consider Augustine. He seems unperturbed to find no discussion earlier than Tertullian.

original and normative baptism of apostolic Christianity. With this principle established, it has also been affirmed that infant baptism needed to be accommodated alongside this missionary baptism as an option.[30] When the world's Catholic, Lutheran, Methodist, and Baptist churches, after extensive Bible study, have coalesced in agreement about this through the 1980s exercise resulting in the document "Baptism, Eucharist and Ministry," conservative Protestants—who admittedly are distrustful of unqualified ecumenical theological discussion—ought to take note lest they, in a kind of "time warp," go on defending matters overdue for careful reconsideration.

The fact that these global families of churches that have participated in the ecumenical discussion on baptism have not, as of yet, fully or properly implemented changes in their baptismal policies that such a common agreement anticipates does not take away from the significance of their common findings. These are that in the apostolic age and for centuries beyond, the missionary baptism of catechumens who answered for themselves remained normative.

A long-term disregard of the now-admitted lack of substantive historical support for the practice of infant baptism in the apostolic and post-apostolic church will doom unbending advocates of this practice into a kind of echo chamber in which the doctrine is argued out and made to stand on the basis of assumptions not shared outside their particular conservative Protestant subculture. In general terms, we already frown at such sectarian theological methods and should be as unprepared to endorse their use in this case as in others.

Abandon infant baptism altogether. In my experience, the "traffic" of persons leaving credobaptist (that is, baptism on profession) communities for those upholding the paedobaptist (that is, infant baptism) position far outnumbers those moving in the reverse direction. Defections from the ranks of paedobaptists for other streams of Christianity are not common, although they do occur.[31] It is likely the case that for those affiliating with

[30]See the discerning discussion of this ecumenical consensus in Wright, *What Has Infant Baptism Done*, 14, and *Infant Baptism in Historical Perspective*, chaps. 22 and 23. The gist of the finding of the "Baptism, Eucharist and Ministry" project regarding baptism was "While the possibility that infant baptism was practiced in the apostolic age cannot be excluded, baptism upon personal profession of faith is the most clearly attested pattern in the New Testament documents."

[31]One notable instance was that of Herbert Carson (1922–2004), who departed from the paedobaptist Church of England in 1964 to assume the pastorate of an independent evangelical congregation. He gave his reasons for the change in *Farewell to Anglicanism* (Worthing, UK: Henry E. Walter, 1969).

churches practicing infant baptism (who were previously in churches with a different practice), baptismal practices are not, in and of themselves, the most prominent issue serving to attract them.[32] Yet for those who leave denominations and churches practicing infant baptism, baptismal doctrine maintains a much higher profile. It is a defining issue.

In the light of the paucity of early evidence for this practice highlighted by Wright and Ferguson, it is certainly conceivable that some persons who were formerly at least sympathetic toward infant baptism will now determine that the remaining arguments (from continuity of God's dealings with humans in both testaments and from post-apostolic tradition) provide insufficient warrant to maintain the practice. From the paucity of evidence in the apostolic and post-apostolic period, they will draw the not utterly unwarranted inference that if this practice was the intention of Jesus and the apostles, these persons failed to make this sufficiently clear both to their contemporaries and to the generation that was to follow them.

However, the Christian who chooses this direction must sooner or later reinvent the wheel (so to speak) by belatedly facing the question, what is the position, before God, of the infant children of Christian believers? In the past, this question has been forced on the church by high infant-mortality rates (now happily reduced) that took many children of Christian parents from the world before their response to the gospel could easily be discerned. But the question forces itself again and again on the church, and it has never yet proved satisfactory to answer the question by merely saying that such children are no different than if raised in pagan families. They are spiritually advantaged children, and such children when brought by their parents to Christ were numbered among the citizens of the kingdom of heaven (Lk 18:17 and parallels). Dare we assume that this principle of infant kingdom membership finds no continuance and no expression in our own day?

Modify infant baptism. Under this heading, there can be grouped together three possible efforts to maintain infant baptism. Each involves adopting a different strategy for its maintenance and preservation.

---

[32]This was the writer's own experience. The Reformed theological tradition, which he entered in his twenties, offered a stabilizing doctrinal and liturgical heritage not available in his earlier years as a young Christian nurtured within a pietistic evangelical setting. The baptism of infants, though this needed to be negotiated as something alien to his background, was part of a larger "package" of beliefs and practices that—taken as a whole—were highly attractive.

Make it an option reserved for the children of those parents who request it. This is the line taken by the highly regarded A. N. S. (Tony) Lane in the recent volume *Baptism: Three Views.*[33] Apparently this policy was followed by whole swaths of the early church in the era prior to infant baptism's becoming so customary. In modern times, it was a point of view recovered at Geneva in 1849 when two congregations—the baptistic Pelisserie congregation (founded 1818) and the paedobaptist Oratoire (founded 1832)—came together to form the Evangelical Free Church of Geneva (Église Évangélique Libre de Genève). In this union, which the church historian Philip Schaff typified as "a Calvinism moderated, simplified, and separated from connection with civil government,"[34] there existed a harmony in which the two points of view existed side by side. Lane noted two American churches, the Evangelical Covenant Church and the Church of the Nazarene, as examples of this dual-baptismal strategy; it represents a kind of an admission that it is not possible for us to know definitively what provisions the early church made for the baptism of the young children of adult believers.[35] Another, the Evangelical Free Church of America (and of Canada), historically provided for such a dual-baptism policy but has largely allowed the baptism of infants to vanish.

That is the one certain thing regarding dual-baptism practice: churches going this route need to be vigilant in seeing that pastors are trained to provide both styles of baptism without disparaging either. Where this pastoral provision is lacking, the system rapidly degenerates from coexistence to one in which one view crowds out the other. Dual-practice baptism requires those who practice it to prize Christian unity in other essentials highly enough that they will forbear from judging fellow believers who differ from them in this matter. Within this framework, infant baptism's advocates need not make any claim for it to be the original or prevalent baptism of early Christianity but only that it was an option present from the beginning.

[33] A. N. S. Lane, "The Dual Practice View," in *Baptism: Three Views*, ed. David F. Wright (Downers Grove, IL: InterVarsity Press, 2009), 139-71. In his contribution, Lane draws attention to his earlier article, "Did the Apostolic Church Baptize Babies? A Seismological Approach," *Tyndale Bulletin* 55, no. 1 (2004): 109-30.

[34] The reference is found in Schaff, *The Creeds of Christendom* (New York: Harpers, 1919), 3:781. The spiritual awakening that led to the creation of the two individual congregations (eventually united) is detailed in Kenneth J. Stewart, *Restoring the Reformation: British Evangelicalism and the Francophone Réveil, 1816–1849* (Carlisle, UK: Paternoster, 2006), 109-10.

[35] Wright, *What Has Infant Baptism Done*, 16.

Defend the baptism of infants on grounds that hitherto have not been used. If one is ready to depart from the principle enunciated at the opening of this chapter—that is, that we should insist wherever possible on historical corroboration for Christian beliefs and practices—then a range of other possibilities open up before those who are desirous of maintaining the practice of infant baptism. One could hold, for instance, that infant baptism is an "unwritten" tradition of the apostles and that it emerged over time in accordance with the unrecorded but real intentions of the apostles themselves. Or one could hold to a view of doctrinal development according to which it was legitimate for doctrines to emerge over time in the life of the church on the basis of their being a legitimate extension of something implicitly contained in earlier teaching. Are we not close here to the line of thinking set out in the provocative little book of I. Howard Marshall, *Going Beyond the Bible?*[36] In my own judgment, such a line of advocacy is vulnerable to the criticism that developments in doctrine can sometimes represent a corruption or declension as well as an advance. This principle, by itself, seems an inadequate grounding for a practice upheld by those who are pledged to uphold the supremacy of Scripture.

Defend the baptism of infants by a renewed attention to the household baptisms of Acts 16 and 1 Corinthians 1:16.[37] Mention has been made already of Wright and Ferguson's combined readiness to dismiss these cases as a foundation on which the current practice of infant baptism might rest. While agreeing that there is an element of "argument from silence" entailed in the use of these passages by both the defenders of paedo- and credobaptism (after all, the children's ages are not named), it is not necessary to let the matter rest there.

[36]I. Howard Marshall, *Going Beyond the Bible?* (Grand Rapids: Baker, 2004). In this stimulating volume, Marshall, having demonstrated doctrinal development from Old Testament to New and within the NT writings, suggests that further doctrinal development can be expected beyond the NT, while of course no further authoritative Scriptures will be added. See especially chapters 2 and 3. I find the same type of argumentation evident in the essay of Peter Leithart, "Infant Baptism in History: An Unfinished Tragicomedy," in *The Case for Covenantal Infant Baptism*, ed. Gregg Strawbridge (Phillipsburg, NJ: P&R, 2003), 246-62. Leithart maintained that while infant baptism was endorsed and practiced by the apostles, it dropped out of practice during the second century, recovered somewhat in the third, and was vindicated by Augustine in the fourth. On this view, the eventual utter dominance of infant baptism was none other than the desire of the apostles.

[37]The language of household in connection with baptism is also echoed in Acts 10:48, 11:14, and 18:8.

Joachim Jeremias, depending in part on the older scholarship of Ethelbert Stauffer, showed quite effectively in his later volume *The Origins of Infant Baptism* (1962) that German scholarship had misjudged matters badly in the first half of the twentieth century in its readiness to conclude that infant baptism was a relative novelty in the time of Tertullian.[38] Jeremias combated this understanding by drawing fresh attention to the *oikos* word group across the New Testament and its antecedents in the Old.[39] Its use is not limited to the three well-known passages in Acts and 1 Corinthians that all parties admit describe family baptism of *some* kind (1 Cor 1:16; Acts 16:15, 33); it extends also to many passages in the Gospels and the remainder of the New Testament in which the gospel is embraced by "houses," or families. The embrace of the gospel by the *oikos* is characteristic of both Jewish and Gentile families (for example, Lk 19:9 and Acts 18:8; Jn 4:53; and Acts 11:14); this welcome of the gospel by whole families was associated with the ministries of Jesus, Peter, and Paul.

While it so happens that the three instances of the salvation of families explicitly entailing baptism (the others implicitly did so insofar as the apostolic church upheld baptism as normative for the saved) were associated with the ministry of Paul *outside* Judea, there is no reason to suppose that the baptism of "houses" knew any such geographical limitation. If we seek a plausible explanation of how the baptism of infants in apostolic times survived to be commented on in the age of Hippolytus, Tertullian, and Origen, let us find it here.[40]

With this attempt to historically locate infant baptism in the century intervening between the apostles and Tertullian comes two challenges. First is the question of whether we are ready to accept that infant baptism in the

---

[38]His earlier volume, *Infant Baptism in the First Four Centuries* (1958; repr., English trans., London: SCM, 1960) had been heavily criticized by fellow German Kurt Aland in *Did the Early Church Baptize Infants?* (1961; repr., English trans., London: SCM, 1963) for its too-free inferences.

[39]Joachim Jeremias, *The Origins of Infant Baptism* (1962; repr., London: SCM, 1963), chap. 2.

[40]I applaud the measured re-enunciation of the *oikos* idea by Jonathan Watt in the essay, "The Oikos Formula," in Strawbridge, *Case for Covenantal Infant Baptism*, 70-84, esp. 81. According to Watt, "The church has historically practiced infant baptism. The use of household language in the biblical world opens up the possibility of the baptism of infants, but by itself may not decide the matter." See also Dan McCartney, "Household, Family," in *Dictionary of the Later New Testament and Its Developments*, ed. Ralph P. Martin and Peter H. Davids (Downers Grove, IL: InterVarsity Press, 1997), 511-13, esp. 511. The standard critique of this viewpoint was supplied by G. R. Beasley-Murray, *Baptism in the New Testament* (Grand Rapids: Eerdmans, 1974), 312-20.

second century as we find it in historical witnesses was, as David Wright aptly termed it, "the minority report." After all, was it ever more than this in the years reflected in the Acts of the Apostles? I very much fear that standard writing in favor of infant baptism in the last two centuries has advocated it not on this basis but on the basis of what it eventually became—the dominant baptismal practice of European and Mediterranean Christendom for more than a millennium.

My challenge to fellow paedobaptists is this. What would it require of us to see infant baptism occupy this more modest place in our churches today? I think that the answer is obvious. We would need to commit ourselves to reversing the proportions of those baptized in infancy (the vast majority in today's paedobaptist churches) and those baptized out of the world (the clear minority today). Does not the very frequency with which infant baptism is practiced in our churches practically obscure our failure to evangelize and baptize from the world?

For this position there also remains the second challenge of resolving a question that has been debated for at least two centuries. That is, is the New Testament theology of baptism one worked out primarily with a view to the majority who received baptism of a missionary kind (in which case the reality figured in baptism is in very many cases enjoyed by infants only *prospectively*, as and when they too respond in faith), or is the New Testament theology of baptism one that applies as fully to *any* recipient of any age? Concretely, is the spiritual reality associated with baptism in Scriptures such as Romans 6:1-14 and 1 Peter 3:21 the possession of all who are baptized, or the prospective possession of those who have yet to answer for themselves? Protestants practicing infant baptism are more and more disadvantaged by their failure to resolve this question. It could just be that an acceptance of the non-dominance of infant baptism in the earliest Christian centuries would make it easier for us to agree with the nineteenth-century Scottish theologian James Bannerman, who wrote:

> The true type of Baptism, from examining which we are to draw our notions of its nature and efficacy, is to be drawn from the adult Baptisms in the early days of Christianity and not in the only Baptism now commonly performed in the professing church, the Baptism of infants. . . . Both among the enemies and friends of infant baptism the neglect of this distinction has been the

> occasion of numberless errors in regard to the import and effects of the sacrament. It is abundantly obvious that adult Baptism is the rule and infant Baptism the exceptional case. . . . The ordinance of Baptism is no more to be judged of in its ministration to children than is the ordinance of preaching to be judged of in its ministration to children.[41]

In consequence, our discussions of infant baptism would be carried on at lower altitudes than is often the case, and to the benefit of all.

In sum, David Wright and Everett Ferguson, both known for their evangelical sympathies, have served as admirable models of how evangelical Christians today carry on the noble heritage of bringing the resources of early Christianity to bear on the Christian movement of the present day.

QUESTIONS FOR DISCUSSION

1. If your home congregation does include the infant children of believers in baptism, what grounds or basis are named in the baptism service as providing a foundation for the practice? Are any of those grounds called into question by Wright and Ferguson?
2. If your congregation does not include such infant children in baptism, are there ever grounds or reasons provided as to why they are not, and if so, what are those? Do Wright and Ferguson raise any questions about your congregation's practice that deserve further thought?
3. One way or the other, can you see ways that the baptismal practices of your home congregation could be improved in light of the issues Wright and Ferguson raise?

[41]James Bannerman, *The Church of Christ*, 2 vols. (1869; repr., London: Banner of Truth, 1960), 2:108-9.

9

Theological Exegesis, Biblical Theology, and the History of Interpretation

ONE VERY NOTEWORTHY DEVELOPMENT in the world of biblical and theological studies in the twentieth century was the rise of theological exegesis. This movement originated in the first half of the twentieth century as a thoughtful reaction to the excesses and arid methods of biblical interpretation that had been gaining the upper hand for a century. In the first half of the twentieth century, critical exegesis had rendered the Old and New Testament Scriptures to be of diminished value for the faith communities that looked to them for guidance.

Writing in 1948, Floyd V. Filson defended the recently coined terminology of "theological exegesis" by maintaining that it was a needed corrective against what had by then come to be the dominant approach in biblical studies. This approach had, in his words, at least permitted "a personal aloofness of the interpreter from the message which dominates the writing under study."[1] The kind of biblical studies that Filson wished to surpass concentrated largely on the history of the biblical text and on its textual

[1]Floyd Filson, "Theological Exegesis," *Journal of Bible and Religion* 16, no. 4 (1948): 212.

variants; in consequence, this method left those wanting to learn the text's application to their lives and situations disappointed and frustrated.

THE BIRTH OF MODERN THEOLOGICAL EXEGESIS

The "theological exegesis" movement, described by Filson as in progress in 1948, was in fact rooted in a period of theological reassessment following the Great War (1914–1918). Karl Barth's commentary on Paul's epistle to the Romans, first published in that postwar climate in 1919 and revised for a second edition in 1922,[2] is reckoned to have marked a swing of the pendulum in a way that heralded a return to treating the Scriptures, in Filson's phrase, "in the context of divine revelation." Filson was reasserting a frankly supernaturalist conception of Scripture. He wrote, "Only he who gives a sense of the powerful working of God is doing justice to (the) passage."[3]

Yet, he was at the same time keen to safeguard this more hopeful approach from being misunderstood. He did not mean to suggest that under a theological exegesis, the Scriptures would be interpreted merely the way ecclesiastical confessions of faith had earlier construed them; this would have been so reiterative as to render any fresh efforts at interpretation of questionable value. He did not mean to suggest either that biblical interpretation, in the future, should come into an unhealthy dependency on some subjective quality of intuition or empathy on the part of the interpreter (as desirable as such sensitivity is), as if that were the key to insight and understanding. He instead looked for interpreters to function as *theologians* who reckoned that the "biblical message speaks concerning the ultimate issues of faith and life."[4] On this understanding, responsible interpretation of Scripture would both require theological reflection by the interpreter and spark similar reflection on the part of the reader or listener.

THEOLOGICAL EXEGESIS AS EXPRESSED IN THE BIBLICAL THEOLOGY MOVEMENT

This postwar attempt to rekindle responsible biblical interpretation soon interacted with another venture: what has come to be called the "Biblical

---

[2]T. H. L. Parker, *Karl Barth* (Grand Rapids: Eerdmans, 1970), chap. 2.
[3]Filson, "Theological Exegesis," 214.
[4]Ibid.

Theology" movement. Today we associate the rise of this movement with past scholars such as G. Ernest Wright and Brevard Childs. Responding to similar atomistic trends in advanced biblical studies, the Biblical Theology movement encouraged and practiced theological reflection on distinct units, genres, and themes of biblical literature.[5] Thus, in due course there appeared titles such as Floyd V. Filson's *The New Testament Against Its Environment,* G. Ernest Wright's *The Old Testament Against Its Environment,* Joachim Jeremias's *Jesus' Promise to the Nations,* and Johann Jakob Stamm's *The Ten Commandments in Recent Research.*[6]

THE REBIRTH OF THE HISTORY OF INTERPRETATION

In still more recent times, we can observe a convergence of these trends in biblical and theological study with a third. There has grown up among Christians of various branches of the Christian family a conviction that biblical and theological studies have been impoverished by the neglect of the history of interpretation.[7] Roman Catholic students of Scripture have had as definite interest in this pursuit as have others. Twentieth-century Catholic biblical studies, having eventually embraced the same critical methods of Scripture study that had earlier provoked the reaction of Protestant post-WWI theological exegesis, has itself in recent times turned fresh attention to the history of interpretation in an attempt to assist in the drawing of theological meaning from Scripture.[8] Fresh engagement with the biblical text in its original languages as well as a new focus on patristic studies had received strong encouragements from the deliberations of the Second Vatican Council (1962–1965).

[5]One of the enduring monuments to this movement was the launching of a series titled "Studies in Biblical Theology," of which Floyd Filson and four others joined, commencing in 1950, to edit at least 110 slender volumes. The series was jointly published by SCM Press, London, and Alec R. Allenson, Naperville, Illinois.

[6]The titles were jointly released by SCM Press, London, and Alec R. Allenson, Naperville, Illinois, in 1950, 1957, 1959, and 1967.

[7]See the seminal article of David C. Steinmetz, "The Superiority of Pre-Critical Exegesis," *Theology Today* 37, no. 1 (1980): 27-38. Some important works that have signified fresh attention to the history of interpretation are Beryl Smalley, *The Study of the Bible in the Middle Ages* (Oxford: Blackwell, 1952); Robert M. Grant, *A Short History of the Interpretation of the Bible* (New York: Macmillan, 1958); and, more recently, Gerald Bray, *Biblical Interpretation: Past and Present* (Downers Grove, IL: InterVarsity Press, 1996).

[8]Illustrated, for example, in such literature as Brian E. Daley, "Is Patristic Exegesis Still Usable? Reflections on the Early Christian Interpretation of the Psalms," *Communio* 29, no. 1 (1974): 185-216.

Broadly evangelical Christianity has not been unaware of these trends; in reality, it too has come to participate in them. Reference works have now been produced that introduce prominent biblical interpreters from across all the Christian centuries.[9] At least two series of biblical commentaries relying on the history of interpretation to draw out the theological significance of the various biblical books are now in the process of publication. These commentary series include (but are not limited to) broadly evangelical contributors.[10] And there is also a growing body of literature demonstrating that the broadly evangelical community is reflecting on the merit and potential of this approach to mining the Scriptures.[11]

EVANGELICAL THEOLOGY'S INTERFACE WITH THESE TRENDS

Yet the question needs to be asked, while the rise of theological exegesis, biblical theology, and studies in the history of interpretation have been beneficial and desirable, do these commendable efforts correct deficiencies that have *also* plagued evangelical Christianity? My answer to this question is "no," "no," and "yes." Such an answer requires to be explained.

Whatever theological and biblical excesses evangelical Christianity may have been guilty of, one of them has not been selling short the theological value of the Bible. Indeed, it has often been alleged that evangelical Christians have shown themselves ready to draw too many dogmatic implications out of the Scriptures rather than too few. The evangelical penchant for theological dogmatism has nowhere been so apparent as in the field of eschatology.[12] And while it is true that in recent times broadly evangelical scholars have shown themselves capable of discussing the text and transmission

---

[9]Donald McKim, *Encyclopedia of Major Bible Interpreters* (Downers Grove, IL: InterVarsity Press, 2007).

[10]The commentary series are the Brazos Theological Commentary on the Bible (Grand Rapids: Baker) and The Church's Bible (Grand Rapids: Eerdmans).

[11]See, for example, Kevin Vanhoozer, ed., *Dictionary for the Theological Interpretation of Scripture* (Grand Rapids: Baker Academic, 2005); John L. Thompson, *Reading the Bible with the Dead* (Grand Rapids: Eerdmans, 2007); Daniel J. Treier, *Introducing the Theological Interpretation of Scripture* (Grand Rapids: Baker Academic, 2008); and J. Todd Billings, *The Word of God for the People of God: An Entryway to the Theological Interpretation of Scripture* (Grand Rapids: Eerdmans, 2010).

[12]To take one example from the writer's own evangelical Presbyterian tradition, J. Oliver Buswell's *Systematic Theology of the Christian Religion* (Grand Rapids: Zondervan, 1962) devoted 258 of its total 983 pages to an exhaustive theological analysis of the Olivet Discourse (recorded in Mt 24, Mk 13, and Lk 21) and Revelation.

of the various portions of the Bible in extended detail, they have not, in the process, neglected theological reflection on the significance of what they have analyzed.[13]

The same might be said regarding evangelical Protestantism and the potentialities of biblical theology. Biblical theology was a discipline being pursued within evangelical Protestantism before and alongside its becoming popular in the wider sphere of theological education. The late Geerhardus Vos (1862–1949) published a work on this theme in 1948 that reflected his decades of teaching in this subject area begun at Princeton Theological Seminary in 1892; the work is still in print. Vos's student at Princeton, the Anabaptist scholar Chester Lehman, outdid his teacher by producing a volume of biblical theology on each testament in 1974. Many pastors with insufficient time to labor through such volumes took up such popular works as the late F. F. Bruce's *New Testament Development of Old Testament Themes* (1969). There now exists an important reference tool, the *New Dictionary of Biblical Theology,* and there is currently in production an extended broadly evangelical series, *New Studies in Biblical Theology.*

Yet, the evangelical interest in biblical theology was noteworthy in a particular respect: it had proceeded from a robust commitment to the unity and overarching authority of the Scriptures. Meanwhile, the new mid-century surge of interest in biblical theology was very often content only to draw out the theological significance of select portions or single themes of Scripture (for example, the Ten Commandments, or humanity in the Old Testament).[14] Valuable as these were, such pursuits did not necessarily bespeak a confidence in the overarching theological authority of the Bible. At times, there was the conception that while constructing systematic or dogmatic theology that was extensively grounded in Scripture was becoming almost impossible, biblical-theological reflection on single themes or single issues still remained within the realm of the possible. All this is to say that the two movements—theological exegesis and biblical theology—while worthy of praise, were not themselves aimed at correcting deficiencies especially manifested in evangelical biblical studies.

---

[13]One thinks of the fourteen current volumes of the *New International Greek Testament Commentary* copublished by Eerdmans and Paternoster, coedited by I. Howard Marshall et al. See also the massive two-volume Luke commentary by Darrell L. Bock (Grand Rapids: Baker Academic, 1996). This work extends to 2,150 pages.

[14]These were the actual volumes composed by J. J. Stamm (1967) and Walther Eichrodt (1970).

But this disclaimer cannot be made with anything like the same confidence when we consider the third related movement—the recovery of interest in the history of interpretation. In my view, the single greatest deficit the twentieth century exposed in evangelical biblical and theological work was the neglect of the history of biblical interpretation across the Christian centuries. In my own theological studies in the 1970s, the two standard works on the history of interpretation that were regularly recommended came from the 1880s and the 1940s.[15] Not very much headway was made in this area of theological studies by evangelicals until the release, in 1996, of *Biblical Interpretation: Past and Present.*[16] Since that year, the same publisher has embarked on two ambitious publication series, each of which addresses this neglect, the Ancient Christian Commentary and the Reformation Commentary on Scripture.[17] In candor, it needs to be admitted that this range of historic commentary resources has seldom, if ever, been available previously to Christians who lacked access to a well-stocked academic theological library. And this lack of access has affected a much wider spectrum of Christians than evangelical Christians alone. Such publication series as these, especially in digitalized form, have brought this Christian learning of the ages within the reach of so many more students of Scripture than formerly.

A case study to illustrate. Perhaps it can be said that the evangelical neglect of studying the history of biblical interpretation has proved to be an area of special concern just because of the double evangelical penchant for "proving" points of doctrine from Scripture and the preference shown for delivering consecutive expositions of Scripture. I can recall a distinct episode where neglect of the history of interpretation led to what I can only call interpretative blundering.

The year was 1973, and the scene was a prominent evangelical congregation in the university district of a major North American city. The preacher

[15]The works were F. W. Farrar, *The History of Interpretation* (1886; repr., Grand Rapids: Baker, 1961); and Robert M. Grant, *A Short History of the Interpretation of the Bible* (1948; repr., New York: Macmillan, 1966).

[16]Gerald Bray, *Biblical Interpretation: Past and Present* (Downers Grove, IL: InterVarsity Press, 1996).

[17]The Ancient Christian Commentary on Scripture was launched as a project by InterVarsity Press in 2001 under the general editorship of Thomas Oden. The Reformation Commentary on Scripture was launched as a project by the same publisher in 2011.

(who was a notable minister assisting that congregation during its pastoral vacancy) had chosen to expound the verses in Acts chapter 1 where the remaining apostles, under the direction of Peter, cast lots so as to determine God's designating one of two candidates (Barsabbas and Matthias). Each was a qualified replacement for the traitorous Judas. In short, the preacher said, the whole exercise was a mistake; Peter had erred in urging the remaining apostles to fill a place that—had he only known it—the Holy Spirit had already reserved for the future apostle Paul. It was an example of hasty action, too little prayed about. Upon hearing this exposition, my jaw dropped.

The theological implications of what the preacher was saying cascaded through my mind as I listened. Were not the apostles and others doing just as Jesus instructed: waiting in Jerusalem? Did not the text describe them as having gathered to pray? Was not the one taking the lead in that gathering Peter, widely understood to have functioned as the leader of the apostles? Was not Peter's stated motive that of replenishing the number of eyewitnesses of Jesus' earthly ministry? And yet, the one who interpreted the Scripture on that Sunday in 1973 was saying that the whole thing, superintended by Peter, had been a *colossal error*. I thought to myself that there had to be another, better way of understanding this passage and the action of the gathered apostles—one that did not call so many seemingly evident things into question. And so, as time passed, from time to time I read interpreters of Acts, asking the question, what credible interpreter of Scripture had *ever* faulted Peter and the apostles for their choosing Matthias, after prayer and the drawing of lots, to take the place of Judas?

It proved a long search. There followed an examination of patristic commentaries, Reformation commentaries, Puritan commentaries, Victorian commentaries, and twentieth-century commentaries.[18] No writer I could locate offered a shred of support for the interpretation that I had found so troubling. There came a surprise, however, when one of the latter group, a commentary on Acts by F. F. Bruce (1910–1990), traced this idiosyncratic interpretation to someone who, in that period of my life, I had come to revere as a pulpit giant.[19] This was the former preacher of Westminster

[18]I owe a special debt of gratitude to my student research assistant in 2015–2016, Sarah Grace Kay, for helping me to complete this long quest.

[19]This was the "New International Commentary on the New Testament," a series originally edited

Chapel, Buckingham Gate, London, G. Campbell Morgan (1864–1945).[20] Bruce identified what was in fact Morgan's stated view with these words:

> It has sometimes been suggested that the apostles were wrong in co-opting Matthias to complete their number; that they should have waited until Paul was ready to fulfill the vacancy in God's good time. This is a *complete mistake* [emphasis added]. Paul did not possess the qualifications set out in vv. 21ff.[21]

So, with the source identified, I went on to inspect Morgan's own treatment of the passage. And there it was:

> The election of Matthias was wrong. Their [the disciples'] idea of what was necessary as a witness to the resurrection was wrong. They said that a witness must have been with them from the baptism of John. They thought a witness must be one who had seen Jesus prior to His ascension. As a matter of fact the most powerful incentive to witness was the seeing of Christ after resurrection, as when He arrested Saul of Tarsus on his way to Damascus. So their principle of selection was wrong. Their method of selection was also wrong.[22]

What is illustrated by this anecdote is that in the twentieth century, eccentric biblical interpretation was a not-uncommon feature of mainstream evangelical life. The pulpit giant, Campbell Morgan, had circulated this view in the 1920s; I had heard it repeated a full half century later. Had Campbell Morgan snatched this eccentric interpretation from thin air? So far as can be known, he may have actually borrowed this opinion from a respected nineteenth-century German writer, Rudolf Stier (1800–1862), whose work *The Words of the Apostles* was available in English translation by 1869.[23]

---

by N. B. Stonehouse and later edited by Bruce himself. The series was published simultaneously by Marshall, Morgan, and Scott in the UK and by Eerdmans in the US. The Acts volume of Bruce was first published in 1954 and is still in print in revised form.

[20]G. Campbell Morgan (1863–1945), known in the United States for his lecturing at Moody Bible Institute, Chicago; Biola University, Los Angeles; and the then Gordon Divinity School, Beverly Farms, Massachusetts, as well as for brief pastorates, was minister of Westminster Chapel, London, during two periods: 1904–1917 and 1935–1943.

[21]F. F. Bruce, *The Acts of the Apostles* (Grand Rapids: Eerdmans, 1954), 52. Using a footnote, Bruce identified Morgan as the advocate of the view he critiqued.

[22]G. Campbell Morgan, *Acts of the Apostles* (New York: Revell, 1924), 19.

[23]Rudolf Stier, *The Words of the Apostles*, translated from the second German edition by G. H. Venables (Edinburgh: T&T Clark, 1869), 12-13. Bruce mentions Stier along with Morgan as exponents of the view about apostolic error. It is entirely likely that Morgan made use of the 1869 work.

Now the point of this is simply that it illustrates both that eccentricities of biblical interpretation have been associated even with those of reputation in the evangelical tradition and that such eccentricities can be curbed by an increased awareness of how a particular biblical passage has been understood across the history of the church. I still have a very high opinion of G. Campbell Morgan, and I now know that as a traveling Bible expositor, he habitually took with him a trunk containing Bible study tools.[24] He was not an utterly irresponsible interpreter. But by the time he put his lectures on Acts into print, he surely had had the opportunity to use a library in one of the several American institutions he briefly lectured in so as to test the interpretation that he (in probable reliance on Stier) had been circulating up to that point.[25] He could certainly have prevented the poor sermon I heard five decades later.

Many such anecdotes could be furnished from the century that is now passed. I would stress, however, that historic evangelical Christianity has very often done much better than this. To take just two examples that come readily to mind, one could first consider the seven-volume devotional series on the four Gospels by late Victorian Anglican bishop J. C. Ryle (1816–1900). If one consults any volume of Ryle's *Expository Thoughts on the Gospels,* one finds him making regular reference to Bible commentators, including church fathers, across the Christian centuries.[26] A second example, drawn from the early decades of the twentieth century, is an apologetic work of 1930, *The Virgin Birth of Christ,* by J. Gresham Machen (1881–1937). Written in a period when historic understandings of Christian doctrine were being abandoned, Machen established by extensive reliance on patristic writings that the orthodox Christian understanding of the virginal conception of Jesus Christ was the understanding in closest conformity to the views of the early Christian fathers of the second century.[27]

---

[24]His daughter and biographer, Jill Morgan, supplies this interesting detail in *A Man of the Word* (New York: Revell, 1951), 258.

[25]At various points, while residing in the US, Morgan had lectured extensively in the Bible Institute of Los Angeles (now Biola University) and the then Gordon Divinity School (now Gordon Conwell Theological Seminary).

[26]The Ryle series was first released between 1856 and 1869. The volumes were reprinted as recently as 2007. See, for example, his *Luke*, vol. 1, where he lists the patristic as well as other materials employed in writing his expositions (ix). Listed are Ambrose, Theophylact, Euthymius, Augustine, and Corderius.

[27]J. Gresham Machen, *The Virgin Birth of Christ* (New York: Harper, 1930), chap. 1, "The Virgin Birth in the Second Century." Writers interacted with include Justin Martyr, Aristides, Ignatius, and the anonymous author of the Shepherd of Hermas.

Two caveats. Once we grant that heeding the history of biblical interpretation is vital, we still have challenges to face. For the history of interpretation can display divergence of opinion as well as consensus. This problem can be illustrated by appeal to the famous passage in Paul's letter to the Galatians, where the subject is the face-to-face confrontation of the apostles Paul and Peter (2:11-16). In our discussion of the disputed passage in Acts 1, we confronted the fact that a "rogue" commentator found fault with Peter (and his fellow apostles) when the Scripture narrative itself did not. But in the Galatians passage, by contrast, we find the apostle Paul charging his contemporary, Peter, with clear inconsistency. Peter's refusal to engage in table fellowship with the Gentile converts of Antioch could not be squared with the conclusion to which he gave voice in the dramatic breakthrough of the Gospel to the Gentile family of Cornelius, the Roman centurion of Caesarea (Acts 10). Then and there, Peter had articulated the drastic change in his own understanding with the words,

> I now realize how true it is that God does not show favoritism, but accepts men from every nation that fear him and do what is right. . . . Can anyone keep these people from being baptized with water? They have received the Holy Spirit just as we have. (Acts 10:34-35, 47 NIV 1984)

As we noted in an earlier chapter, Martin Luther, while in process of writing an exposition of this Pauline epistle, found that church fathers Jerome (ca. 347–420) and Augustine (354–430) were not in agreement in their understanding of Peter's role in this episode.[28] Jerome, because of a pre-commitment to the primacy of Peter among the apostles and to an accompanying notion that Peter was kept from erring, sought to deflect Paul's reproof of Peter at Antioch. Augustine, by contrast, while still reverencing Peter in his apostolic role, was more inclined to let Paul's rebuke of Peter stand. Thus, the mere antiquity of an opinion about a major Scripture does not render it infallible. It must still be tested against other Scriptures and against the doctrinal framework (the analogy of faith) we have had passed on to us by those who taught us the Christian faith.

---

[28]See chapter 5.

If it needs to be admitted that consulting earlier interpreters does not, in and of itself, automatically rule out blunders in biblical interpretation, there is also an even more fundamental admission needing to be made. And that is that depending on where the Christian believer of today is situated on the globe, resources offering help in the history of interpretation may be well-nigh nonexistent. The difficulty is admitted, and yet there are signs of hope. To take an example, much of the African continent now has access to the substantial one-volume *Africa Bible Commentary*, prepared by African biblical interpreters who concerned themselves with well-grounded Scripture interpretation. This volume, geared to English-speaking Africa, is also available in French, Portuguese, Swahili, Hausa, and Malagasy.[29] A similar, though distinct, volume is now available for both Southeast Asia and Russian-speaking regions.[30] And for those with computer access, there are massive collections of commentaries on Scripture from across the centuries accessible at no charge from such sources as the Christian Classics Ethereal Library.[31] Collections such as the late nineteenth-century Ante-Nicene, Nicene, and Post-Nicene Fathers series have been digitalized so as to make them available where library facilities are minimal or nonexistent.[32]

QUESTIONS FOR DISCUSSION

1. Can you, like the writer, recall an occasion when a preacher's biblical interpretation seemed fanciful or plainly off base? How did you react? What do you think the preacher might have done differently?
2. It is easier to assert the idea that one's biblical interpretation ought to take into account exemplary interpretation from earlier centuries than

---

[29]Tokunboh Adeyemo, ed., *Africa Bible Commentary: A One-Volume Commentary Written by 70 African Scholars* (Nairobi, Kenya: WordAlive; Grand Rapids: Zondervan, 2010). Though published in the United States, such study tools are often distributed in Africa by Christian charities such as the Langham Trust.

[30]Brian Wintle, ed., *South Asia Bible Commentary: A One-Volume Commentary on the Whole Bible* (Udaipur, India: Open Door; Grand Rapids: Zondervan, 2015). As with the *Africa Bible Commentary*, this is distributed internationally by the Langham Trust. The same agency released the *Slavic Bible Commentary* in late 2016. See the details at www.e-n.org.uk/2017/01/world-news/ukraine-bible-commentary/?search=1.

[31]See www.ccel.org/.

[32]See Early Church Fathers, Protestant edition, from Logos Bible Software, www.logos.com/product/5771/early-church-fathers-protestant-edition.

to ensure that Christians around the globe have the wherewithal to make that happen. What practical steps can make this "best practice" more attainable?

3. Are evangelical Christians vulnerable to the charge that they try to prove too many things from Scripture? Does Scripture itself indicate that it is focused more on some matters than others?

PART III

SOME CONTEMPORARY EXAMPLES THAT SHOULD GIVE US PAUSE

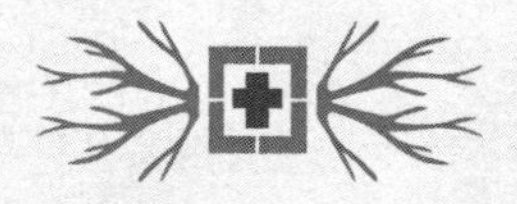

10

Short-Changed for Lack of the Apocrypha?

THUS FAR IN THE BOOK, you will have noticed quite frequent reminders of the curiosity evangelical Christians have today to delve into the literature and practices of the early Christian church. It is important that we grasp that these investigations—innocent enough as they are in themselves—can result in our being seriously misled. So beginning here, and in two chapters following, we will take up contemporary examples of quests that are tending to generate confusion and misunderstanding.

Have you noticed any or all of the following: A mail-order catalogue of household bric-a-brac encouraging you to buy and read "the missing books of the Bible"? A Christian folk troubadour offering for sale a CD of songs "taken from Scripture and the Apocrypha"? The book store displays of Bibles with choices that include and exclude a center section of writings located between Malachi and Matthew? All the signs point to the reemergence of the Old Testament apocryphal writings as a body of religious literature claiming the attention of evangelical Christians.

Bible translations associated with evangelicalism, such as the NIV, the NASB, and the NLT, continue—as before the rise of this recent push to re-appropriate the Apocrypha—to circulate without these additional materials. How did evangelical Christianity come to be in this situation, in which it is regularly asked to give consideration to ancient books that have, by its own way of reckoning, all but dropped out of sight? Answering this question will take us on quite a circuitous route.

First, a definition is in order. Consult a standard reference work such as the *Oxford Dictionary of the Christian Church* and one finds that by the term "apocrypha" is meant "the Biblical books received by the early Church as part of the Greek version of the O.T. but not included in the Hebrew Bible, being excluded by the non-Hellenistic Jews from their canon. Their position in Christian usage has been somewhat ambiguous."[1]

If anything, this definition understates the layers of ambiguity associated with the proper classification of this intertestamental literature that had been composed over a period extending between 300 BC and AD 100. This is a body of literature including 1 and 2 Esdras, Tobit, Judith, Additions to Esther, Wisdom of Solomon, Ecclesiasticus (Ben Sira, or Sirach), Baruch, Letter of Jeremiah, Prayers of Azariah and the Three Young Men, Susanna, Bel and the Dragon, the Prayer of Manasseh, and 1 and 2 Maccabees.[2]

THE SIXTEENTH-CENTURY REFORMATION SHOULD NOT BE BLAMED

Many people today, upon learning that modern evangelical Christianity has neglected this literature, are instinctively inclined to blame the Reformation era. Was it not during that period of time that the German Lutherans and the Swiss Reformed codified their churches' relationship to these books by placing them in a sort of appendix to the Old Testament, printed between Malachi and Matthew?[3] But one does not need to explore the matter in any great depth to find that this development in the sixteenth century was far from the beginning of wrangling over the status of these books. That wrangling had begun in Christianity's earliest centuries, growing out of the Gentile Christian church's belated discovery that the Old Testament in

[1]F. L. Cross, ed., *Oxford Dictionary of the Christian Church* (London: Oxford University Press, 1957), s.v. "Apocrypha," 68. This definition remains unchanged in the ODCC third edition of 1997.

[2]I have utilized the list provided in the article "Apocrypha" by John J. Collins in *Encyclopedia of Early Christianity*, ed. Everett Ferguson (New York: Garland, 1990), 61-62.

[3]Note the especially helpful chapters by Klaus Dietrich Fricke, "The Apocrypha in the Luther Bible," and Wilhelm Neuser, "The Reformed Churches and the Old Testament Apocrypha," in *The Apocrypha in Ecumenical Perspective*, ed. Siegfried Meurer (New York: United Bible Societies, 1991).

Greek (the Septuagint, or LXX), which was the standard employed by Christians and Jews outside Palestine, did not correspond perfectly with the Hebrew Scriptures.

In about AD 180, Melito, a Greek bishop from Sardis in what is today western Turkey, determined to go to Palestine—on behalf of an acquaintance—to "learn the precise facts about the ancient books, particularly their number and order."[4] What he found among the Jewish teachers he consulted must have been somewhat unsettling: on the one hand, the list of books did not extend to nor include any of the books we have come to call "apocrypha." On the other hand, the list of books then vouched for by the Jewish authorities did not perfectly replicate the Old Testament as we now know it. Esther was nowhere to be seen, indicating that at that date, late in the second century, Jewish discussion about the status of this book was still ongoing. In any case, Melito, by his research, had laid down a kind of a marker; notice had been served that the Hebrew Old Testament and the prevalent Christian Old Testament in Greek were at variance.

Meanwhile, events were moving in a direction that would make an impartial adjudication of this question even more difficult. On the one hand, Christians were moving away from the use of the traditional scroll format that had long been used for holy books. In the same second century in which Melito undertook his Palestinian investigation, Christian Scriptures and other literature were increasingly copied and circulated employing the bound "codex" format in which leaves—first of papyrus sheets, later of parchment—were bound together in a book format.[5] This made possible the production of Septuagint Old Testament collections that bound together these intertestamental writings with the Hebrew books; the former seemed validated by their inclusion with the latter. This closer physical association lent greater credence to the notion that the two types of writings were to be equated.

---

[4]As recorded in Eusebius, *The History of the Church*, trans. and ed. G. A. Williamson (New York: Dorset, 1965), 27.6.

[5]The Christian role in the shift of preference from papyrus scrolls to codices (made of papyrus or parchment) is described in Everett Ferguson, "Codex," in *Encyclopedia of Early Christianity*, 219-20; and by T. C. Skeat, "Early Christian Book Production: Papyri and Manuscripts," in *The Cambridge History of the Bible*, ed. G. W. H. Lampe, vol. 2, *The West from the Fathers to the Reformation* (Cambridge: Cambridge University Press, 1969), 554-79.

On the other hand, the use of Greek (which had earlier necessitated the use of the Septuagint) was declining in the western Mediterranean region. This required the gradual translation of the Septuagint, intertestamental writings, and New Testament writings from Greek to Latin. This work, which may have been centered in North Africa or Milan, produced a range of translated texts collectively known as the Old Latin Version.[6] In this way also, the intertestamental literature passed into the west Mediterranean churches in the closest possible association with the books constituting the Hebrew canon and the expanding collection of New Testament writings. Bruce Metzger could accordingly write:

> It is not strange, therefore, that Greek and Latin Church Fathers of the second and third centuries, such as Irenaeus, Tertullian, Clement of Alexandria and Cyprian (none of whom knew any Hebrew), quote the Apocrypha with the same formulas of citation as they use when referring to the books of the Old Testament.[7]

Yet all the while, the discrepancy between the received collection of Hebrew sacred books and these same books translated into Greek with intertestamental writings reflected in the Septuagint, noted first by Melito, became apparent to others who were also situated in the Greek-speaking East. One such was Origen (ca. 185–251), who in compiling his six-column Bible, the *Hexapla*, was confronted with the same evidence of discordant collections as Melito had seen. Athanasius (ca. 300–373), also of Alexandria, admitted the same distinction between the Hebrew canon of the Old Testament and the Greek collection that was reflected in the Septuagint. Accordingly, such other Eastern fathers such as Cyril of Jerusalem (d. 387), Gregory of Nazianzus (ca. 329–390), and Amphilochius (ca. 340–394) drew up formal lists of the Old Testament Scriptures in which the Apocrypha do not appear.[8]

In the West, there was no clear spokesman for this position of reserve (regarding the composition of the canon) before Jerome (ca. 347–420). Already adept in the Greek and Roman classics, he accepted the commission

[6]C. S. C. Williams, "The Text and Canon of the New Testament to Jerome," in *Cambridge History of the Bible*, 2:37-39.
[7]Bruce Metzger, *An Introduction to the Apocrypha* (New York: Oxford University Press, 1957), 178.
[8]Ibid., 179.

of Pope Damasus in 382 to improve the Old Latin Vulgate. In pursuit of this (a project that extended well beyond the death of that pope), Jerome went east and employed a series of tutors by whom he learned Hebrew; his fresh translation of the Old Testament occupied him from 389 to 405. Already by the year 390, he was focusing solely on the Hebrew canon and defended this position by an appeal to what he called "the Hebrew verity."[9]

He elaborated his new understanding of the relative values of the Septuagint and Hebrew Old Testament in *Hebrew Questions on Genesis*; this made clear that Jerome's fresh interpretation of Genesis had been amply enriched by his reliance on Hebrew study and on rabbinic commentary.

Now in the end, everything that had previously been included in the Old Latin Bible (including the Apocrypha) was reproduced in the improved Vulgate. Jerome indicated in prefatory comments to books in the Vulgate his own conviction that the Hebrew canon of the Old Testament should be deferred to. However, over time, his cautions were not heeded.[10] Yet Jerome had put the discussion of the proper role of the Apocrypha in a new framework—that is, he maintained that these writings were suitable for devotional reading but should not be made the foundation for Christian doctrine. When criticized for his stance, he drew attention to the fact that he was upholding a position earlier staked out by Origen. Indeed, his own work had been carried out in reliance on Origen's multicolumn Bible, the *Hexapla*.[11]

JEROME'S DEBTORS

The mainstream church in the West did not heed Jerome's instruction about the superiority of the Hebrew canon over the canon as reflected in the tradition of the Septuagint and Vulgate. His advice would have designated the apocryphal writings as "ecclesiastical books" distinct from canonical books. No one opposed his views more vociferously than did Augustine (354–430); it was Augustine's, not Jerome's, view of things that was ratified at the Council of Carthage in 397. Yet there were important Christian thinkers who gravitated toward the view Jerome had championed. One was

---

[9]Terence G. Kardong, "Vulgate," in *Encyclopedia of Early Christianity*, 932-33; and J. N. D. Kelly, *Jerome: His Life, Writings and Controversy* (New York: Harper & Row, 1975), chap. 15.

[10]Metzger, *Introduction to the Apocrypha*, 180; and David A. deSilva, *Introducing the Apocrypha* (Grand Rapids: Baker Academic, 2002), 37.

[11]Kelly, *Jerome*, 157-58.

his contemporary and sometime friend, Rufinus of Aquileia (ca. 345–410). Among those who later followed Jerome's view were Pope Gregory the Great (540–604), John of Damascus (ca. 675–749), Hugh of St. Victor (ca. 1096–1141), and finally the great Franciscan Hebraist, Nicholas of Lyra (ca. 1270–1340).[12] The general principle illustrated in these who followed Jerome's example was that Christians who had gained knowledge of the Semitic world and had been exposed to the study of Hebrew regarded the Apocrypha as distinct, as a "second" or "ecclesiastical" collection separate from the canon shared with Judaism.

THE *AD FONTES* MOVEMENT OF THE EUROPEAN RENAISSANCE

We are not yet at Luther and the age of Reformation, and for good reason. For the cultural Renaissance that characterized first Mediterranean and then northern Europe relied in large part for its momentum on the recovery of ancient languages. The acquisition of these (a purer Latin, Greek, and Hebrew) would (it was believed) make it possible for aspiring Europeans to write and to speak persuasively, having drawn from the wells of antiquity. Most obviously, the process can be seen to be under way in Renaissance Florence where, by 1397, the Byzantine Greek scholar Manuel Chrysolorus was lecturing in Greek. Chrysolorus was such a sought-after scholar that he was soon enticed away to Bologna and beyond there to Venice and Rome. In his wake arrived the equally important John Argyropoulos (1415–1487). Such Greek study had not been available in western Europe for more than half a millennia.[13] This instruction was soon drawing students from across western Europe. As for classical Greek, which by extension enriched biblical study, so ancient Hebrew, when made available in western Europe, had the same enriching effect.

As it had been with Jerome, western Europeans of the Renaissance era—in order to acquire Hebrew—needed to obtain the services of Jewish teachers. The German humanist Johann Reuchlin (1455–1522), already an

---

[12]deSilva, *Introducing the Apocrypha*, 37. For further detail on Hugh of St. Victor and the abbey in which Hebrew studies were so encouraged, see F. F. Bruce, *The Canon of Scripture* (Downers Grove, IL: InterVarsity Press, 1988), 99-100.

[13]Jonathan W. Zophy, *A Short History of Renaissance and Reformation Europe*, 4th ed. (Upper Saddle River, NJ: Pearson Prentice Hall, 2009), 75.

accomplished Graecist and Latinist, acquired Hebrew with help from a Jewish physician; by 1506, he was able to publish a Hebrew grammar.[14] In Spain, another center of Hebrew study, *conversados* (persons converted from Judaism) became the authoritative Christian Hebraists; they took on pupils, and there was such a proliferation of those eager to study this language that a new university, the University of the Alcalá, had from its founding in 1499 professorial chairs in Latin, Greek, and Hebrew.[15] From this Spanish university would emerge by 1520 the Complutensian Polyglot multicolumn Bible offering the Latin Vulgate, Greek, Hebrew, and (where applicable) Aramaic.[16] The sponsor of this massive, multiyear project was the Roman Catholic cardinal and Franciscan monk Jiménez de Cisneros (1436–1517). We should not be surprised to find that his orientation to Hebrew study had led him to embrace Jerome's conception of the role of the Apocrypha. At its publication in 1520 the Complutensian Polyglot placed the Apocrypha in an appendix.[17]

Jiménez de Cisneros was not alone as a Roman Catholic authority holding this conviction in this period. Another, also devoted to the biblical languages, was the Italian-born Santes Pagnino (1470–1541), a Dominican scholar who produced a fresh revision of the Latin Vulgate, in reliance on the Hebrew and Greek, at Lyons in 1527. This edition, titled *Veteris et Novi Testamenti nova translatio,* honored the conception of Jerome in separating the Apocrypha from the Hebrew books of the Old Testament. His taking this stance did not prevent his gaining the written endorsements of two contemporary popes, Adrian VI (reigned 1522–1523) and Clement VII (reigned 1523–1534), for his edition.[18] Another, who like Cisneros attained the rank of cardinal, Thomas Cajetan (1469–1534), was—like him—both a friend of the literary renaissance and a supporter of Jerome's approach to the Apocrypha.[19]

[14]Lewis W. Spitz Jr., *The Religious Renaissance of the German Humanists* (Cambridge, MA: Harvard University Press, 1963), chap. 4.

[15]Erika Rummel, *Jiménez de Cisneros: On the Threshold of Spain's Golden Age* (Tempe, AZ: Center for Medieval and Renaissance Studies, 1999), chap. 4.

[16]Basil Hall, "Cardinal Jiménez and the Complutensian Bible," chap. 1 in *Humanists and Reformers: 1500–1900* (Edinburgh: T&T Clark, 1990).

[17]Metzger, *Introduction to the Apocrypha*, 180.

[18]Ibid.

[19]Ibid.; deSilva, *Introducing the Apocrypha*, 37. Martin Luther was to stand before Cardinal Cajetan at Augsburg in 1518. Given his reputation as a friend of scriptural reform, Luther was disappointed when told by Cajetan to renounce his Ninety-Five Theses without discussion.

THE SIXTEENTH-CENTURY REFORMATION, WITH SUCH FOUNDATIONS, PRESSED THIS POSITION

The leading personalities in the Protestant Reformation of the sixteenth century were, by and large, participants in this cultural and linguistic renaissance that, by 1517, was more than a century old. The reacquisition of Greek and Hebrew were highly important to them, and such studies were offered in an increasing number of universities by their day. Universities offering these studies were said to be participating in the "new learning." But those who emerged as Protestant Reformers were not just linguists; they were people who cared very much for the discussions about the composition of the Bible that had, by then, been going on for centuries. It was of very great significance that an authoritative edition of the *Works* of Jerome (letters and treatises) was published from Basel in 1516.[20]

Though Martin Luther did not release his translation of the complete Old Testament (comprising six volumes) until 1534, the constituent parts of this project had been available in individual volumes much earlier. In 1522, the year when his New Testament translation first appeared, he also released the first volume of the Old Testament translation project. That volume, constituting the books of Moses, contained a table of contents of what was to come in all future volumes. Already at this point, Luther made clear that he intended to segregate the apocryphal writings in a separate volume (whereas earlier they had appeared interspersed among the biblical books of the Hebrew canon). This intention was in fact realized when, in 1534, the full "Luther Bible" was available to the public.[21] Luther had not only segregated the Apocrypha from scriptural writings but had taken the liberty of drastically changing the order in which they had usually followed one another, interspersed among books of the Old Testament. The Apocrypha was now available in the vernacular language as pious reading material yet distinct from the canonical books.

The conviction implicit in this change found formal expression in 1580 in the first section of the *Formula of Concord*: "We believe, teach, and confess

---

[20]Eugene F. Rice, *Saint Jerome in the Renaissance* (Baltimore: Johns Hopkins University Press, 1985), 118-19.

[21]Klaus Dietrich Fricke, "The Apocrypha in the Luther Bible," in Meurer, *Apocrypha in Ecumenical Perspective*, 48-51.

that the prophetic and apostolic writings of the Old and New Testaments are the only rule and norm according to which all doctrines and teachers alike must be appraised and judged."[22]

In Reformed Zurich in German-speaking Switzerland, things moved just as fast as in Lutheran Wittenberg. By 1529, in a way clearly dependent on the new way of viewing the Apocrypha advanced by Luther earlier in the decade, Leo Jud (1482–1542) published his own freestanding translation of the Apocrypha. "These are the books which the Fathers did not count among biblical Scripture, and which are not found among the Hebrews" proclaimed the title page of Jud's collection. Availability yet disassociation were now the order of the day. Having appeared in this separate volume, apocryphal writings subsequently appeared as a collection within the large *Zurich Bible* of 1531.[23] One can observe a note of concession toward a cantonal population just recently swept into the jurisdiction of a Reformed church in this preface prepared for this Bible:

> These books, here appended to the biblical books, are printed by us, not because they should be held as equal to Holy Scripture in value and esteem, but so that those who have read them and like them should have no reason to complain that they are lacking and so that anyone may find something to his taste.[24]

The same attitudes entirely are found in prefaces to Bibles published at Geneva in 1540 and 1546.[25] The Protestant confession produced in the Low Countries, the Belgic Confession (1561), took the same approach; while allowing that the apocryphal books "may certainly be read," the confession insisted on differentiation. "They do not have such power and virtue that one could confirm from their testimony any point of faith."[26] Only slightly more accommodating were the *Articles of Religion*, approved for the Church of England in 1562. Insisting that the Apocrypha could not be used to establish any doctrine, it was still allowed that they were to be read "for

---

[22]"Formula of Concord I.1," as printed in *The Book of Concord: The Confessions of the Evangelical Lutheran Church*, trans. and ed. Theodore G. Tappert (Philadelphia: Fortress, 1959), 464.

[23]Wilhelm Neuser, "The Reformed Churches and the Apocrypha," in Meurer, *Apocrypha in Ecumenical Perspective*, 88-89.

[24]Deutsche Bibel 12.23n5, quoted in Neuser, "Reformed Churches and the Apocrypha," 90.

[25]Neuser, "Reformed Churches and the Apocrypha," 95.

[26]Belgic Confession, article 7, as printed in the *Psalter Hymnal* (Grand Rapids: CRC Publications, 1987), 820.

instruction of life and manners." Provision was still made for their inclusion in the cycles of public Scripture readings.[27] The Apocrypha was kept accessible and yet disassociated from the canonical writings.

In the background of all this determination to make distinctions was the fact that supporters of the Reformation cause were conscious that Roman Catholicism was still relying on the apocryphal writings for support for practices that Protestants opposed as lacking actual biblical support. These were prayers for the deceased (understood to be warranted by appeal to 2 Macc 12:43-45) and the acquisition of merit by the performance of good works (Tob 12:9; Ecclus 3:30; 2 Esdr 8:33; 13:46).[28] A delicate line was being walked: early Protestantism must signal to its adherents that the *religious* use of the Apocrypha was still appropriate while at the same time upholding the principle that there was no *doctrinal* value in these same writings. This somewhat calibrated standoff might have held for some time except that there came about an escalation of the debate, the repercussions of which have lasted for centuries. That escalation took place in the fourth session of the Council of Trent (1546).

HOW THE COUNCIL OF TRENT ALTERED THE EQUATION

As recently as the 1520s, scholarly Roman Catholics had been affirming the distinction drawn by Jerome between what he called the "Hebrew verity" of the books recognized by Jews and the intertestamental books. Jiménez de Cisneros, Santes Pagnino, and Thomas Cajetan, participants in the Christian humanist movement, had made this distinction and suffered no hardship for doing so. But in that fourth session of the Council of Trent, the cardinals and theologians of Rome affirmed what had not previously been claimed: that all the books of the Old and New Testament (apocryphal writings included) had been "dictated either by Christ's own word or by the Holy Ghost and preserved in the Catholic Church by a continuous succession." All the books of the Hebrew canon, the apocryphal texts, and the standard New Testament writings were then named individually. These books were to be received as they had been circulated

[27]Owen Chadwick, "The Significance of the Deuterocanonical Writings in the Anglican Tradition," in Meurer, *Apocrypha in Ecumenical Perspective*, 116-17.
[28]Metzger, *Introduction to the Apocrypha*, 181.

in the traditional pre-Reformation Latin Vulgate. Those who taught otherwise were subject to the Church's anathema.[29] The stating of this position entailed a raising of the stakes in the theological debate of that time. Protestants had been allowing for the devotional reading of the intertestamental writings while insisting that Christian doctrines might not be proved from them.

For almost a century following the Council of Trent, the Protestant position of restrained use of the Apocrypha would continue. Even so, a new note began to be detected in discussion. Trent had claimed an undifferentiated divine inspiration for all the works considered to be sacred writings. Was this a defensible position? Already in 1547, John Calvin had expressed his strong misgivings. He insisted that by this decree, Rome had paved the way for the continued maintenance of doctrines not supported in the truly canonical Scriptures.[30] The *Westminster Confession of Faith* (1647), the doctrinal articles on the basis of which the religious unity of England and Scotland was sought, reflected this more stringent position. The books of the Old and New Testament were enumerated as alone inspired of God; the Apocrypha was pointedly excluded as having "no authority in the Church of God." They were to be "approved and made use of no more than other human writings."[31]

Meanwhile, Protestant Bibles on the Continent and in Britain maintained the practice commenced in the earliest decades of the Reformation: the Apocrypha continued to appear in an appendix at the close of the Old Testament. This was true of the many editions of the Geneva Bible (1560) and all the early versions of the King James or Authorized Version of 1611. Their continued use in this period is reflected in the oft-told story of the persecuted Baptist, John Bunyan (1628–1688). Bunyan wracked his memory, without success, to find the location of a quotation that had consoled him in a time of distress. The statement, "Did ever any trust in the Lord and was

---

[29]"Decree Concerning the Canonical Scriptures," 4th session, April 8, 1546, as reprinted in *Creeds of Christendom*, ed. Philip Schaff, vol. 2, *The Greek and Latin Creeds* (1877; repr., Grand Rapids: Baker, 1977), 79-81.

[30]Neuser, "Reformed Churches and the Apocrypha," 98, 99, draws attention to Calvin's 1547 "Antidote to the Decrees of the Council of Trent." This treatise is available in English translation in *Calvin's Tracts and Treatises*, trans. Henry Beveridge, vol. 3 (Edinburgh: Calvin Translation Society, 1851).

[31]Westminster Confession of Faith, 1.2 and 3 (Glasgow: Free Presbyterian Publications, 1966).

confounded?" was eventually located by him not within the sixty-six books of the Protestant canon but in the apocryphal Ecclesiasticus. Evidently, Bunyan had at some past time in his life heard the Apocrypha or read these writings himself.[32] Yet gradually over time, three forces called this transitional arrangement into question.

First was the question of economy in book production. Not every Protestant Bible purchaser cared for the added bulk of pages necessitated by the insertion of the Apocrypha as an appendix between Malachi and Matthew. Printers found they could lower the price of Bibles that excluded this content. One could say that market forces took charge so that over a two-century period Protestants grew steadily less familiar with the Apocrypha and their contents. Second, in Britain and her colonies, the promotion of the use of the Apocrypha in church life came to be closely associated in the public mind with the unpopular religious policies of the Stuart monarchy; these seemed to move the national churches steadily in a less robustly Protestant direction. Accordingly, the second half of the seventeenth century was one in which those of Puritan and Nonconformist sympathies pressed steadily for the elimination of the Apocrypha from both printed Bibles and liturgical use.[33]

By the early nineteenth century a third factor came into play: the massive role exercised in the circulation of the Bible by various Bible societies. While such societies had been founded by German Pietists in the seventeenth century,[34] the great dynamic force in early nineteenth-century Bible distribution was the British and Foreign Bible Society, founded in London in 1804. While German Pietist Bible societies had consistently circulated Bibles with the Apocrypha (in an appendix) in a way consistent with European Protestant practice since the Reformation, this was not true for Bibles distributed by the London society. Partly for reasons of economy of production and partly because the British evangelical constituency supportive of the society had learned to live without the apocryphal writings in the preceding 150

---

[32]The story, recounted in Bunyan's *Grace Abounding to the Chief of Sinners* (1666), is reported by Metzger, *Introduction to the Apocrypha*, 199. Ecclesiasticus 2:10 was the reference.

[33]Owen Chadwick, "Significance of the Deuterocanonical Writings," in Meurer, *Apocrypha in Ecumenical Perspective*, 121.

[34]Douglas Shantz, *An Introduction to German Pietism* (Baltimore: Johns Hopkins University Press, 2013), chap. 8.

years, the British and Foreign Bible Society did not make a priority of circulating Bibles including them.[35]

British and Continental Protestant practice came into conflict in the period after 1804, during which time the London-based society attempted to help affiliate societies in the various major cities of Europe by supplying them with affordable copies of vernacular Scriptures for distribution. Affiliate societies in Francophone and Germanic Europe explained to the British society that their constituencies looked with suspicion on Scriptures omitting the Apocrypha. The British society then explored the idea of producing copies of the Bible that met this expectation for European distribution but pulled back from this resolve when a concerted minority of its constituency balked and withdrew to form a rival society. Yet across the span of the nineteenth century, German Bible societies grew more tolerant of the British concept and gradually offered for sale Scriptures with and without the Apocrypha in appendix.[36]

FROM THE LATE NINETEENTH CENTURY TO TODAY

Though the revision of the King James Version as the English Revised Version (completed 1885) was followed by a fresh translation of the Apocrypha (1896), the American expression of this fresh translation, the American Standard Version (1901), was not so followed.[37] North American Protestant attitudes toward the Apocrypha were, if anything, cooler than could be said to be true in Britain and Europe. Though Bibles with and without the Apocrypha had been published within the United States since the Revolutionary era, demand for access to the Apocrypha was not high.[38] The American Bible Society, founded in New York in 1816, generally followed the policy of the sister society at London; its own reluctance to circulate the Apocrypha with the Scriptures of the Old and New

---

[35]See the helpful overview of Wilhelm Gundert, "The Bible Societies and the Deuterocanonical Writings," in Meurer, *Apocrypha in Ecumenical Perspective*, 134-50.

[36]Gundert, "Bible Societies and the Deuterocanonical Writings," 137, 138. See also Kenneth J. Stewart, *Restoring the Reformation: British Evangelicalism and the Francophone Réveil, 1816–1849* (Carlisle, UK: Paternoster, 2006), 60, 176-77.

[37]F. F. Bruce, *The English Bible: A History of Translations* (Oxford: Oxford University Press, 1961), 138-39.

[38]Jack P. Lewis, "Some Aspects of the Problem of the Inclusion of the Apocrypha," in Meurer, *Apocrypha in Ecumenical Perspective*, 161.

Testament meant that its Scripture distribution in Latin America encountered some resistance.[39]

So far as the twentieth-century American Protestant world is concerned, renewed interest was sparked especially by the translation effort of E. J. Goodspeed (1871–1962), who with J. M. Powis Smith produced *The Complete Bible: An American Translation* (1938), which contained a new translation of the Apocrypha.[40] The *Revised Standard Version* of the Bible (OT, 1946; NT, 1952) supplied a fresh translation of the Apocrypha as a supplement in 1957. As an indication of the level of unease that this last development generated, by way of anticipation, Princeton Theological Seminary's 1956 Stone Lectures were devoted to questions about the Protestant canon. The perspective of the lecturer toward the Apocrypha was not one of hospitality.[41]

That being so, it was not surprising that the production of late twentieth-century Bible translations oriented to the evangelical Protestant world such as the New International Version (1984, 2011) and the New American Standard Bible (1960, 1995) reflected this skeptical point of view. But of a piece with earlier American efforts resulting in the Revised Standard Version (1946, 1952), British initiatives of 1947 leading to the release of the New English Bible (1961, 1970) were intended from the start to supply the Apocrypha as an appendix to the Old Testament.

The New Revised Standard Version (1989) was more ambitious still: it was intended from the start that it be made available in a Protestant-only format (lacking the Apocrypha), a Roman Catholic format (with the Apocrypha in their traditional interspersed positions among the Old Testament writings), and a common format (including all the writings honored by Protestants, Roman Catholics, and Eastern Orthodox).

In that same era of thawed relationships between Protestants, Catholics, and Orthodox (largely attributable to the emphasis on ecumenicity within the Roman Catholic Second Vatican Council [1962–1965]), two new Bible versions, distinguished by their reliance on Greek, Hebrew, and Aramaic,

---

[39]Ibid., 163.

[40]Ibid., 165.

[41]The lectures in their published form, Floyd V. Filson, *Which Books Belong in the Bible: A Study of the Canon* (Philadelphia: Westminster, 1957), remains a most helpful statement of the question as it was judged in the mid-twentieth century.

were produced by scholars within Roman Catholicism. These, the Jerusalem Bible (1966, 1985) and the New American Bible (1970, 2012), preserve the Roman Catholic custom of interspersing the apocryphal books across the Old Testament canon. In prefaces to these books, acknowledgment is given to the fact that Protestants do not recognize them (as not being part of the Hebrew canon) and at the same time the repeated insistence, first made at the Council of Trent, that these writings are "inspired in the same way" as all biblical writings.

ASSESSING WHERE WE STAND IN THE TWENTY-FIRST CENTURY

Our concerns can be fairly summed up in the following ways. First, there should be no debate at all as to the value of these intertestamental writings in their ability to shed light on the religious and social setting in which the Jewish people lived after their return from exile. Everyone interested in the period when the Jewish people were dominated by Persians, Greeks, and Romans can learn valuable things by becoming familiar with this literature. And yet it needs to be said that the body of recovered intertestamental literature in our possession today now considerably *exceeds* these books (because of ongoing discoveries), whose place in the canon has been for so long a matter of discussion and debate. Why should some of this intertestamental literature be privileged above others?

Second, there should equally be no debate at all that this intertestamental literature formed part of the thought-world of Jesus and the writers of the New Testament. The first Greek New Testament I acquired as a student indicated in its indices that there are at least 130 places in the New Testament where literary affinity exists between the words of the New Testament and the wording found in intertestamental writings.[42] And yet it needs to be said that even in the few places where the New Testament writers quote intertestamental literature directly (e.g., Jude 14, 15) the formula of quotation does not identify the intertestamental source as Scripture.[43]

---

[42]*The Greek New Testament*, 2nd ed., ed. Kurt Aland et al. (New York: United Bible Society, 1968), 918-19.

[43]On this point, note the emphasis of Patrick J. Harrigan, SJ, "The O.T. Apocrypha in the Early Church and Today," in *The Canon Debate*, ed. Lee Martin McDonald and James A. Sanders (Peabody, MA: Hendrickson, 2002), 200.

Third, far from it being the case that it is just recalcitrant Protestants holding out against an otherwise unified front of Roman Catholic, Eastern Orthodox, and other Christians on the question of the status of these intertestamental writings, one finds on closer examination that not even Roman Catholicism and Eastern Orthodoxy are in agreement as to which intertestamental writings should be approved. Moreover, Eastern Orthodoxy has not declared the Apocrypha (which it prefers to call the deuterocanonical books) to be divinely inspired; it has not approved them to be read in churches.[44] And Eastern Orthodoxy (which has actually allowed open discussion of these matters up to the present) stands on different ground when estimating the deuterocanonical literature than does the "Church of the East" (Assyrian Orthodox), the Ethiopian Orthodox, and the Coptic (Egyptian) Orthodox Church. When one is confronted by this bewildering array of attitudes on this question, it becomes clear that a coexistence of convictions rather than a capitulation of convictions should be the appropriate stance.[45]

Fourth, it is far from the case that only Protestants have raised questions about the historicity and accuracy of the intertestamental writings. Modern Roman Catholic scholarship seems to be caught in the dilemma of, on the one hand, maintaining with the Council of Trent that these writings share a common inspiration with all the other biblical writings, and on the other, allowing that serious historical inaccuracy mars some of these writings. The writer John J. Collins utilizes terms such "elements of fantasy" to describe 2 Maccabees, "fictional" to describe Judith, and "folk tale" to describe Tobit.[46] P. J. Harrington concludes, "It is generally futile to try to discover and defend the historical details in these books. We are on somewhat firmer ground with I Esdras and I & II Maccabees."[47] Unless one is ready to suppose that divine inspiration ensures *nothing* as to the quality and accuracy of writing, this conflicted Roman Catholic position appears to be unsustainable.

---

[44]The distinctive Eastern Orthodox approach to these questions is described by Elias Oikonomous in "Deuterocanonicals in the Orthodox Church," in Meurer, *Apocrypha in Ecumenical Perspective*, 24, 25.

[45]This is exactly the point made by Jack P. Lewis, "Some Aspects of the Inclusion of the Apocrypha," in Meurer, *Apocrypha in Ecumenical Perspective*, esp. 186-88.

[46]John J. Collins, "Apocrypha, Old Testament," in *Encyclopedia of Early Christianity*, ed. Everett Ferguson, 61-62.

[47]Harrigan, "O.T. Apocrypha," 208.

Fifth, as at the era of sixteenth-century Reformation, it is worth considering again that Roman Catholicism continues to maintain distinctive doctrines and practices that lean for support on places and statements found only in these intertestamental writings. Jack P. Lewis encapsulates the problem thus:

> Opponents of the inclusion of the Apocrypha remain as concerned about the content of this literature as they have been at least since the time of the Reformation. Included in areas of concern are the historical veracity of some of the books and the doctrinal contents of others. Concern continues about ideas of purgatory and prayers for the dead (2 Macc: 12:46), the merit of works (Tobit 4:10; 12:9; 14:10-11), exorcism (Tobit 6:7, 11) and almsgiving atoning for sin (Sirach 3:30).[48]

Sixth and last, we need to consider that ongoing pleadings on behalf of the role to be played by the Apocrypha today have a considerable "romantic" element to them. All branches of the Christian church lament the curse of biblical illiteracy and a lack of familiarity with the story line of redemptive history. In some branches of the church the difficulty is that a former, impressive biblical literacy is evaporating; in other branches the difficulty is that the legacy of centuries of restriction of personal Bible ownership and private Bible study have not easily been erased. Where does Apocrypha literacy fit into this major challenge? Surely no one will maintain that it is as urgent as biblical literacy itself. Even liturgically oriented churches that have allowed a place for the voluntary reading of Apocryphal writings in church services have observed this option going largely unexercised.[49] Those who pine over the diminished role of the Apocrypha compared to a half millennium ago need to take care that they are not venerating an imagined past.

QUESTIONS FOR DISCUSSION

1. Does the Bible you regularly use include the apocryphal books? Are these interspersed among the Old Testament writings or grouped together after the prophet Malachi? Is there explanation added that distinguishes these, singly or together, from the undisputed Old Testament writings?

---

[48]Lewis, "Problems of Inclusion," 186.

[49]Chadwick, "Significance of the Deuterocanonical Writings," 127-28.

2. Have you ever been present when the apocryphal writings were used as part of the reading for a given service of worship? Were comments made that distinguished these writings from others, or were all treated the same?
3. It was late in the second century before Greek-speaking Christians (like Melito of Sardis) learned that their Old Testament collection did not correspond to the collection honored by Judaism. What ground or grounds kept Greek-speaking (and later Latin-speaking) Christians from accepting the judgment of Judaism on this question?
4. How do you grapple, comparatively, with the need to reverse growing biblical illiteracy and the desirability of at least greater familiarity with the apocryphal writings? Are these distinguishable issues or a single issue needing a remedy?

11

Bringing Back Monasticism?

EVANGELICAL CHRISTIANITY SHOULD BE MORE familiar with the various branches of Christian monasticism, both male and female. When one considers that both movements have sought to elevate the standard of Christian living and devotion in times when mainstream Christianity has been lax and that both have regularly sought the global expansion of the faith through missionary labor, one is entitled to wonder why these two expressions of Christianity have not become better friends.

The answer to this question, from the evangelical Protestant side, surely has to do with the early Protestant era. Ex-monastics such as Martin Luther (1483–1546) of Wittenberg (who married the former nun, Katie von Bora), Martin Bucer of Strasbourg (1491–1551), and Peter Martyr Vermigli of Florence (1500–1562) were at the forefront of efforts to lead in the reform of European Christianity.[1] These and others (such as John Calvin) with no monastic past argued that monasticism was part of late medieval Christianity's malaise rather than any part of its remedy.[2] It was not only monasticism's tendency to entropy that troubled them (the institutional church

[1]On this fascinating point, see Scott Hendrix, *Recultivating the Vineyard: The Reformation Agendas of Christianization* (Louisville, KY: Westminster John Knox, 2004), 24-28; and Owen Chadwick, *The Early Reformation on the Continent* (Oxford: Oxford University Press, 2001), chap. 8.

[2]It remained the case in many Protestant territories that preexisting monasteries and convents were permitted to continue to function, usually with the stipulation that no new recruits would be permitted. Kirsi Stjerna, *Women and the Reformation* (Oxford: Blackwell, 2008), chap. 2.

displayed this also); rather, it was the foundational assumptions of a movement that urged that singleness was superior to marriage and family and that monastic life cultivated a personal sanctity beyond the reach of Christians in society.[3]

Though this Protestant critique stuck, the making of it did not require the Reformers to ignore the positive contributions made by a number of earlier monk-theologians. The Dominican Johannes Tauler (ca. 1300–1361) influenced the young Luther;[4] the Cistercian Bernard of Clairvaux (1090–1153) was a favorite writer of Calvin;[5] the Benedictine Ratramnus of Corbie (d. 868) enabled English reformers Thomas Cranmer (1489–1556) and Nicholas Ridley (1500–1555) to understand the Lord's Supper in a different way.[6]

We now speak regularly of climate change and mean by it melting glaciers and rising temperatures. But we can as appropriately speak of another climate change. In our time, some Catholic bishops came to urge their flocks to support Billy Graham crusades, while concurrently numerous evangelical Protestants began to visit monasteries for prayer retreats. Protestants are now busy exploring the various forms of monasticism that, instead of expiring under the barrage of criticism focused on it five centuries ago, has persevered and adapted. Yet the current rekindling of the evangelical imagination regarding monasticism (in both its male and female expressions) is not without perils, the chief of which is myopia—that is, a poor ability to discern things at a distance. Myopia is a common affliction among Christians who are novices in any branch of the Christian family with which they

---

[3]See, for example, Martin Luther's treatise "On Monastic Vows," in *Luther's Works*, ed. James Atkinson, vol. 44, *Christian in Society I* (Philadelphia: Fortress, 1966), and the critical references to developments in monastic life in the Augsburg Confession, art. 27. See Theodore G. Tappert, ed., *The Book of Concord* (Philadelphia: Fortress, 1959), 70-80. See also the discussion on monastic vows in Melanchthon's 1521 *Loci Communes*, Willhelm Pauck, ed., *Melanchthon and Bucer*, Library of Christian Classics, vol. 19 (Philadelphia: Westminster, 1969), 59-61.

[4]Luther's early fascination with German mystics such as Tauler is highlighted by his republishing of "The German Theology," attributed to Tauler. On this point see James Kittelson, *Luther the Reformer* (Minneapolis: Augsburg, 1986), 76-78. The treatise of Tauler is reprinted in Ray C. Petry, ed., *Late Medieval Mysticism* (London: SCM, 1957), 321-50.

[5]A. N. S. Lane, *John Calvin: Student of the Church Fathers* (Grand Rapids: Baker Academic, 1999), chap. 4.

[6]The treatise of Ratramnus, "Christ's Body and Blood," was republished in George R. McCracken, ed., *Early Medieval Theology* (London: SCM, 1957), 109-47. For Ratramnus's Reformation-era influence, see A. G. Dickens, *The English Reformation* (London: Batsford, 1964), 186, 248; and Felicity Heal, *The Reformation in Britain and Ireland* (Oxford: Oxford University Press, 2003), 324.

are newly acquainted. This difficulty, when expressed in a different way, is that it is too easy to fall prey to an idealized notion of the Christian past.

WHICH MONASTICISM?

By stressing the need to discern things at a distance, I do not mean that monasticism can be studied only in connection with its ancient origins; after all, the phenomenon of monasticism persists to this day. I do mean to stress, however, that we cannot properly appraise the distinct parts of monasticism without some idea of the whole progression. Three recent inquiries into monasticism by evangelical Christians have concentrated on the parts of monasticism without furnishing us with any larger picture.

Dennis Okholm's *Monk Habits for Everyday People* provides a window into this Azusa Pacific professor's more than two-decades-long fascination with Benedictine monasticism.[7] He indicates that he is among thousands of Benedictine oblates who have espoused the way of Benedict while married and at large in society.[8] Now, the monastic movement itself, originally associated with the desert regions of eastern Egypt, Sinai, and Syria, had spanned the Mediterranean world and reached as far west as Ireland. There was two-way traffic involving Easterners such as Athanasius who, when exiled to the West in AD 336, took with him his eventual spiritual classic about the desert monastic patriarch, *The Life of Antony,* and curious westerners such as John Cassian who went to the eastern deserts circa AD 385 to observe the movement firsthand.

Benedictinism, the expression of monasticism that Okholm investigated through long association, represents the attempt by Benedict of Nursia (480–550) to adapt this monasticism of the desert to a different society, a different climate, and a different temperament. If desert monasticism represented the daring, the heroic, and the bold, European Benedictinism (the term "Benedictine" only came into common use after AD 1300) represented a monasticism that kept clear of extremes; it offered a stable, housed, communal life characterized by work, prayer, and devotion. It was a fairly

---

[7]Dennis E. Okholm, *Monk Habits for Everyday People: Benedictine Spirituality for Protestants* (Grand Rapids: Baker, 2007).

[8]As defined in the *New International Dictionary of the Christian Church*, ed. J. D. Douglas (Grand Rapids: Zondervan, 1974), an oblate is a person "who shares in the common life of a monastery without taking the vows."

comfortable life and drew its recruits not from the margins of society but from the center. Serfs and vassals needn't apply.

Okholm, who traveled a trajectory that led him from Pentecostal roots and a Baptist phase into mainline Presbyterianism, finds in Benedictinism a kind of access point to an early, pre-papal Christian antiquity. In its ordered devotion, he finds an antidote for the superficial froth that characterizes so much evangelical spirituality; in its communal life and deliberation, he finds an alternative model for the way in which Christians should weigh matters of import. To his credit, Okholm devotes an appendix of his book to the long-standing Protestant critique of the monastic life.[9]

But left unanswered is the paramount question, why select Benedictinism and not the still earlier desert monasticism? After all, desert monasticism was the *original*. Or why not the hardy life of the Irish monks, who dwelled in beehive-like stone shelters (their own desert-like existence) on their Atlantic-facing coasts and islands? Or why not the later Cistercians (a group *I* take to be exemplary), who followed later, carving productive monastery farms from swamp and forest? Notably, these Cistercians proposed to improve on Benedictinism's seeming default tendency to get comfortable and to acquire wealth and property.

By contrast, Karen Sloan, a campus minister at Quinnipiac University, Connecticut, was drawn to the form of monasticism that took its rise in the thirteenth century under the leadership of Dominic (1170–1221). Her extended look at Dominicanism is provided in *Flirting with Monasticism*.[10] A mainline Presbyterian like Okholm, Sloan for her own part was drawn to investigate this variety of monastic life because—when already open to sampling various forms of Christian spirituality—she met a handsome recruit (novice) who was entering the probationary year during which it would be determined how well he fit the Dominican order. During the time Sloan spent hoping that the novice would find the Dominican order a poor fit (leaving him, in consequence, available for an ongoing relationship), she gradually became a perceptive interpreter of his order. The novice did find his calling in Dominican life (the Dominicans approved), but the chagrined

---

[9]See Okholm, *Monk Habits*, 115-29.

[10]Karen E. Sloan, *Flirting with Monasticism: Finding God in Ancient Paths* (Downers Grove, IL: InterVarsity Press, 2006).

Sloan nevertheless pressed on to understand this way of life more fully. It is to her credit that she did not walk away, crestfallen.

But there are loose ends in her narrative. We are told repeatedly that the Dominicans are an order of friar-preachers; that is, rather than being pure contemplatives, they serve the Christian world as priest-pastors of churches. But Sloan, rather like Okholm in his admiration of the Benedictines, was most fascinated by the order's contemplative devotion. She can acknowledge that in the Dominican past there was energetic outward ministry: the order's known theological prowess (illustrated by theologians such as Thomas Aquinas) was at times turned to the dubious purpose of assisting the medieval Inquisition in its hounding of Jews and of Christians of doubtful orthodoxy. One suspects that a Dominican writer would enumerate the distinctives of this order differently than Sloan has done and lay much more stress on acts of ministry and mission carried out *beyond* cloister and church walls. Savonarola, the turbulent monk-reformer of Florence (1452–1498), would be one such striking example of Dominican activism. One also suspects that Sloan, who writes with an admirable clarity, would have utilized her keen powers of observation and description just as happily on the Benedictines or Cistercians if she had been providentially introduced to a handsome novice oriented to such an alternative order.

With the volume of Scott Bessenecker, *The New Friars,*[11] we move beyond the commending of monastic devotion and community to a consideration of the possibility that monasticism might serve as a pattern for evangelical activism. The friars, whether Franciscan, Dominican, or Carmelite, were itinerant, rather than cloistered, and they championed activism in society on behalf of the unevangelized and needy. Bessenecker means to appropriate the preacher-friar aspect of monasticism for the equipping of a new generation of evangelical missionaries to the urban slums and garbage-heap communities of the developing world. It is not monastic dress, communal life, or styles of devotion that fires the imagination of this author, but the model of a voluntary, celibate, impassioned ministry to the poorest and neediest that he sees displayed in the careers of Francis of Assisi (1181–1226), Bartolomé de las Casas (1474–1566), and Mother Teresa (1910–1997).[12] Like

[11]Scott A. Bessenecker, *The New Friars* (Downers Grove, IL: InterVarsity Press, 2006).

[12]Considerable support for this idea of the appropriating of monastic ideas for today's evangelical

the above-named writers who chose to concentrate on one particular expression of monasticism, Bessenecker does not show an awareness of the equally disciplined Celtic and Benedictine missionaries who evangelized regions of northwest Europe half a millennium before the age of the thirteenth-century friars.[13]

His "apologia" for friar-monasticism is the more intriguing inasmuch as he, a former Roman Catholic, saw enough slackness in an Iowa Franciscan monastery he once visited as a teen to permanently cure him of any romantic notion that monasticism represented the definitive way of living the Christian life. It is the present utility of aids such as the ancient monastic "rule" (code) of Augustine of Hippo (354–430) that alone commends them for present use. Bessenecker's interest is not in pursuing any cloying conformity to patterns of monasticism as it once was; he simply desires to extrapolate practices from the missionary-activist side of monasticism to assist evangelicalism (long known for its activism) to recover a zeal to help the unlovely.

The question begging to be asked (yet left unaddressed by all three authors) is that of what is the larger whole of which these particular expressions of monasticism (Benedictine, Dominican, and Franciscan) are only parts. When one considers that these various monastic movements originally represented, and to some degree still represent, attempts to improve on the track records of other, earlier expressions, monasticism must be seen in this big-picture format. Who will provide it since they do not?

VIEWING THE "BIG PICTURE" OF MONASTICISM

Curious readers will want to know of some classic treatments on the larger subject of monastic history. I do not know of any compact work that surpasses the overview provided by the late Benedictine scholar and Cambridge

missionary efforts was lent by *Christianity Today* magazine in its September 2005 issue, available at www.christianitytoday.com/ct/2005/septemberweb-only/52.0.html?start=2. I think it is fair to say that this utilitarian approach, which aims to locate elements from monasticism capable of being applied in new settings, is the one most worthy of attention. See this reflected in two recent books: Graham Cray, Ian Mosby, and Aaron Kennedy, eds., *New Monasticism as Fresh Expression of Church* (Norwich, UK: Canterbury, 2010); and Wes Markofski, *New Monasticism and the Transformation of American Evangelicalism* (New York: Oxford University Press, 2015).

[13]This ministry is helpfully discussed in Ian Wood, *The Missionary Life: Saints and the Evangelization of Northern Europe, 400–1050* (New York: Longman, 2001).

University professor David Knowles, *Christian Monasticism*.[14] For its compactness, vivid detail, and clear illustration it stands alone. Jean Leclercq's volume *The Love of Learning and the Desire for God* provides a reliable and satisfying window into the medieval Benedictine world.[15] For those who have begun with Knowles's compact volume, next in line surely is the splendid work of medievalist C. H. Lawrence. His *Medieval Monasticism: Forms of the Religious Life in the Middle Ages* is superb in every way and offers a sympathetic blend of narration and deft criticism.[16] Also excellent, and with a special interest in the distinctive interplay between the particular ideals of the various orders of monks and the kinds of buildings and grounds they created, is the fine volume of another British medievalist, Christopher Brooke. His *The Age of the Cloister: The Story of Monastic Life in the Middle Ages* is a fine blend of narrative and interpretation of the story.[17]

Not to be neglected either are two older works produced by early twentieth-century Protestants. Especially notable because of his empathetic treatment of the monastic story is the work of H. B. Workman, a British Methodist, whose insightful *The Evolution of the Monastic Ideal: A Chapter in the History of Christian Renunciation* first appeared in 1913.[18] Workman helpfully demonstrated that the springing up of the distinguishable monastic movements in successive centuries must be understood as the pursuit of an ideal that was altered from one period to the next. The conviction of the earliest monks was that a lonely desert life of renunciation and contemplation was the best way of emulating the life of the apostles of Jesus. But this was not any longer the ideal being pursued by the European Benedictines a half millennium later in their massive abbeys, where formal liturgical worship eventually came to reign supreme.

[14]David Knowles, *Christian Monasticism* (New York: McGraw-Hill, 1969).

[15]Jean Leclercq, *The Love of Learning and the Desire for God*, 3rd ed. (New York: Fordham University Press, 1992).

[16]C. H. Lawrence, *Medieval Monasticism: Forms of the Religious Life in the Middle Ages*, 3rd ed. (London: Routledge, 2000). A fourth edition is now available. The same author has also provided an additional title, *The Friars: The Impact of the Mendicant Movement on Western Society* (New York: Longman, 1994).

[17]Christopher Brooke, *The Age of the Cloister: The Story of Monastic Life in the Middle Ages* (Mahwah, NJ: Paulist Press, 2002).

[18]Herbert B. Workman, *The Evolution of the Monastic Ideal* (1913; repr., Boston: Beacon, 1962). It is especially notable that the 1962 reprint included a largely commendatory preface by the Benedictine author David Knowles.

The friars of the thirteenth century who went begging and preaching in the new cities of Europe represented yet another conception of what the apostolic life demanded. Had not Jesus sent the apostles into the world preaching? This new monastic ideal pursued by the friars was one of activism rather than contemplation and withdrawal. Today's popular literature directing our attention to various single strands of the monastic story falls short by failing to address the fact of this steady adaptation.

If the Methodist Workman could be said to have written on monasticism with empathy, one would not use this term to describe the appraisal of monasticism supplied by another British medievalist (a modernist-leaning Anglican), C. G. Coulton, whose multivolume *Five Centuries of Religion* provides ample evidence that all was not sweetness and light in the medieval cloister. Monasticism, on Coulton's view, was a phenomenon that needed to be outgrown and relegated to the past.[19]

Happily, Protestant writing about the monastic life—taken as a whole—did not end with these writers, spread over the last century. Evangelical Protestants have begun to tackle this canvas. More recently, an evangelical author, Greg Peters, has produced two volumes. His *Reforming the Monastery* demonstrates that Protestant Christianity did not terminate all consideration of the potential of monastic life with the onset of the Reformation era.[20] Forms of monasticism lived on, both because of the degree of toleration extended to existing religious houses in Protestant territory and because of the useful roles that male and female religious orders still provided for those who sought entry.[21] It needs to be said, however, that Peters focuses largely on Protestant writers post-1800 who could offer at least qualified support for monastic life. Forthright modern critics of the movement such

[19]C. G. Coulton, *Five Centuries of Religion*, 4 vols. (1923–1950; repr., New York: Farrar, 1980). His withering views on monasticism were also set out in shorter compass in *Ten Medieval Studies* (1910; repr., Boston: Beacon, 1959). Coulton's writing career is reviewed by Gerald Christianson, "The Medieval Historian as Controversialist," *The Catholic Historical Review* 57, no. 3 (1977): 421-41.

[20]Greg Peters, *Reforming the Monastery: Protestant Theologies of the Religious Life* (Eugene, OR: Cascade, 2014).

[21]This is a question on the minds of many who have followed the influential BBC/PBS television serial *Call the Midwife* since 2012. The story line involves midwife-nurses drawn both from the Anglican monastic order of St. John the Divine (founded 1849) and from the National Health Service (founded 1948).

as Coulton are not consulted.[22] Peters's second volume, *The Story of Monasticism,*[23] stands alone as an attempt by a modern evangelical Protestant to provide a history of monasticism, taken as a whole. Yet the ambition of the author to both commend the monastic life as well as to narrate monastic history means that we find less critical evaluation of the flow of monasticism than is readily available in the treatments provided by medievalists such as Workman, Lawrence, and Brooke.

In sum, with such an abundance of resources available to us, no one should today mistakenly think that when they have once observed a Benedictine, Dominican, or Franciscan religious house, they have a picture of monasticism as a whole. Monasticism's component parts need to be viewed in relation to this larger, moving story.

WHY NOT CONSIDER MONASTICISM AS A PARACHURCH MOVEMENT?

This suggestion may initially seem disconcerting. But is it not possible that beyond whatever affinities evangelicals may have with the concern of monastic orders to deepen devotion and to carry the gospel to the unbelieving, there is yet another affinity—that is, a readiness to second-guess the institutional church as an effective matrix for nurture and Christian action?

Monasticism from its earliest times represented an expression of less-than-robust trust in the zeal and adequacy of the institutional church. As he entered his local church, Antony of Egypt heard the reading of the gospel story of the rich young man who "went away sad" rather than part with his wealth;[24] but the net effect of Antony's sense of calling was that *he* went away, leaving that church for the desert.[25] And this was not the supine, comfortable church, at ease with the empire in the aftermath of Constantine's eventual

[22]Most impressive are the analyses of monasticism's strengths and weaknesses offered by Karl Barth and Dietrich Bonhoeffer (chap. 3) and Donald Bloesch (chap. 4).

[23]Greg Peters, *The Story of Monasticism* (Grand Rapids: Baker, 2015). I have reviewed "Is Evangelical Monasticism an Option?," Peters's two volumes at The Gospel Coalition, January 4, 2016, www.thegospelcoalition.org/article/book-reviews-is-evangelical-monasticism.

[24]The reference is to Matthew 19:22.

[25]Athanasius, "The Life of Antony," in *The Life of Antony and Letter to Marcellinus*, ed. Robert C. Gregg (New York: Paulist Press, 1980), 31-32. This protesting character against the institutional church does not seem to be recognized adequately by Rod Dreher, author of *The Benedict Option* (New York: Sentinel, 2017). See the excerpt of Dreher's book under the title "The Christian Village" in *Christianity Today* 61.2 (March 2017): 34-41.

edict of toleration in the year 313—no, it was the church still vulnerable to imperial persecution.[26] Nevertheless, the institutional church was perceived by Antony to be lacking something that desert monastic life could supply. Evangelical Protestants instinctively know this story of Christian agencies, "arms of the church" we call them, that out-do the church at select tasks such as youth ministry, discipleship, evangelism, and missions.

True enough, the institutional church did eventually restrain monasticism's tendency to go it alone. Basil of Caesarea (330–379) is credited with obliging the monks in his region to leave their wilderness retreats and come to communal facilities in towns to serve in trades, schools, and hospitals.[27] But the issue was not settled so quickly in the church at large. Early Benedictine monasteries in western Europe were brought under episcopal jurisdiction only with difficulty; Christian donors were as likely to remember monasteries with bequests and grants as they were the institutional church. Even when, in time, all new monastic orders were required to gain a papal charter, the fact remained that the men and women who sought entry to them were, as surely as old Antony, seeking affiliation with a variant of the church that seemed more likely to assist in the pursuit of salvation and sanctity. The institutional church, having established the point that monastic life could no longer exist without reference to the church's superintendence, does not seem to have cared to challenge the premise that monastic life provided benefits not so readily available in the local parish church. So, whether our contemporary writers are urging our appropriation of the insights of one branch of monasticism or of several taken collectively, the question remains: why the monastery and not the church?

MONASTICISM'S DECLINING NUMBERS

There are plenty of reports that in the global south, Catholic monasteries and convents are doing very well; we hear this particularly of such countries as Nigeria.[28] But this is not what we hear about Europe and North America.

---

[26]See the "Edict of Milan" in *Documents of the Christian Church*, ed. Henry Bettenson and Chris Maunder, 3rd ed. (New York: Oxford University Press, 1999), 17.

[27]The role of Basil in monastic history is described by Lawrence, *Medieval Monasticism*, 8-10; and Peters, *Story of Monasticism*, 54-55.

[28]See this trend reported in various sources: "Catholic Nuns and Monks Decline," BBC, February 5, 2008, news.bbc.co.uk/go/pr/fr/-/2/hi/europe/7227629.stm, reports on the global decline in recruitment to monasteries and convents. David Gonzalez in the *New York Times* has drawn attention to the closing of monastic institutions of long-standing: "After 146 Years, a Brooklyn

The Dominicans, whom Sloan observed at such close quarters, number less than one thousand in North America; the laid-back Franciscan monastery in Iowa that Bessenecker visited in his teens is now no more. That under these straightened circumstances we have evangelical writers rediscovering and commending monastic ideals does not require us to suspect that they are deluded. But once more, we are entitled to ask whether the parts of the story are being seen in right relation to the whole.

Seeing the whole will require us to understand that over centuries, any marked decline in monastic recruitment has been an indicator of weakness in the church constituency from which recruits come. Conversely, a flood of recruits (and still more, the chartering of new orders) has generally been a reflection of some heightened vitality in the church at large, which lends to monasticism its keenest. There is reason to suspect that our evangelical writers have not grasped the wider complexity of the situation they describe as deserving of our emulation.

CAN WE SMILE AT THE FOIBLES?

In an old cowboy ballad, there was a line about "skies are not cloudy all day." There are few clouds in the monastic sky depicted in Okholm, Sloan, Bessenecker, and Peters. I have credited Okholm with acknowledging the critique of monasticism given in the early Protestant era; Sloan admits that the Dominicans were not on the side of the angels in supporting the Inquisition; Bessenecker has never forgotten the Iowa Franciscans who so shattered his expectations in a monastery visit in his teens. But what one needs to see acknowledged also, in such favorable accounts as these, is that criticisms of the monastic life have been a regular feature of *Catholic* life. Without this admission, one is left with the impression that only Protestantism has been faultfinding.

When Benedictine monasticism at Cluny grew opulent, it was the puritanical Cistercian Bernard of Clairvaux (1090–1153) who aimed sarcastic criticism at Cluny.[29] Francis of Assisi (1181–1226) had the preexisting monastic orders (Benedictine and Cistercian) in mind when he forbade his own

---

Covent Is Closing," December 16, 2008, www.nytimes.com/2008/12/17/nyregion/17convent.html. Peters in *Story of Monasticism*, 255-58, notes that the decline has accelerated markedly since the Vatican II era.

[29]See Bernard's "Apologia for Abbot William," in *The Cistercian World: Monastic Studies of the Twelfth Century*, trans. and ed. Pauline Tommaso (New York: Penguin, 1993), 44-58.

recruits to receive gifts of coin and discouraged the use of books.[30] Giovanni Boccaccio (1313–1375) found easy targets, both monks and nuns, when he composed his *Decameron*. The early Renaissance humanist Lorenzo Valla (1407–1457), credited with exposing the fraudulent *Donation of Constantine* and preparing (in manuscript) "Annotations on the New Testament,"[31] composed his own review of monasticism as he saw it. Valla would not accept that the term "religious" could be reserved for monks in contrast to lay Christians. He maintained that the religious orders held an inflated conception of the superiority of monastic compared to lay Christian life.[32] To crown it all, Erasmus of Rotterdam had poked fun at the various mendicant (begging) monastic orders by describing how they sent their emissaries into a dying man's bedroom; there each friar jockeyed with the other in hope of seeing his own religious order written into the man's will.[33]

If loyal Catholics have pointed to monasticism's foibles, can we not at least smile with them? To fail to do so suggests that we are settling for a kind of sterilized understanding of the monastic story that does not mesh with the story that older forms of Christianity (which have been hospitable to monasticism) have helped to write.

DISCERNMENT, DISCERNMENT

In this chapter, we have focused especially on authors who are evangelical Protestants—writers seeking to appropriate elements within monasticism for the strengthening of the devotion, community life, and mission-outreach of their fellow evangelicals. But in order to serve the evangelical constituency well, some basic theological landmarks need to be maintained. This is true especially in reviewing the sacramental practices that are a regular feature of life in the monastic orders. Okholm, while he does not openly endorse the Catholic understanding that after consecration the elements of bread and

---

[30]See "Rule of St. Francis," in Bettenson and Maunder, *Documents of the Christian Church*, 141.

[31]Valla's "Annotations" were posthumously published by Erasmus in 1505. See Christopher S. Celenza, "Lorenzo Valla's Radical Philology: The 'Preface' to the *Annotations to the New Testament* in Context," *Journal of Medieval and Early Modern Studies* 42, no. 2 (2012): 365-94.

[32]Lorenzo Valla, "The Profession of the Religious," in *The Profession of the Religious and Selections from the Falsely-Believed and Forged Donation of Constantine*, trans. and ed. Olga Zorsi Pugliese (Toronto: Center for Renaissance and Reformation Studies, 1994).

[33]See "The Funeral," in *Erasmus: Ten Colloquies*, trans. and ed. Craig Thompson (Indianapolis: Bobbs-Merrill, 1977), 92-112.

wine are transformed into the body and blood of Christ (physical appearances notwithstanding), nevertheless bluntly indicates that the elements *are* the body and blood.[34] Not only is this not the view of evangelicalism, broadly conceived, but it is not the view of his own adoptive Reformed tradition. In this tradition, we may speak of a real presence of the heavenly Jesus Christ in the Supper facilitated by the agency of the Holy Spirit. Although Sloan, who stands in the same broadly Reformed theological tradition, refrains from participating in the Dominican administration of the Mass, she makes no theological evaluation of the Catholic devotional practice of the "adoration of the host" in which she regularly participates; this practice, however, presupposes transubstantiation to be actual.[35] A high Marian devotion, similarly, is observed but given no theological evaluation.

In a similar way, Bessenecker gives an extended defense of the view, popularized by Mother Teresa, that in serving the destitute, we serve Christ unseen. He might have acknowledged that this is a problematic interpretation of Matthew 25.[36] These books are intended as "windows" into monasticism for evangelical Protestants who are utterly new to the subject; to do this effectively would require the exercise of more theological discernment than they have shown.

WHY NOT RECIPROCITY?

Finally, if one accepts the suggestion made at this chapter's beginning that there are actual affinities between monasticism and evangelical Protestantism, should we not then expect that exemplary forms of evangelical spirituality would hold a degree of fascination for large-hearted Catholics—monastics among them—as surely as features of monasticism draw evangelical admiration? This is not a "phantom" notion. I am thinking of the story of the evangelist D. L. Moody (1837–1899), who while preaching in Britain in 1875 received an effusive letter from a Welsh Roman Catholic monk; he

[34]Okholm, *Monk Habits*, 40.

[35]Sloan, *Flirting with Monasticism*, 64.

[36]Bessenecker, *New Friars*, 87-88. A much more defensible understanding of this Scripture, which squares with the New Testament emphasis on salvation by faith, was provided in *Christianity Today* in March 2015. See Andy Horvath, "What You Probably Don't Know About 'The Least of These': A More Biblically Accurate Understanding of Jesus' Words in Matthew 25," March 5, 2015, www.christianitytoday.com/ct/2015/march-web-only/what-you-probably-dont-know-about-least-of-these.html.

wrote assuring Moody of his prayers for God's blessing on his evangelistic preaching.[37] In our own century, the evangelical student ministry Campus Crusade for Christ (now Cru) has been welcomed into Poland to assist the Roman Catholic Church there with student evangelism and discipleship.[38]

I do not observe this idea of mutuality surfacing in the evangelical books under consideration. Instead, their collective tendency is to suggest a unidirectional fascination in which evangelicals *alone* must appropriate from the other tradition. As one who himself accepts that evangelical Protestant movements originated as movements of the Spirit, it seems to me that this unidirectional fascination betrays the very evangelical identity crisis that this book is aiming to dispel as something inaccurate and misleading.[39] We should affirm that our movement began as a movement of the Spirit *and* that there were also earlier initiatives of the Spirit to renew the church; by such an affirmation we have a basis for reciprocal curiosity. So, let this conversation about evangelicalism and monasticism undergo some needed fine tuning, and then continue.

QUESTIONS FOR DISCUSSION

1. Have you ever visited a monastery or convent for a prayer retreat or to find personal solitude? Share your impressions and recollections.
2. Where in the family history of monasticism did this monastery or convent fit? Was it part of the Benedictine "wave"? The "wave" of reform illustrated by the Cistercians? The "wave" of the urban, circulating friars (Dominican and Franciscan)? Were the monks or nuns themselves conscious of why they were of one allegiance compared to another?
3. What interpretation do you place on the fact that monasteries and convents are largely in decline in western Europe and North America?
4. What do you make of the efforts by evangelical Protestants to borrow monastic ideas and practices as a means of ministry to the urban poor, whether in North America or elsewhere?

---

[37]The story is recounted in Lyle Dorsett, *A Passion for Souls: The Life of D. L. Moody* (Chicago: Moody Press, 1997), 239-40.

[38]Erin Dienst, "Sharing the Gospel with 1 Million Youth in Poland," Campus Crusade for Christ International, accessed January 17, 2017, www.cru.org/communities/locations/europe/poland/sharing-the-gospel-with-1-million-youth-in-poland.html.

[39]See the opening chapter of this book.

12

A Tale of Two Newmans

"To be deep in history is to cease to be Protestant." Perhaps you have noticed this statement of John Henry Newman being bandied about recently.[1] Type these words into any search engine and prepare for a deluge; my own search generated almost 41,000 hits.[2] Those who quote this saying are just a bit gleeful when using it, for it seems to be a ready-made put-down of Protestantism from an eminently quotable source. Francis Beckwith, a Christian philosopher, utilized this adage as part of an explanation of why he left evangelical Protestantism for the Roman Catholicism of his upbringing.[3]

Soundings like these go some distance to explain why no modern historical figure's name is invoked as often as that of John Henry Newman (1801–1890) in evangelical Protestantism's current fascination with Roman Catholicism and Orthodoxy.[4] This man of the nineteenth century—the

---

[1]The author records his gratitude to Dr. Andrew Atherstone and Dr. Brian Tabb for commenting on earlier versions of this chapter.

[2]Roughly 40,700 references to this sentence appeared when the writer conducted an online search on February 22, 2014.

[3]Francis J. Beckwith, *Return to Rome: Confessions of an Evangelical Catholic* (Grand Rapids: Brazos, 2009), 73. Beckwith stands apart from the myriads (both Roman clergy and others) online. He, at least, can trace the Newman statement to its origin in *Essay on the Development of Christian Doctrine* (London: Tooley, 1845).

[4]See, for example, Thomas Howard, who placed J. H. Newman first among those to whom he dedicated *Evangelical Is Not Enough* (San Francisco: Ignatius, 1984). Second in the dedication list was R. A. Knox, discussed in this chapter. See also Christian Smith, *How to Go from Being a Good*

Anglican college don and clergyman who embraced Catholicism in 1845—has become a kind of "poster child" for wavering Protestants who find themselves steadily more perturbed with the perceived shortcomings of evangelical Christianity. And just as it is for Newman the man, so it is also for his books. Among this restive sort of Protestant, no piece of literature is alluded to so often as Newman's autobiographical *Apologia Pro Vita Sua*, published in 1864.[5]

However, this appetite for the aphorisms of Newman and his *Apologia* dodges a range of questions. For starters, the "deep in history" statement, made by Newman in 1845, was part of a book that caused grave concern to the Catholic authorities who were in the process of welcoming him from Anglicanism. Newman consented, in publishing his *Essay on the Development of Christian Doctrine,* to declare that the contents of this book were reflective of his Anglican years. He himself was still a Protestant at the time of writing.[6] The larger argument of which the "deep in history" statement was a part was problematic across the churches in 1845 and for years thereafter.[7] At the very least, that context requires that there should be more restraint today in using Newman's statement for polemical purposes. Do those in the process of abandoning evangelical Christianity who use it as a great one-liner have a conception of Newman's larger argument? As for Newman's still popular *Apologia*, where is the recognition that these reminiscences of his life up to 1845 are not simply those of a reflective man but are the efforts of one whose integrity had been seriously challenged? Of Newman, it had been said that he had been a closet Roman Catholic for years before his reaffiliation and turned numerous others in a Rome-ward direction before following suit himself.[8] The *Apologia* is still a contested piece of writing.

Evangelical to a Committed Catholic in Ninety-Five Difficult Steps (Eugene, OR: Cascade, 2011), 39; and Michael Harper, *The True Light: An Evangelical's Journey to Orthodoxy* (London: Hodder & Stoughton, 1997), 162.

[5]The current demand for his *Apologia* is illustrated by the fact that a consulting of Amazon.com in January 2014 found no fewer than twenty-two English-language editions (many of which were reprints-on-demand) offered for sale.

[6]See his acknowledgement of this in *Essay on the Development*, xi.

[7]We have considered the unsettling effects of this book in chapter 4.

[8]These insinuations had been made most forcefully by Charles Kingsley in his *And What Does Mr. Newman Mean?* (London: Macmillan, 1864).

Concerns of this sort warrant the opinion that we are today really dealing with *two* John Henry Newmans. There is the *first* Newman popularized in the decades immediately following the 1864 publication of his *Apologia*; this is the "heroic" Newman who is lionized by today's disenchanted. To seekers like these, this is the "real" Newman. But there is also a *second* Newman, distinguishable from the first, who has been subject to closer investigation by those, both Catholic and Protestant, who have been less motivated by what might be called partisan concerns.

THE FIRST NEWMAN

The man I refer to as the "first" Newman is not a make-believe figure. He is in fact the character portrayed in writing by Newman himself. Before his passing in 1890 Newman, the man of letters, had taken considerable pains to secure his personal legacy. He had revised his *Apologia* of 1864 twice (in 1865 and in 1886); in the process of revision, he had omitted the original heated and terse exchanges with his critic, Charles Kingsley.[9] He had left a tremendous trove of correspondence (meticulously organized) extending back decades as well as an unpublished autobiographical account (distinct from the *Apologia*) datable to the 1870s.

Consistent with Newman's concern as to how he would be remembered, soon after his passing in 1890, the curious could read an edited selection of his early *Letters*.[10] They could also digest a treatment of the dawn of the movement with which Newman had been so closely associated in his Anglican years.[11] They could also take in hand a two-volume biography composed by his long acquaintance, Wilfrid Ward; this biographer utilized many of the materials preselected for this purpose by Newman himself.[12] This was John Henry Newman in his own and others' words in the first period of his influence. Critics there were, to be sure.[13] But the truly dominant voices

[9]Martin J. Svaglic, "The Revision of Newman's *Apologia*," *Modern Philology* 50, no. 1 (1952): 43-44.

[10]Edited by his sister, Anne Mozley, *Letters and Diaries of J. H. Newman* (London: Longmans Green, 1890).

[11]R. W. Church, *The Oxford Movement: Twelve Years, 1833–1845* (London: Macmillan, 1891).

[12]Wilfrid Ward, *Life of J. H. Newman*, 2 vols. (London: Longmans Green, 1912). Wilfrid Ward was son of a former close associate of Newman, W. G. Ward.

[13]One of particular note in this late Victorian period was the Scottish preacher and writer, Alexander Whyte (1836–1921). In preparing his *John Henry Newman: An Appreciation* (Edinburgh: Oliphant, Anderson and Ferrier, 1901), Whyte had actually interviewed Newman at his Birmingham

were Newman himself and the circle of admirers to whom he entrusted materials pertaining to his life.

THE SECOND NEWMAN

Yet here we are aiming to identify an approach to Newman that is distinguishable from the first. There is a body of literature that is, so to speak, out from under the Newman "cloud." We can take as our starting point 1933, when a century had passed since Newman and a circle including John Keble, E. B. Pusey, and R. H. Froude had, by launching a series of pamphlets, commenced what came to be called the "Oxford" or "Tractarian" movement. This series of pamphlets had eventually reached to number 90 in 1841, at which point the Anglican bishop of Oxford intervened to forbid any further publication.

At the 1933 Tractarian centennial. By 1933, Newman had been dead for forty years. By that year, there was a steady decline even of the number of those of a younger generation who could claim any personal acquaintance with him. And yet five publications appeared in connection with that centenary year, which were motivated by some "affinity factor."

E. A. Knox (1847–1937), author of *The Tractarian Movement: 1833–1845*,[14] was, by 1933, the retired Anglican bishop of Manchester long known as an outspoken evangelical. He had studied in Oxford two decades following Newman's departure for Rome in 1845, had become a fellow of Merton College and entered a long and distinguished ministry in the Church of England. As a bishop holding evangelical principles, he was a stalwart in opposing the Anglo-Catholic revision of the *Book of Common Prayer* in the 1920s. Of still greater relevance was the sobering fact that the youngest of his six children, distinguished scholar Ronald Arbuthnott Knox (1888–1957), had spurned the evangelical upbringing provided in his home to embrace initially the Anglo-Catholic expression of Anglicanism before eventually entering the Roman communion.[15] A second son, Wilfred Lawrence Knox (1886–1950), who was also academically gifted, similarly brought disappointment to his parents by embracing Anglo-Catholicism.

---

oratory. Additional late Victorian Protestant analysis of Newman is provided by E. G. Rupp in his *Just Men* (London: Epworth, 1977), chap. 9, "Newman Through Nonconformist Eyes."

[14]E. A. Knox, *The Tractarian Movement: 1833–1845* (London: Putnam, 1933).

[15]We have considered the important anti-evangelical work of R. A. Knox, *Enthusiasm* (Oxford: 1950), in chapter 2.

But far from Edmund Knox's book of 1933 being a kind of a rejoinder to Tractarianism, the careful reader finds that it is instead a thoughtful intellectual history of Newman and his circle; it explored the strong affinities of the English Tractarians with their French Catholic contemporaries, the Ultramontanist party.[16] Each party in its own way was seeking to exalt the primacy of religious authority over the authority of the modern state; each saw dangers in the expansion of popular democracy. Knox portrayed Newman and the Tractarians as Romantics.

By contrast, the Anglo-Catholic party of the Church of England (as the Tractarian movement had come to be known) used the 1933 centenary to celebrate the attainments of a movement that had not only persisted but steadily grown in strength, despite Newman's 1845 secession to Rome.[17] The celebratory volume produced for that year under the editorship of Oxford professor Norman P. Williams bore the somewhat ostentatious title *Northern Catholicism: Studies in the Oxford Centenary and Parallel Movements.*[18] Though the title was taken by at least one reviewer as an indicator of a kind of pretension—that is, that it was advancing a claim that Anglicanism exercised a wide sphere of influence analogous to that of Rome or Eastern Orthodoxy—there was more substance to this implied claim than the American reviewer was ready to grant.[19] At that near-zenith stage of the British Empire, Anglo-Catholicism had been able to extensively replicate its emphases wherever Anglicanism had extended itself across the British Empire.

A writer who would be associated with the Anglo-Catholic movement throughout his long academic career, Frank L. Cross,[20] produced in that same centenary year an insightful overview of our subject, *John Henry*

[16]Knox (ix) acknowledged that the writer, Wilfrid Ward (see n12), had earlier developed this theme in *W. G. Ward and the Catholic Revival* (London, 1893).

[17]The very large-scale celebration observed at the 1933 centenary has recently been explored by Andrew Atherstone in "Evangelicals and the Oxford Movement Centenary," *Journal of Religious History* 37, no. 1 (2013): 98-117.

[18]Norman P. Williams, *Northern Catholicism: Studies in the Oxford Centenary and Parallel Movements* (London: SPCK, 1933).

[19]Thomas Kelly Rogers, reviewing *Northern Catholicism* in the *Anglican Theological Review* 16, no. 3 (1934): 231-33.

[20]We remember Cross (1900–1968) today most of all for his editorship of the *Oxford Dictionary of the Christian Church*, 1st ed. (Oxford: Oxford University Press, 1957). In 1933 he was the librarian of Pusey House, the Anglo-Catholic house of study at Oxford, founded in 1884. Cross went on to become Lady Margaret Professor of Divinity in 1944.

Newman.[21] Most striking from a writer who stood in the stream of Anglicanism tracing its origin to the movement of the 1830s was the readiness of this author to question the historical accuracy of Newman's *Apologia* of 1864. Cross proposed that it was Newman's sense of having been severely rebuffed in the furor generated by his *Tract 90* in 1841—rather than a sustained line of reading and reflection (as Newman suggested in his *Apologia*)—that had set Newman on the trajectory that eventually saw him received into the Church of Rome in 1845. The furor generated by the release of *Tract 90,* on Cross's reading, put Newman in the position of being an exile within the very Anglican communion in which he had been raised and to which he had given the better part of twenty years.[22] When a rising Anglo-Catholic scholar such as Cross, writing empathetically about his subject, was ready to take such a critical look at the *Apologia*, something of great significance was under way.

Again in 1933 there appeared a striking volume, *Oxford Apostles,* which despite its title was chiefly about Newman.[23] The author, Geoffrey Faber (1889–1961), wrote as a distinguished Oxford graduate and as the grand-nephew of J. H. Newman's fellow traveler to Rome, the hymn writer Frederick W. Faber (1814–1863). It was a matter of historical record that F. W. Faber, a devoted follower of Newman both while at Oxford and in his reaffiliation to Rome, was treated with brusqueness by Newman in the years following. Skillfully written by one who became the cofounder of a publishing house bearing his name and with a dash of irreverence toward the hallowed memory of his subject, Faber's volume attempted an account of Newman's career that focused on a number of unresolved conundrums. Faber, influenced by Freudian psychology, took a particular interest in Newman's prolonged and unrelenting relationship with his mother, his claimed determination from age fifteen to follow a life of celibacy, his overwhelming preference for male company (long before his reaffiliation to Rome), his recurring tendency to have severe health crises when confronted by great tasks, and supremely his self-absorption. Faber strongly implied the existence of

[21]Frank L. Cross, *John Henry Newman* (London: Philip Allan, 1933).

[22]Ibid., 132-33.

[23]Geoffrey Faber, *Oxford Apostles* (London: Faber, 1933). The work is still in print from its original publisher.

dark psychological forces at work in the Tractarian hero. In modern parlance, we might call *The Oxford Apostles* a piece of psychohistory. Faber was, at the same time, a good scholar and a lucid writer.

This work understandably aggravated Newman loyalists, and so within a year there appeared from the pen of the rising young Catholic historian Christopher Dawson (1889–1970) a kind of rejoinder titled *The Spirit of the Oxford Movement.*[24] Dawson, no less than Faber, had a "horse in the race." If Faber wrote influenced by the conviction that Newman encouraged his grand-uncle into secession from the Church of England only to treat him shabbily afterward, Dawson—himself an adult convert to Rome from Anglo-Catholicism—was determined to "buff" Newman's reputation back to a restored luster.[25] It is not too much to call Dawson's work defensive. Yet its literary merits were such that the book was reprinted in 2001.

Contextual studies in mid-century. The decades following the 1933 centennial were not characterized by quite the same high interest in Newman and the movement he had helped to found. Yet the flame was kept alive by four notable volumes. Henry Tristram, a twentieth-century member of the Birmingham Oratory (the monastery-like residence presided over by Newman until his passing in 1890), assembled for publication a collection of materials from Newman's own hand. These all had bearing on aspects of Newman's life and were published in 1957 as *John Henry Newman: Autobiographical Writings.*[26] Here at the very least was hard evidence confirming something remarked on by Newman biographers: Newman was a man who was very solicitous as to how he would be portrayed by biographers and had marked the way for them by an extensive preselection of materials. Of special interest in the volume is Newman's little-known *Autobiographical Memoir* of 1874, which relates the story of his life in a markedly different fashion from that of his rather stylized *Apologia Pro Vita Sua* of 1864. While the latter told Newman's life up to his reaffiliation to Rome in 1845 with a view to rehabilitating his tattered reputation in the eyes of English Protestant readers, the *Autobiographical Memoir* told the story as Newman wished it

---

[24]Christopher Dawson, *The Spirit of the Oxford Movement* (London: Sheed and Ward, 1934). The work was reissued with a fresh introduction in 2001 from the London publisher St. Austin Press.

[25]Dawson makes explicit reference to Faber's "psychological" approach in introducing his own work. See ibid., vi.

[26]Henry Tristram, *John Henry Newman: Autobiographical Writings* (New York: Sheed and Ward, 1957).

to be passed on to readers of a later time. Notably, Newman's debt to the evangelicalism of his youth (a prominent part of the *Apologia*) was largely omitted in the later account.[27]

A striking development in the next year (1957) was the release of Owen Chadwick's insightful volume *From Bossuet to Newman: The Idea of Doctrinal Development.*[28] Chadwick elaborated the story of how, in the post-Reformation period, Catholic apologists such as Jacques Bossuet (1627–1704) had labored to maintain the traditional claim that the Roman Catholic Church had maintained an unbroken doctrinal conformity with the church of the earliest centuries. Catholic apologists such as Bossuet therefore maintained that innovation and declension in doctrine was the unique legacy of Protestantism. Newman, on the other hand, while a young Protestant scholar had maintained the opposite—that is, it was Rome that had clearly declined from an original, less-encumbered stance toward Christian doctrine. The young Newman maintained that Protestantism *had* been warranted in making a fresh appeal to Scripture and the Fathers at the Reformation. Yet in the 1840s, Newman reversed himself by coming to hold that while Catholic doctrine had indeed undergone a kind of "evolution," this was consistently of a defensible and organic type. Chadwick's book of 1957 succeeded in putting the question of doctrinal development back on the "menu" of Protestantism as it had not been for half a century.

At the centenary of the release of Newman's* Apologia *(1864). As with the year 1933, the year 1964 was seen as especially significant as it marked the centenary of the original release of Newman's autobiographical sketch of his life up to 1845, the *Apologia.* A series of volumes appeared that consciously related to the approach of this centenary mark. The trend was signaled as early as 1961 when Oxford University Press began to issue the *Letters and Diaries of John Henry Newman,* a series eventually reaching thirty-one volumes.[29] The editorial lead for this project was

[27]On the marked differences between the two accounts, see Kenneth J. Stewart, "Newman Versus Newman: The *Apologia Pro Vita Sua (1864)* and later *Biographical Memoir* Compared," *Scottish Bulletin of Evangelical Theology* 26, no. 1 (2008): 57-67.

[28]Owen Chadwick, *From Bossuet to Newman: The Idea of Doctrinal Development* (Cambridge: Cambridge University Press, 1957).

[29]The series reached a completion in 2008.

taken by C. S. Dessain, the archivist of the very Birmingham Oratory established by Newman in 1848.[30]

Next, there appeared a two-volume biography by the English writer Meriol Trevor. Herself a successful author of children's literature and various historical novels, Trevor had converted to Catholicism in 1950 and turned to the subject of Newman (as had other such converts, such as Dawson) with *Newman: The Pillar of the Cloud* (1961) and *Newman: Light in Winter* (1962).[31] On the strength of the acclaim that this biography generated, Trevor was shortly to be involved in the editing of a short collection of essays published in 1965, *Newman: A Portrait Restored; An Ecumenical Evaluation.*[32] Here Roman Catholic and Church of England contributors collaborated and made it their business to assess Newman in a fresh way. This took into account both the century that had passed since the first release of the *Apologia* and the fact that the Second Vatican Council (where Newman's ideas were receiving fresh attention) was in process in the years 1962–1965.[33]

In these same years Owen Chadwick was joined by a second author in producing volumes in which Newman and the Tractarian movement were set in context by samplings of its literature. This was achieved by providing anthologies of the writings of Newman and those associated with him up to his reaffiliation in 1845. Chadwick, for his part, assembled representative excerpts from the writings of the Tractarians (very largely culled from the ninety publications of the *Tracts for the Times series*). This volume enables one to observe—without any necessary access to the original *Tracts* (eventually bound in four volumes)—just what were the opinions of the Tractarians regarding the Church of England in her relation to the state, the relation of her episcopate to the original apostles,

---

[30]From Dessain's editorial labors also emerged the compact Newman biography of 1966, *John Henry Newman* (London: Nelson, 1966). Of its third edition (1980) Newman scholar Owen Chadwick said, "It is the unadorned survey of one who is the most recent master of its subject." *Newman: A Short Introduction* (Oxford: Oxford University Press, 1983), 79.

[31]Meriol Trevor, *Newman*, 2 vols. (New York: Doubleday, 1961, 1962).

[32]John Coulson, A. M. Allchin, and Meriol Trevor, eds., *Newman: A Portrait Restored; An Ecumenical Evaluation* (London: Sheed and Ward, 1965).

[33]In this volume, A. M. Allchin, the author of the second chapter, "The Via Media: An Anglican Revaluation," asked the very interesting question of how much of Newman's earlier Protestantism had been taken with him into the Roman communion. He answered his own question by affirming that Newman's thought was still extensively Protestant after his reaffiliation.

and the meaning of her sacraments. This volume was *The Mind of the Oxford Movement.*[34]

A volume resembling it but containing fewer, more extensive excerpts was Eugene R. Fairweather's *The Oxford Movement.*[35] This anthology concentrated not so extensively as the prior volume on samplings from the periodic *Tracts for the Times* (commenced in 1833) but from independent theological writings produced by those in sympathy with the movement that sponsored the *Tracts*. Writers included Isaac Williams, Robert Wilberforce (son of the advocate for the abolition of slavery), and W. G. Ward, whose reaffiliation to Rome had preceded that of Newman himself.

Last of all, mention can be made of a helpful volume reflecting the author's research late in this mid-century period. William Robbins's *The Newman Brothers: An Essay in Comparative Intellectual Biography* attempted an evaluation of John Henry Newman through an extended comparison with his younger brother—the equally gifted Francis Newman (1805–1897).[36] The younger brother had in his adolescence shared the evangelical commitment acknowledged also by John, his senior. The younger brother had outperformed John, having done brilliantly at Oxford, and then had served for a time as a missionary to Syria in connection with the early Plymouth Brethren movement. Finally, Francis had turned in the latter half of his life to religious liberalism and eventually Unitarianism. Through the eyes of Francis, John Henry Newman was perceived to be something of a "prig" who was extremely self-absorbed. Yet in the eyes of the older brother John, Francis—who was drifting from orthodox Christian belief—personified the secularizing tendency of their era that the established Church of England seemed powerless to arrest.

Newman in the era of Vatican II. It is an intriguing fact that Newman came into his own (so to speak) within the Roman communion only through the vehicle of the Second Vatican Council, sessions of which were held each autumn in Rome from 1962 to 1965. Until that era, Newman's view that the Roman communion had been party to an extended legitimate evolution of

[34]Owen Chadwick, *The Mind of the Oxford Movement* (Cambridge: Cambridge University Press, 1960).

[35]Eugene R. Fairweather, *The Oxford Movement* (New York: Oxford University Press, 1964). The volume comprised part of Oxford University Press's series Library of Protestant Thought.

[36]William Robbins, *The Newman Brothers: An Essay in Comparative Intellectual Biography* (Cambridge, MA: Harvard University Press, 1966).

Christian doctrine from the age of the apostles forward received no official approbation by Roman theologians. There had, in fact, been steady Roman Catholic apprehensiveness regarding Newman's theological position from the time of his reception by Rome. His treatise of 1845, *Essay on the Development of Christian Doctrine,* was—at the time of his reception—understood to be incongruent with Catholic teaching.[37] There had been no actual change in this assessment of Newman's views on this subject by the early twentieth century.

However, this was precisely the trajectory followed in the collaborative work of 1967, *The Rediscovery of Newman: An Oxford Symposium.*[38] Now, Newman was being "rediscovered" in multiple senses: (1) there was fresh attention given to the influences contributing to the development of his thought; (2) there was assessment offered of Newman's influence (as a Catholic) in three regions of northern Europe as well as on English Nonconformity;[39] and (3) there was a concluding essay that explored the belated influence of Newman on the Second Vatican Council—just then concluded three quarters of a century after his death. The author of the latter essay, Cuthbert Butler, credited Newman's theological posture with being a contributing factor in the Vatican Council's enlarged attention to biblical theology as a counterweight to dogmatic theology, and to the role of the whole people of God in assessing the boundaries of the faith as a counterweight to the nineteenth-century ultramontane insistence on papal infallibility and the dominant role of the hierarchy.[40]

The *Rediscovery* volume was by no means the only indicator that fresh interest in Newman was emerging in that post-Vatican era. By 1969, the American Roman Catholic historian Marvin R. O'Connell (then already known for his study of sixteenth-century Counter-Reformers), had produced *The Oxford Conspirators: A History of the Oxford Movement, 1833–1845.* This book constituted the first full attempt to describe the birth of the

---

[37]On this point, see Frank M. Turner, *Newman: The Challenge to Evangelical Religion* (New Haven, CT: Yale University Press, 2002), 558-59.

[38]John Coulson and A. M. Allchin, eds., *The Rediscovery of Newman: An Oxford Symposium* (London: Sheed and Ward, 1967). It is important to note that it was not the volume of 1967 but of 1964 that had established the precedent of Roman Catholic-Protestant dialogue regarding Newman.

[39]Especially worthy of comment are the contributions by Protestants Gordon Rupp and Hubert Cunliffe-Jones.

[40]Coulson and Allchin, *Rediscovery of Newman*, 236-44.

movement (and Newman's place in it) since the 1933 work of the Anglican evangelical E. A. Knox. It was certainly the largest work of its kind written to that point by any American writer.[41]

In this same period Nicholas Lash of Cambridge University revisited the theme earlier highlighted in Chadwick's 1957 study, *From Bossuet to Newman*. Lash's volume was *Newman on Development: The Search for an Explanation in History*.[42] This valuable study had as its particular strength an analysis of the reception (or resistance to reception) of Newman's thought within Roman Catholic theology across the first half of the twentieth century. This mixed reception had come about in large part through the appropriation of Newman's thought by French representatives of Catholic Modernism, which gave rise in the minds of conservative Catholics to a kind of guilt by association for Newman.[43] Only after the mid-twentieth century did the Roman communion consider his thought more dispassionately.

Two other works that emerged in the post–Vatican II era showed that evangelical Protestantism was also reexamining the Tractarian movement and its period. Peter Toon's insightful *Evangelical Theology, 1833–1856: A Response to Tractarianism* (1979) shed fresh light on how Anglican evangelicals responded to Newman and his movement in the years preceding *and* following his reception by Rome.[44] Names with which we might have been much more familiar, such as William Goode (1801–1868), emerge in this volume as vigorous champions of the evangelical Protestant position, which by this period in the nineteenth century had grown exponentially within the Church of England. As if to make more accessible some of the controversial literature of the era highlighted by Toon, Elisabeth Jay provided a 1983 anthology of writers from this period, *The Evangelical and Oxford Movements*. The book featured excerpts from Tractarian (Oxford)

---

[41]Geoffrey Bromiley, reviewing *The Oxford Conspirators* in *Christianity Today* 13, no. 21 (1969): 26 questioned whether O'Connell had actually added anything new to the record with this volume.

[42]Nicholas Lash, *Newman on Development: The Search for an Explanation in History* (Shepherdstown, WV: Patmos, 1975).

[43]See "Newman's *Essay on Development* in Twentieth-Century Theology," chap. 7 in Lash, *Newman on Development*.

[44]Peter Toon, *Evangelical Theology, 1833–1856: A Response to Tractarianism* (London: Marshalls, 1979). The work was jointly issued by John Knox Press (Atlanta). It is worthy of mention that in this same period, Toon produced a valuable short study, *The Development of Doctrine in the Church* (Grand Rapids: Eerdmans, 1979). It has been drawn on in chapter 4.

writers Isaac Williams, John Keble, J. H. Newman, and E. B. Pusey as well as their critics Francis Close and William Goode.[45] The Jay anthology performed a real service in making accessible what had long been very hard to access.

Some credit has already been paid to the significant contribution to Newman scholarship made by the Cambridge historian Owen Chadwick. How fitting then that when Oxford University Press wished to commission a small volume for its *Short Introduction* series, it turned to Chadwick. The 1983 volume of eighty-three pages is not a biography but an introduction to Newman's thought.[46] A synopsis and evaluation is provided for each of Newman's major writings, and the volume closes with an annotated guide to further reading. The Latin phrase *multum in parvo* (much in small space) is perfectly illustrated in this little volume, which provides an ideal point of departure for those just beginning Newman studies.

Also notable is a volume produced by the then-chaplain of Keble College, Oxford, Geoffrey Rowell—*The Vision Glorious: Themes and Personalities in the Catholic Revival in Anglicanism* (1983).[47] As one of the foremost modern Anglo-Catholic authorities on Newman and the Tractarians, Rowell here provided deft interpretations of the significance of the three primary Tractarian leaders of the 1830s: Keble, Newman, and Pusey. His overview of Newman's growth in understanding of the development of doctrine, encapsulated in his work of the same name in 1845, will prove helpful. By 1986, Rowell had edited a fine compendium of essays reflecting an academic conference held at Oxford in 1983 to mark the 150th anniversary of the Oxford movement: *Tradition Renewed: The Oxford Movement Conference Papers*.[48] The range and quality of presentations from an international range of Protestant as well as Roman Catholic contributors show this volume to represent a kind of high-water mark of ecumenical consideration of Newman and this

---

[45]Elisabeth Jay, *The Evangelical and Oxford Movements* (Cambridge: Cambridge University Press, 1983).

[46]Owen Chadwick, *Newman: A Short Introduction* (New York: Oxford University Press, 1983). I have consulted the reissue of 2010.

[47]Geoffrey Rowell, *The Vision Glorious: Themes and Personalities in the Catholic Revival in Anglicanism* (Oxford: Oxford University Press, 1983). In November 2013, Rowell completed a term as Anglican bishop of Gibraltar in Europe, which commenced in 2001.

[48]Geoffrey Rowell, ed., *Tradition Renewed: The Oxford Movement Conference Papers* (London: Darton, Longman and Todd, 1986).

movement up to that time. A healthily critical perspective is in evidence in many essays, with Newman and his circle subjected to searching analysis from all points of the theological compass.[49]

Associated with the centenary of Newman's death (1990). As at the centenary of the launch of the Tractarian movement (1933) and of the initial release of the *Apologia* (1864), so also did the approach of the centenary of Newman's passing in 1890 serve as a stimulus to writers. The release of Ian Ker's *John Henry Newman: A Biography* (1988) was heralded as a development of great moment.[50] Ker, then at the University of St. Thomas, Minnesota, and latterly of Oxford University's Blackfriars Hall, was by this era establishing himself as one of the world's leading authorities on Newman and his thought.[51] His massive biography of 745 pages had taken full advantage of the serially published *Letters and Diaries of Newman,* which had been in production since 1961. To its credit, this biography spent two-thirds of its pages on Newman's Anglican phase to 1845 (an approach that makes it possible to recognize continuities between Newman the Anglican and Newman the Roman Catholic). And yet it may be asked whether Ker's very immersion in the literary remains of his subject—such that one reviewer could speak of Ker's volume as providing "Newman on Newman"[52]—did not deflect the biographer from securing the necessary critical distance from his subject. The same author in the centenary year published a volume of essays, *The Achievement of John Henry Newman.*[53] Freed from the biographer's focus on chronology, these essays focus on five select aspects of Newman as educator, philosopher, preacher, theologian, and writer, and synthesize the contributions of his career by theme.

In the same centenary year, the recognized Newman authority, Owen Chadwick, released a volume of essays, *The Spirit of the Oxford Movement:*

---

[49]Note especially the chapters of S. W. Sykes and S. W. Gilley, "No Bishop, No Church! The Tractarian Impact on Anglicanism"; Peter Toon, "Anglicanism in Popish Dress"; Gordon Wakefield, "A Mystical Substitute for the Glorious Gospel"; and W. S. F. Pickering, "Anglo-Catholicism: Some Sociological Observations."

[50]Ian Ker, *John Henry Newman: A Biography* (Oxford and New York: Oxford University Press, 1988).

[51]This college within Oxford was of medieval foundation, suppressed in 1538 under the Henrician Reformation, and reestablished in 1921. It, of course, did not exist in the early Victorian Oxford of Newman's day.

[52]Reviewer Andrew F. Weisner in *Currents in Theology and Mission* 17, no. 4 (1990): 312-13.

[53]Andrew F. Weisner, *The Achievement of John Henry Newman* (Notre Dame, IN: University of Notre Dame Press, 1990).

Tractarian Essays.[54] Though some of the chapters had been written as recently as 1987, the book taken as a whole was a kind of gathered harvest of Chadwick's writings on Newman—some from as long before as 1954. The essay that provided the book with its title, "The Spirit of the Oxford Movement," had originally prefaced Chadwick's 1960 anthology of Tractarian writings, *The Soul of the Oxford Movement.* Chadwick's aim in that centenary year was to make available essays that—because they were scattered across a range of periodicals inaccessible to most—would be otherwise unobtainable. In my opinion there is no writer on Newman and Tractarianism who represented such a balance of empathetic interpretation and critical distance as did Chadwick. This era was crowned by a highly impressive compendium of essays edited by Ian Ker and Alan G. Hill, *Newman After a Hundred Years.*[55] Here, a collaboration of Protestant and Roman Catholic contributors[56] drew attention to Newman's stature as a man of literature, a former university head, a patristic theologian, and a source of influence on the Second Vatican Council.[57]

In a new century. After the space of a decade, there appeared an important new treatment of Newman that was notable in several respects: Avery Dulles's *John Henry Newman* (2001).[58] Dulles, like his subject, had been raised a Protestant and embraced Catholicism in his adulthood. The author (1918–2008), a distinguished Jesuit theologian associated with Fordham University, New York, was also (like Newman) raised to the cardinalate at an advanced age.[59] But as an outworking of these affinities, Dulles laid stress not on the biographical aspects of his subject's career (which had been related many times over) but on the development of his theological

---

[54] Owen Chadwick, *The Spirit of the Oxford Movement: Tractarian Essays* (Cambridge: Cambridge University Press, 1990).

[55] Ian Ker and Alan G. Hill, eds., *Newman After a Hundred Years* (Oxford: Clarendon, 1990).

[56] Notably, the volume embraced the contributions of non-Anglican Protestant writers (as well as Roman Catholics), including Colin Gunton, theologian within Kings College, University of London. Among notable Anglican writers were Rowan Williams (later archbishop of Canterbury) and S. W. Sykes, Cambridge University.

[57] The latter essay, on Newman and the Second Vatican Council, was provided by Christopher Lash, whose 1975 volume *Newman on Development* has been commented on above.

[58] Avery Dulles, *John Henry Newman* (New York: Continuum, 2002).

[59] Avery Dulles was the son of the secretary of state under Dwight D. Eisenhower, John Foster Dulles (1888–1959). Avery Dulles was elevated to the cardinalate in 2001, above the age of eighty years.

thought. Dulles was one of the Catholic participants in the "Evangelicals and Catholics Together" initiative of 1994, and his elevation as cardinal had taken into account that and other involvements.

Dulles's treatment of Newman accordingly stressed the way in which he had taken with him into Catholicism emphases such as the need for scriptural exegesis, the ultimate superiority of Scripture to tradition, and the legitimate role of biblical criticism. Newman's distinctive emphases, when eventually disseminated, assisted his new communion to come to terms with non-Roman Christianity and the changed situation of the twentieth century. Newman was, on such an accounting, a facilitator of a later post-WWII ecumenism.[60]

Within a year, there appeared a massive work that has managed to alter the landscape of Newman studies for the foreseeable future. I refer to historian Frank M. Turner's *John Henry Newman: The Challenge to Evangelical Religion*.[61] Here, in massive detail, Turner challenged Newman's own heavily stylized account of his pilgrimage from his evangelical youth, into a sacramentalist Anglicanism, and into the embrace of Rome. According to Turner, Newman's autobiographical writings—while they portrayed the trajectory of his life as a battle against political and theological liberalism—intentionally obscured his underlying opposition to evangelicalism (whether within or beyond the Church of England). On such an understanding, the stylized *Apologia Pro Vita Sua* of 1864 (an account of his life to the year of his entry into the Church of Rome) was a determined effort by Newman to rehabilitate his reputation as an alleged Protestant traitor in the minds of an evangelical Protestant public that he all the while genuinely disdained.

A careful reading of the Turner volume raises many of the questions earlier posed by the Victorian writer Charles Kingsley who, because he alleged that Newman had long concealed Roman Catholic sentiments while still a minister of the Church of England, provoked Newman to write his *Apologia* of 1864. The Turner volume creates in the mind of the reader the lingering impression that Newman's "persona" was one he carefully cultivated during his

[60]Dulles, *John Henry Newman*, 25, 68, 130.
[61]The present writer reviewed this work in the *Calvin Theological Journal* 38, no. 2 (2003): 414-17.

long life and that this "preferred" reading of his life and career is the one that has lived on into the century beyond his departure.[62]

Two anthologies close our survey of Newman literature since 1933. The first, edited by Ian Ker and Terrence Merrigan, *The Cambridge Companion to John Henry Newman* (2009),[63] provides a most helpful survey of Newman's career by Sheridan Gilley and some very fine overviews of Newman's thinking about various theological themes.[64] Yet one is struck in reflecting on the range of contributors to this anthology that this *Cambridge Companion* has taken a step backward from the pioneering efforts made between 1964 and 1990 to make the scholarly discussion of John Henry Newman transconfessional. The *Cambridge Companion* is an overwhelmingly Roman Catholic collaboration produced by theological writers who give scant attention to historical factors.[65]

Finally, there is the interesting volume of 2012, *The Oxford Movement: Europe and the Wider World.*[66] This work seeks to do again, at the space of eighty-five years, what was attempted in the 1933 volume *Northern Catholicism*—that is, to demonstrate the transnational and transoceanic influence of that movement with which Newman's Oxford but pre-Roman Catholic years were so actively intertwined. While the 1933 volume, compiled while Britain still maintained an empire, had more of a global scope, the 2012 version is more concerned with the Oxford movement's influence within the United Kingdom (there are chapters on Wales and Scotland) and on Britain's former Australian colony as well as on the Continent, where various affinity movements are found to have existed across the nineteenth and early twentieth centuries.

---

[62]See the rousing, affirmative review of the Turner volume in the *Guardian*: Tristram Hunt, "Cardinal Spin," January 3, 2003, www.theguardian.com/books/2003/jan/04/biography.philosophy.

[63]Ian Ker and Terrence Merrigan, eds., *The Cambridge Companion to John Henry Newman* (Cambridge: Cambridge University Press, 2009).

[64]Keith Beaumont, review of *The Cambridge Companion to John Henry Newman*, ed. Ian Ker and Terrence Merrigan, *Catholic Historical Review* 97, no. 1 (2011): 159-60.

[65]See the trenchant remarks on this imbalance in Simon Skinner, "History Versus Hagiography: The Reception of Turner's *Newman*," *Journal of Ecclesiastical History* 61, no. 4 (2010): 784. Two modern anthologies produced since 1980—the Rowell-edited *Tradition Renewed* and the Ker-Hill edited *Newman After a Hundred Years*—are by contrast exemplary in their transconfessional and interdisciplinary perspectives.

[66]S. J. Brown and Peter Nockles, eds., *The Oxford Movement: Europe and the Wider World* (Cambridge: Cambridge University Press, 2012). The present author has reviewed this volume in *Themelios* 38, no. 3 (2013): 493-95.

CONTEMPORARY SIGNIFICANCE OF THE "TWO NEWMANS" PHENOMENON

This chapter has sought to demonstrate that there are two conceptions of John Henry Newman in circulation today. There is the somewhat "privileged" conception of Newman left over from the late Victorian era, according to which Newman was most of all a courageous man, a seeker after light, and a man of such religious resolve as to be worthy of all praise. There is also a more "accessible" Newman who is subject to ongoing investigation by both Protestants and Roman Catholics and who is much less easily pressed into service for polemical purposes.

We are seeing and hearing too much of the first Newman these days and need more of the second. It is as though those enamored with Newman the "poster child" are *first* Newman people; they do not show sufficient awareness of the *second*. By contrast, those familiar with the *second* Newman had to acquire knowledge of the *first* in order to make their way. The consequences of this neglect are quite serious. Let me encapsulate some difficulties that have ensued.

First, those who are ready to employ the words and example of John Henry Newman as a kind of a ready "jawbone" against evangelical Protestantism need to demonstrate that they are conscious that Protestants in general (including Protestants of evangelical sympathies) have been working in the field of Newman studies for well over a hundred years. If they are not yet familiar with the investigations and writings of Edmund Knox, Owen Chadwick, E. R. Fairweather, Geoffrey Rowell, Gordon Rupp, and Peter Toon (to name but a few) on Newman and the Tractarian movement, they should be. By reason of Protestants never having abandoned the field of Newman studies, those who today imagine that Newman represents some kind a "trump card" waiting to be played against unsuspecting evangelical Protestants have badly misjudged the situation. In this, as in so many other cases we have examined, today's restive sort of evangelicals demonstrate that they are unaware of Protestant Christianity's past engagements.

Second, those enamored with the power of Newman's example in renouncing evangelical Protestantism will find—if they look into it—that Newman's decades in his adoptive Roman Catholic communion raise some difficult questions for those who are thinking of following his example. Both in his native England and at Rome, Newman was initially treated with extreme wariness by many Roman Catholic authorities. It was not that Newman's sincerity in seeking admission to the Roman communion was questioned; it was that he was properly sized up as a theological thinker and writer who was still extensively Protestant in his outlook. The question became one of where Newman could be "posted" in his homeland and given meaningful tasks to do while withholding all possibility that he would ever function as a theological lecturer (his former role as a Protestant). His biographer, Dessain, speaks of Newman's "leaving the mainstream and entering a rivulet."[67] That rivulet was the Birmingham Oratory (which he directed from its foundation in 1848). True enough, he was invited to Dublin in 1854 to become the rector of a new Catholic university.[68] Yet Newman—though producing the stimulating book *The Idea of a University* while in Dublin—did not find any great concurrence with those ideals among traditional Irish Catholics and relinquished the post. Newman was then similarly rebuffed in his efforts to establish a branch of his Birmingham Oratory at Oxford; the Catholic sentiment opposing him did not wish Catholic young men to be encouraged to study in Protestant Oxford. What was initially intended to be an extension of the Birmingham Oratory at London eventually broke its link with Newman and Birmingham. The resident priests at London—many of whom had followed Newman in converting to Rome—had adopted an "Italianate" outlook on what constituted proper Catholic devotion; they came to consider themselves more wholehearted converts than Newman, whom they faulted for his relative independence of outlook.[69] Newman had to relinquish the editorship of the Catholic literary magazine *The Rambler* because of insular English Catholic attitudes.[70] From the frustrations stemming from what can only be called imposed horizons, Newman was delivered only in 1879 when Pope Leo XIII nominated him as a cardinal. Only in that final period of his life was he accorded the measure of respect that his new communion might have extended much sooner. Then, as now, distinctions are

---

[67]Stephen Dessain, *John Henry Newman* (London: Thomas Nelson, 1966), 89. On his thwarted ambition to teach Catholic theology in England, see p. 99.

[68]This new foundation at Dublin eventually became University College, Cork.

[69]Dessain, *John Henry Newman*, 93.

[70]Ker, *John Henry Newman*, 477-78.

drawn between those raised in the Catholic faith and those who affiliate at later stages of life. Newman was a man with Protestant baggage.

Third, and related to the second, is the fact—commented on with increasing frequency in the twentieth century—that Newman carried with him into Roman Catholicism certain definite convictions that were more Protestant than Catholic. Roman Catholic commentators have themselves drawn attention to his advocacy of the importance of biblical exegesis for theology (something not yet adequately acknowledged in nineteenth-century Catholic theology), the ultimate supremacy of Scripture over tradition, and the limitations of conceiving of churchly authority primarily in terms of the functioning of the hierarchy.[71] If it is maintained that Newman represents an example of one who came to submit himself to the claims of a changeless holy church and its hierarchy, it must also be maintained that Newman was an agent for theological change in the church that received him. Newman's stance is not properly appraised if it is described as mere conformist.

Fourth, it needs to be recognized that in the building up of the conception of this "second" Newman (in the period since 1933) there has been a highly important role played by converts to Roman Catholicism. The names Christopher Dawson, Meriol Trevor, and Avery Dulles are in a way like those who today choose the Church of Rome over the churches of their upbringing. Many of today's converts, like them, have composed literary works to tell the world about the reasons for their change of allegiance. But there is this difference: Dawson, Trevor, and Dulles joined discussions about Newman in which the participation of non–Roman Catholics was both obvious and taken for granted. Certainly since the 1960s, ecumenical discussion of Newman has displaced the old, more partisan approach. Today's enthusiasts for Newman need to recalibrate matters and to acknowledge that their own quite legitimate interest in this man of the nineteenth century is only part of this larger discussion that by and large evades polemic.

QUESTIONS FOR DISCUSSION

1. Had you ever heard or read the Newman quotation "To be deep in history is to cease to be Protestant" before reading this chapter? If

[71]See the discussion of Cuthbert Butler, Nicholas Lash, and Avery Dulles above.

you have such a recollection, was the quotation introduced in a disparaging way?

2. If there are some so enthusiastic about the name and legacy of Newman that they can find no fault with him, are there also Protestant and evangelical heroes who receive this same kind of uncritical veneration?
3. Is it difficult or straightforward to accept that Newman, in embracing Catholicism, carried certain Protestant and evangelical ideas? Does this carrying forward still happen today among those who change church affiliations?
4. What is one way in which you now think differently about J. H. Newman, having considered that there are distinguishable images of him in circulation?

PART IV

THREE CHALLENGES THAT REMAIN

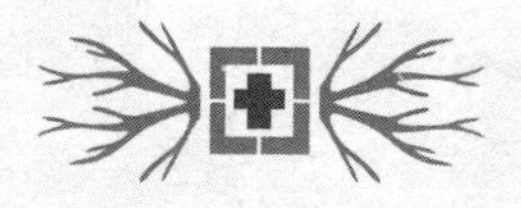

13

Is Christian Unity Dependent on a Central Bishop of Rome?

ON NOVEMBER 6, 2015, a delegation of persons representing the World Evangelical Fellowship was granted an audience with Pope Francis.[1] This meeting could hardly have been contemplated a half century ago when Catholic-Protestant relationships were still "frosty" on both sides. What has changed in the last half century to make such a meeting possible? There are two very obvious factors. First, there has been a "new face" for Catholicism and the papacy since Vatican II. And second, since 1978, there has been a series of popes who have intrigued evangelical Protestants.

ASSESSING AN IDEA: SHOULD CHRISTIANS UNITE UNDER THE BISHOP OF ROME?

Evangelical Protestants who have been part of this considerable "shift" in attitudes regarding the visible leader of the Roman Catholic communion are likely to be encouraged more and more to regard the bishop of Rome as the

[1]The Vatican press release regarding the audience granted to this delegation was accessed on November 7, 2014, and is available at press.vatican.va/content/salastampa/it/bollettino/pubblico/2014/11/06/0823/01747.html.

only figurehead capable of advancing the visible Christian unity that has eluded Christians for a millennium.[2] Protestantism in general and evangelical Protestantism in particular has admittedly contributed to the multiplication of expressions of Christianity. Now, on the one hand, evangelical Christians will likely give thought to the idea of unifying under the pope's leadership because of the evaporation of comparable international leadership from within our own ranks. International evangelical leaders such as Billy Graham and John Stott, who were very prominent in the second half of the twentieth century, no longer fill their former roles and have left no obvious successors.[3]

On the other hand, they will be more open to considering the idea of a unity presided over by the pope because they regularly express appreciation for public statements of recent bishops of Rome made in defense of the sanctity of life, the importance of traditional marriage, and the dangers of moral relativism. The question is, with these merits acknowledged, are the claims to global jurisdiction made by occupants of the office of pope defensible and convincing? What are these claims?

THE HISTORICAL CLAIMS MADE FOR THE BISHOP OF ROME

Claims made in the First Vatican Council (1869–1870). Since the late nineteenth century, the Church of Rome has reiterated its earlier claims asserting the pope to be the direct successor of Peter and the individual who is intended to exercise a dominion over the entire global church. The First Vatican Council affirmed:

> If then, any should deny that it is by the institution of Christ the Lord and by Divine right, that Blessed Peter should have a perpetual line of successors in the Primacy over the Universal Church, or that the Roman Pontiff is the successor of Blessed Peter in this primacy; let him be anathema.[4]

Claims of this magnitude were taken note of in 1870 beyond Roman Catholicism; this was, after all, a time when the bishop of Rome was attempting—

---

[2]We acknowledge here that the Christianity of the eastern Mediterranean became estranged from that of the west Mediterranean in AD 1054.

[3]Evangelist Billy Graham (b. 1918) has curtailed all public ministry since 2006. The UK Anglican John Stott (1921–2011), who was often associated with Graham, withdrew from public ministry in 2007.

[4]"The First Dogmatic Constitution on the Church of Christ: Pastore Aeturnus," chap. 2, accessed June 30, 2014, available at www.catholicplanet.org/councils/20-Pastor-Aeternus.htm.

with some difficulty—to assert his ongoing influence in a Europe increasingly inclined to popular democracy, and in a reunified Italy that took from him of all the territories he had held for a thousand years.[5] The great concern of that First Vatican Council was to reassert the indispensability of the papacy in a radically changing world.

Such claims were again reiterated in the Second Vatican Council (1962–1965). Without in any way muting this existing emphasis, a new collegial note was sounded in the second council: "He (Christ) formed after the manner of a college or a stable group, over which He placed Peter, chosen from among them."[6]

And yet this welcomed emphasis on the place for mutual interchange between the bishop of Rome and bishops around the globe did not make outmoded the earlier emphasis on the solitary prerogatives of the pope. On the contrary,

> the college or body of bishops has no authority unless it is understood together with the Roman Pontiff, the successor of Peter as its head. The Pope's power of primacy over all, both pastors and faithful, remains whole and intact. In virtue of his office, that is as Vicar of Christ and pastor of the whole Church the Roman Pontiff has full, supreme and universal power over the Church.[7]

And that the central role of the pope as regards the diverse Christians of the world (now kindly regarded as "separated brethren") was not intended to be diminished was made plain in the Decree on Ecumenism: "Jesus Christ, then, willed that the apostles and their successors—the bishops with Peter's successor at their head—should preach the Gospel faithfully, administer the sacraments, and rule the Church in love."[8]

---

[5]These territories, extending from Rome to the northeast, had long been known as the Papal States and were the basis of the pope's longstanding claim to be a head of state. The bishop of Rome had first come into possession of these territories in the ninth century.

[6]"Dogmatic Constitution of the Church: Lumen Gentium," November 21, 1964, paragraph 19, available at www.vatican.va/archive/hist_councils/ii_vatican_council/documents/vat-ii_const_19641121_lumen-gentium_en.html.

[7]"Dogmatic Constitution of the Church: Lumen Gentium," paragraph 22.

[8]"Decree on Ecumenism: Unitatis Redintegratio," November 21, 1964, available at www.vatican.va/archive/hist_councils/ii_vatican_council/documents/vat-ii_decree_19641121_unitatis-redintegratio_en.html.

Follow-up claims made by Pope John Paul II in the 1995 encyclical "Ut Unum Sint." Late in his tenure as bishop of Rome, Pope John Paul II attempted to further the Second Vatican Council's intention to foster a greater unity among the diverse Christians of the world. In his seventy-fifth year he issued an encyclical, "Ut Unum Sint" (That We May Be One); this was an attempt at advancing the reunion of Christians.[9] The document was in most major respects strictly in line with the utterances of Vatican I and II regarding the indispensable role of the pope in world Christianity.

> Among all the Churches and Ecclesial Communities, the Catholic Church is conscious that she has preserved the ministry of the successor of the Apostle Peter, the Bishop of Rome, whom God has established as her "perpetual and visible principle and foundation of unity" and whom the Spirit sustains in order that he may enable all the others to share in this essential good.

Yet in another respect, this encyclical was unprecedented in its extending what might be called an "olive branch" to the non-Roman expressions of world Christianity by its acknowledging that

> the Catholic Church's conviction that in the ministry of the Bishop of Rome she has preserved, in fidelity to the Apostolic Tradition and the faith of the Fathers, the visible sign and guarantor of unity, constitutes a difficulty for most other Christians, whose memory is marked by certain painful recollections.[10]

This was an acknowledgement that in the collective experience of non-Roman Christians, the bishop of Rome has often been found to be something *other* than the "guarantor" of unity.

This, in a nutshell, is the dilemma facing evangelical Protestants today. Are we to embrace an "idealist" conception of the bishop of Rome (the one preferred by Rome), according to which he can utilize the *potentialities* of his important role to foster unity among Christians? Or are we to give greatest weight to the historical actuality or "track record" of the papacy, which shows both that the papacy's claims to universal jurisdiction reach

[9]The encyclical is accessible at w2.vatican.va/content/john-paul-ii/en/encyclicals/documents/hf_jp-ii_enc_25051995_ut-unum-sint.html.
[10]"Decree on Ecumenism: Unitatis Redintegratio."

beyond the bounds of what is defensible and that its performance has too often been at variance with these claims? I hold that support for the latter approach far outweighs support for the former. In investigating these questions, special attention will be given to authorities who are themselves sympathetic to traditional Roman Catholic claims.

REASONS FOR NOT EMBRACING THE BISHOP OF ROME AS UNIVERSAL BISHOP

The claimed origins of the papal institution. While it is asserted in official statements issued by the Vatican and reiterated in popular histories of the papacy both that the apostle Peter was the first bishop of Rome and that subsequent bishops were his clear successors, there is good historical reason to question both assertions.[11] It is not that there is much dispute that the apostle Peter, the evident leader of the original twelve, died at Rome around the year 64, as did the apostle Paul—this is widely accepted. But that one or both functioned as first of a succession of "bishops" of Rome is an assertion of a different kind.

In that era, the Christian movement at Rome evidently functioned as a number of house churches (compare Rom 16:5); there was no single major assembly over which a prominent leader might be seen to preside as bishop. In this setting, Peter (with Paul) may very well have supplied pastoral oversight, but there was as yet no bishop there. Such developments awaited the second century—both at Rome and elsewhere. The compiled lists of bishops in the church at Rome do not begin with Peter, but with Linus.[12]

As to the leadership of the churches of the Mediterranean taken as a whole, there is New Testament evidence to suggest that while he lived, James—the brother of the Lord—was reckoned to have an exalted standing

---

[11]So, for instance, the statement from Vatican I (cited above) that Peter "lives, presides, and judges, to this day and always, in his successors the Bishops of the Holy See of Rome, which was founded by him." The modern papal historian John W. O'Malley, in *A History of the Popes* (Lanham, MD: Sheed and Ward, 2010), 11, equivocates over this question, answering it with "yes and no."

[12]Linus, who *may* be the person of this name mentioned in 2 Timothy 4:21, heads various early lists of bishops of Rome. Even though the formal office of bishop may actually have emerged later, tradition reckons him to have been "bishop" in the church at Rome circa AD 80. Michael P. McHugh, s.v. "Linus," in *Encyclopedia of Early Christianity*, ed. Everett Ferguson (New York: Garland, 1990), 539.

(Mk 6:3; Gal 1:19).[13] In the Jerusalem church at least, this standing seems to have been greater than that of Peter.[14] The apostle Paul consulted with the persons reckoned to be "pillars" of the church there (Peter and James among them) in the aftermath of his own conversion to Christ (Gal 1:19). Luke's account of the Jerusalem council (Acts 15:13) portrays a gathering in which James appears to preside; James was still exercising this role in the Jerusalem church when Paul returned there from his missionary journeys (Acts 21:18). Thus, while Jerusalem remained, up to the time of its destruction by the armies of Titus in AD 70, *that* church was esteemed to be the "center" of the Christian world. It was evidently still enjoying this recognition when Peter and Paul perished at Rome.

The rise in the estimation of the importance of other Mediterranean cities of Christian import (Antioch, Ephesus, Alexandria, and Rome—with Carthage to follow) unfolded in the aftermath of the marginalization of the Jerusalem church through the Roman military destruction of the city. And, of these other cities, Rome was not the only one to claim an association with apostles. Antioch, like Rome, had been the scene of the labors of both Peter and Paul (Gal 2:11); Ephesus had been the scene of the labors of both John and Paul (Acts 19 and 20);[15] Alexandria was reckoned by the Coptic churches of Egypt to have been the scene of the labors of Mark, who had been associated with Peter at Rome.[16]

The upshot of this was that while the church at Rome enjoyed a special status as the scene of the martyrdoms of two apostles, until at least the second half of the second century it was only reckoned to be the "seat" of Christianity in the west, as was Antioch to the north and Alexandria to the south. Accordingly, claims for a unique or exalted status for the church at Rome cannot be dated to Christianity's first century, and are first made in

---

[13]Glen A. Koch, s.v. "James," in *Encyclopedia of Early Christianity*, 482, estimates AD 62 as the year of James's martyrdom.

[14]Ibid., 482-83.

[15]The NT itself does not link John to Ephesus. However, by the second century, such a connection was widely believed to exist. Richard Oster, s.v. "Ephesus, Ephesians," in ibid., 302. If it is accepted that the John who wrote the book of Revelation is the apostle John, then the author's imprisonment on the island of Patmos (compare Rev 1:9), a location proximate to Ephesus, comes close to establishing the Ephesian link.

[16]Donald P. Senior, s.v. "Mark," in ibid., 572.

the second half of the second century.[17] And with Jerusalem marginalized on account of the destruction of AD 70, there were the other-named Mediterranean Christian centers, besides Rome, claiming an apostolic association with their founding.

In every case, it was the *church* of the city (rather than any particular current Christian leader) that inherited an exalted status by virtue of such associations.[18] We surely have no foundation here for the traditional claim that the church and bishop of Rome were always intended for supremacy.

The early papacy's modest theological prowess. The customary claims reiterated since 1870 about the universal and perpetual scope of the jurisdiction of the bishop of Rome (reckoned as "successor" of Peter) do not square very easily with the fact that early Christian Rome was a relative "lightweight" in the realm of Christian thought. This lightweight status was not the consequence of the Christian movement at Rome in the second and third centuries being cut off from the east-Mediterranean Christian churches by a linguistic barrier. That barrier (the eventual decline of Greek in the West) had not yet developed. It was simply the case that weighty theological reflection at Rome was still in the future, whereas in the East it was in process.

It was in the east that the hubs of Christian learning would, for two centuries or more, be found chiefly in Alexandria and Antioch. Both of these centers of ancient Christianity were famous early on for their great libraries and the scholars—such as Clement and Origen—who were associated with them. By the opening of the third century, Carthage had begun to come to the attention of the wider church through the writings of Tertullian and Cyprian. But by the third century, Christian Rome was notable only for a schismatic bishop-theologian, Hippolytus (ca. 170–ca. 235).[19] Irenaeus, known to us as associated with Lyons, and who was one of the earliest Christian thinkers to draw attention to the important role of Rome for

[17]Irenaeus in *Contra Haereses* III.3 can state "that very great, oldest and well known church founded and established at Rome by those two glorious apostles, Peter and Paul" makes a statement open to pretty universal qualification in our time. No serious writer affirms the apostles to have been the founders, and no serious writer maintains that the church at Rome has the greatest antiquity. See the text in C. C. Richardson, ed., *Early Christian Fathers* (Philadelphia: Westminster, 1953), 372.

[18]Eamon Duffy, *Saints and Sinners: A History of the Popes* (New Haven, CT: Yale University Press, 1997), 13.

[19]O'Malley, *History of the Popes*, 18.

western European Christianity, was himself of east Mediterranean origin and indebted to the theological learning of the Greek church.[20] When the first ecumenical council was convened at Nicaea in 325, the rising star among the orthodox was Athanasius of Alexandria (ca. 296–373). Sylvester, bishop of Rome (reigned 314–335), like most western bishops, did not attend this important council. He sent two delegates to represent him.[21]

Moreover, far from leading the whole Mediterranean church in theological reflection, a number of earlier bishops of Rome stumbled badly in theological matters. Bishop Victor (reigned 189–198) tried without success to bring the churches of the Italian peninsula to observe a common date for Easter. While the policy Victor urged was the one favored in the churches of the west, his opponents within Italy drew support from the churches of Asia Minor.[22] A later Roman bishop, Marcellinus (reigned 296–304), though eventually dying as a martyr, had earlier surrendered Scriptures to be burned and offered incense to the emperor's image in the Diocletian persecution.[23]

Under extreme political pressure from Emperor Constantius (who favored the ongoing Arian party after the Nicene Council of 325), the imprisoned Pope Liberius (reigned 352–366) had agreed to the excommunication of the orthodox champion Athanasius and signed a formula that "while it did not actually repudiate the Nicene creed, weakened it with the meaningless claim that the *Logos* was 'like the father in being' and in all things." While Liberius endured imperial imprisonment, Constantius put forward the pliable Felix as candidate for pope; he was guaranteed not to obstruct the Arian program.[24]

The heretic Pelagius, having been rightly censured by bishop of Rome Innocent I (reigned 401–417) in conjunction with the Synod of Carthage, turned tables by gaining the patronage of Innocent's successor, Zosimus. Bishop Zosimus (reigned 417–418) needed the Synod of Carthage to abruptly remind him that there was to be no going back on the joint verdict

---

[20]Mary T. Clark, s.v. "Irenaeus," in Ferguson, *Encyclopedia of Early Christianity*, 472. F. L. Cross, *Oxford Dictionary of the Christian Church* (London: Oxford University Press, 1957), 702, notes the indebtedness of Irenaeus to both Justin Martyr and Theophilus of Antioch.

[21]Duffy, *Saints and Sinners*, 23. The Western church as a whole was poorly represented.

[22]Ibid., 11.

[23]O'Malley, *History of the Popes*, 25.

[24]Duffy, *Saints and Sinners*, 25.

against Pelagius, in which his predecessor had concurred.[25] All this is to say that early bishops of Rome, however great their influence may have been while functioning in a role that might be called "patriarch of the west," were hardly able—in these early centuries—to demonstrate that the Mediterranean churches should look to Rome for the best articulation of Christian teaching. Any theological ascendancy that Rome might attain was still in the future.

The recurrence of rival antipopes. The assertion by Pope John Paul II in 1997 that the ongoing succession of bishops at Rome had provided the "perpetual and visible principle and foundation of unity"[26] is a claim with a track record that deserves to be examined. In the abstract, it is of course possible that a single Christian leader (or succession of leaders) strategically located somewhere in the world *might* exercise this kind of a unifying influence.

But upon investigation, one finds that the succession of bishops of Rome have a truly mixed record on this count. For a variety of reasons, recurring contests over *who* should fill the role of bishop of Rome have meant that across the intervening centuries, there have been rival popes or "antipopes" put forward thirty-four times.[27] That is to say that in selecting a bishop of Rome, there have been thirty-four occasions when either a minority party insisted on standing by their man and declaring him to be elected irrespective of the majority's action, *or* when some individual (perhaps a king or an emperor) put forward a candidate who faced a rival candidate preferred by others. A few historical examples will help to make concrete what will otherwise seem bewildering.

The first of the antipopes was Hippolytus (ca. 170–ca. 238), a Roman Christian still remembered for writings such as *The Apostolic Tradition.*[28] At the death of bishop Zephyrinus in 217, the clergy of the city of Rome chose Callistus (reigned 217–222) to succeed him. But Hippolytus, who was supported by a disgruntled minority of the city's clergy, was also declared elected. And as the Christian movement at Rome had no mechanism in place for defusing such a standoff, there was an extended period of time

---

[25]B. J. Kidd, *The Roman Primacy to 461* (London: SPCK, 1936), 88-89.

[26]"Decree on Ecumenism: Unitatis Redintegratio."

[27]This reckoning is made from the comprehensive list of popes provided by Duffy, *Saints and Sinners*, 293-99.

[28]Everett Ferguson, s.v. "Hippolytus," in Ferguson, *Encyclopedia of Early Christianity*, 427.

when the two—Hippolytus and Callistus—competed for the loyalty of the Christians at Rome.

Another notable example of the same type occurred in the year 366, when the election of Damasus as bishop of Rome (reigned 366–384) was countered by the claim of a rival, Ursinus. In this case, supporters of each took to the streets in hand-to-hand combat—137 supporters of Ursinus perished in the fighting.[29]

The classic example, however, of the office of Roman bishop (or pope) serving as a force for division rather than unity came in the period in the fourteenth century we have come to know as the "Babylonian Captivity." A newly elected Francophone bishop of Rome, taking the name Clement V (reigned 1305–1314), by reason of the threat of physical danger at Rome, determined to exercise his reign from Avignon (in what is today the Provençe region of France) rather than the Italian home of the papacy. Thus began an extensive era, lasting until the middle of the next century, where there were four occasions when there was at least one rival pope and one period in which there were two. Of course, each claimed to be the genuine article.[30]

The long association of the papacy with territories that were subject to the king of France (begun in 1309) and the unsuccessful attempts that followed to restore the papacy to its customary Roman home have, as indicated above, been designated the "captivity" of the church.[31] The terminology was meant to communicate the harmful over-association of the papacy with France. Even the return of the papacy (in the person of Urban VI) to Rome in 1378 did not end the ambiguities. For then, a succession of antipopes (all French) began once more to make Avignon their base of operation. This lamentable period known as the "Papal Schism" divided European Christianity inasmuch as Europe's rising nation-states proceeded to show loyalty toward one pope or the other based on whether they were on more friendly

---

[29]Duffy, *Saints and Sinners*, 29. The reputation of Damasus suffered for some time for this reason, as well as others.

[30]Duffy's chronology indicates that in this century and a half there were antipopes in the years 1328–1330, 1378–1394, 1409–1419, 1423–1429, and 1439–1449.

[31]While made subject to the crown of France from the year 1271 onward, by the time of the commencing of papal residence there in 1309, this territory was under the jurisdiction of the Count of Provence. The territory of Avignon was purchased by the papacy in the year 1348 when Clement VI reigned. From that time forward, this territory was reckoned as belonging to the "papal estates," which were primarily situated to the north and east of Rome. Cf. C. W. Previte-Orton, *The Shorter Cambridge Medieval History* (Cambridge: Cambridge University Press, 1955), 2:835.

terms with the king of France (who supported the Avignonese antipopes) or the Holy Roman Emperor (who supported the Roman popes). Thus, Scotland (an ally of France) supported the Avignonese popes while England (enemy to France and Scotland) supported the restored papacy at Rome.

Even though the Papal Schism was ended through the efforts of reforming councils at Constance (1415) and Basel (1439), a terrible cumulative lesson had been communicated: the papacy could just as easily polarize as unite Western Christianity.[32] This was not at all the simple working out of blind ambition on the part of individual popes. It was as much an indication that various parties in western Europe were determined to have "their man" in the papal office so that their own regional interests could be advanced. The combination of the removal of the papacy to Avignon followed (after its return to Rome) by multiple rival popes worked as much as anything to demonstrate that the western churches might need to function without any central papal office whatsoever. In the interim, until the schism was healed, this is just what they attempted to do.

In sum, the ongoing claim that the bishop of Rome serves as a focal point of Christian unity deserves to have a large asterisk set beside it. Thirty-four antipopes in the period up to 1439 require qualifying this claim. And it is *not* simply the existence of rival popes that has at times made the papacy a divisive force.

The attempted "control" of the papacy alternately by Constantinople, by wealthy Roman families, and by Gothic and Frankish kings. Though there is a widespread perception that once the first Christian Roman emperor Constantine relocated his capital from Rome to Constantinople in the year 330 the bishop of Rome was left utterly free to chart his own course, the truth is much more complex. On the one hand, there are the true reports of how—in a period when Roman power in the West was waning—bishops of Rome such as Leo I (reigned 440–461) negotiated with Attila the Hun so as to spare the city of Rome from destruction. On the other hand, it deserves to be better known that in negotiating, Leo was still acting on the urgings of the emperor at Constantinople, Valentinian II.[33] The reduction of the imperial military presence in the west that left Rome under-protected

[32]Geoffrey Barraclough, *The Medieval Papacy* (London: Thames and Hudson, 1968), 180-84.
[33]O'Malley, *History of the Popes*, 40.

against invasion and that made this papal negotiation with the Huns necessary did not yet mean that the bishop of Rome was operating in an autonomous manner. The chief citizen of the city of Rome he had certainly become, but in the year 452 it was not clear that Rome would in the future find no support at all from the imperial capital at Constantinople. As late as the year 537 the Byzantine emperor Justinian was still able to secure the election of his favorite, Vigilius, as the Roman bishop (reigned 537–555).

If imperial influence over choice of popes gradually diminished, there were two other forces closer at hand immediately ready to exert their own power. Since the late fourth century, Christianity had gained a much greater foothold among the patrician classes of old Rome. These had maintained traditional pagan loyalties longer than the population at large. But as imperial influence from Constantinople diminished, Roman patrician families embraced the Christian faith in greater numbers. They grew determined that Rome's bishop should be drawn from their own social strata. This determination, once manifested, would become one of the leading forces influencing the direction of the papacy for the future. The trend was observable in Roman bishops such as Damasus (reigned 366–384), Leo (reigned 440–461), and Gregory the Great (reigned 590–604).

But Rome was also to be increasingly constrained by new overlords who came from the north. These were the Gothic kings led by Theodoric (ca. 455–526), who reigned from a capital at Ravenna. Yet the kingdom established in the Italian peninsula by these invaders was one aligned with heretical Arian Christianity, and the bishop of Rome could come to terms with such kings only with difficulty.[34] This Gothic kingdom could not control the bishop of Rome, but it did work to reduce his sphere of influence by turning northern Italian churches to Arian purposes.

During a subsequent period when Constantinople temporarily recovered the rule of its North African and Italian peninsular territory (a campaign launched in the year 533), the papacy was temporarily drawn back into a much closer relation to the Byzantine emperor. In this period, no individual who was elected pope at Rome could be consecrated to this office without first being confirmed by the emperor at Constantinople.[35]

---

[34]Duffy, *Saints and Sinners*, 37.
[35]Ibid., 57.

Still later, Roman bishops had to learn how to deal with invading Lombards. Even though these invaders were eventually assimilated into mainstream Christianity, they harbored territorial ambitions on Rome and the surrounding territories from which the bishops of Rome drew revenues. The papacy's inability to defend itself against the schemes of the Lombards drove it into an alliance with the rising dynasty of France. The strategy of turning to France was necessitated by the inability of the emperor at Constantinople to make good his claim to continued jurisdiction in the Italian peninsula.[36] The military invasions of the north Italian peninsula by the French king, Pepin, in 754 and 756 restored to the bishop of Rome lands that the Lombards had seized, and provided the basis for the papacy's future tenure over what would be known as the "Papal States" (a tenure superseded only by the absorption of this territory into modern Italy in 1869). From this point onward, supported by Pepin's descendants, the bishop of Rome reckoned himself to be a temporal as well as a spiritual ruler. As a head of state, he would levy taxes; he would also maintain troops loyal to himself.

The sobering principle that emerges from this survey is that ever since the decision of Constantine to legitimize Christianity in the year 313,[37] the bishop of Rome has constantly found it necessary to ally himself with one temporal power or another. Changes brought on by the decline of empire, foreign invasion, or (as in the nineteenth century) nation-building have had the effect of disturbing existing alliances and requiring the papacy to enter into others. As recently as 1929, the papacy entered into a mutual concordat with the nation of Italy, receiving, in return for promises of noninterference, guarantees about the safety of the Vatican and the immunity of persons (both Italian and foreign) directly employed there.[38] The unresolved question is surely that of whether such alliances between the church Jesus founded and various states and dynasties is intrinsic to the church's existence and welfare.

The escalation, over time, of the papacy's honorific claims. The role of the bishop of Rome may be considered as an *office*, filled by individuals, each

[36]Ibid., 69-69; and Previte-Orton, *Cambridge Shorter Medieval History*, 1:300-301.

[37]By the Edict of Milan. See the text as printed in Henry Bettenson and Chris Maunder, eds., *Documents of the Christian Church*, 3rd ed. (New York: Oxford University Press, 1999), 17.

[38]The text of the 1929 accord, technically known as the Lateran Pact, is printed in Frank J. Coppa, ed., *Controversial Concordats: The Vatican's Relations with Napoleon, Mussolini, and Hitler* (Washington, DC: Catholic University of America Press, 1999), 193-205.

of whom is reckoned a successor of St. Peter. When viewed in this way, the virtues and shortcomings of the individuals who have filled the office can be compared in interesting ways.[39] We find individual bishops who are worthy of our Christian admiration as well as those whose dissolute lives make us rub our eyes in utter disbelief.

Yet the role of the bishop of Rome may also be viewed as an *institution* that has been required to adapt itself to change and circumstance not of its own making. Empires may rise and fall, dynasties may fade, and autocracy may give way to popular democracy. It is the papacy's response to such changes that concerns us here, for as we examine this phenomenon we find that over time, changes in circumstances have contributed to a questionable escalation of what bishops of Rome claim about themselves.

Prior to the extending of toleration to Christianity in the Edict of Milan in 313, the self-understanding of the bishops of Rome seems to have been that while they were on par with the patriarchs at Antioch and Alexandria, there was one notable difference. Because Peter and Paul had been martyred at Rome, the other chief centers of Christianity were willing to grant a kind of honorific precedence to Rome and its bishop. But this did not carry with it any precedence of power.[40] Barraclough has aptly described this state of affairs as "a federation of episcopal churches, each with its own customs and usages, loosely ruled by synods."[41]

Until the latter half of the third century, it was unusual for the argument to be made that Jesus' statement recorded in Matthew 16:18-19, "You are Peter, and on this rock I will build my church. . . . I will give you the keys of the kingdom," applied narrowly to bishops of Rome. Roman bishop Stephen (d. 257) was the first to argue for this narrow application of the pledge of Jesus to his own office. Stephen was also the first to speak of his papal office as the "chair of Peter."[42] His contemporary, Cyprian of Carthage, resisted such a narrow application of Jesus' words.[43] Only over time did Stephen's view gain traction.

---

[39] Thus, the provocative title of Eamon Duffy's history of the papacy, *Saints and Sinners*.

[40] Duffy, *Saints and Sinners*, 5.

[41] Barraclough, *Medieval Papacy*, 17.

[42] Ibid., 16.

[43] Ibid., 15; Duffy, *Saints and Sinners*, 16; and Hans von Campenhausen, *Ecclesiastical Authority and Spiritual Power in the Church of the First Three Centuries* (1969; repr., Peabody, MA: Hendrickson, 1997), chap. 11.

The eventual removal of the imperial seat of government from Rome to Constantinople (AD 330) meant, for one thing, that the bishop of Rome would eventually find an ecclesiastical counterpart in that new capital, as was already the case in Carthage, Alexandria, and Antioch. At the Council of Constantinople (AD 381) it was affirmed that the bishop of the new capital would "have the pre-eminence in honor after the Bishop of Rome, for Constantinople is the New Rome."[44] The access of the bishop of Rome to the Christian emperor that had been savored for just over a decade at Rome was now to characterize the role of a new patriarch in the empire's new capital.

And it was in this context that bishops of Rome began to articulate a further case for heightened authority for their own office. The earlier insistence of Sylvester that Rome's bishop was the direct inheritor of promises recorded in Matthew 16 was now reiterated. Rome, moreover, claimed to have a supremacy over the churches by the provision of Christ himself.[45] Mid-fifth-century bishop of Rome Leo I (reigned 440–461) pressed matters further by claiming to "stand in the place of Peter," using current Roman legal understanding to argue that each pope was a direct successor and legal executor of Peter's original mandate.[46]

The issue of the relative "rankings" of the various patriarchs of the Mediterranean church (introduced by the Council of Constantinople, 381) was still rankling bishops of Rome a century later. With a patriarch long installed at Constantinople, Pope Gelasius I (reigned 492–496) wrote the Byzantine emperor Anastasius to impress on him the dual principle that spiritual authority trumped the temporal power of emperors and that the physical location of that earthly spiritual power resides in the papacy.

> If the hearts of the faithful should be submitted to all priests in general who rightly administer divine things, how much more should assent be given to the bishop of that see which the Most High God wished to be preeminent

[44]Duffy, *Saints and Sinners*, 25. Rome clearly found the implication of the decree of Constantinople objectionable, for it implied that Rome—no less than Constantinople—derived its ecclesiastical significance from proximity to imperial power.

[45]O'Malley, *History of the Popes*, 38.

[46]Walter Ullmann, "Leo I and the Theory of Papal Primacy," *Journal of Theological Studies* 11 (1960): 25.

over all priests and which the devotion of the whole church has honored ever since.[47]

There was still one more important development, however. The just-elected Pope Innocent III (reigned 1198–1216) was no longer content to state what predecessors had claimed before him. His articulation of the papal status was that "we are the successor of the prince of the Apostles, but we are not the vicar of any man or Apostle, but the vicar of Jesus Christ himself."[48]

At this point, a bridge had been crossed. To an already disputable claim that only Rome's bishop stood in direction succession to Peter was added another: Rome's bishop was the supreme earthly representative of Jesus Christ. It was this kind of claim that provoked the complaint that such grandiose language arrogated to Rome's bishop what no single Christian believer should dare to claim. Such a claim was stupendous when one man uttered it. The day was not far off when as many as three individual claimants to the "chair of Peter" would make the same claim simultaneously.[49]

A PERSPECTIVE FOR THE FUTURE

Evangelical Protestants, while dealing with the bishop of Rome or his representatives, need not be overawed by lofty claims made about the antiquity and universal role of the papacy. Instead, we do well to center on those aspects of the papacy that are not a matter of dispute. I refer here to such factors as this individual's being

- the chosen Roman Catholic bishop of Rome and the person recognized within global Roman Catholicism as having preeminence over all other Roman bishops and
- the bishop of Rome, who accordingly (whether in person or by his delegates) is able to represent the Roman Catholic communion in dialogues with other expressions of Christianity, non-Christian religious traditions, or heads of state.

[47]Gelasius I, "Letter," in Marvin Perry, Joseph R. Peden, and Theodore H. Von Laue, eds., *Sources of the Western Tradition* (Boston: Houghton Mifflin, 1999), 1:189-90. The "see" referred to was Gelasius's own city of Rome. It is hard to avoid the implication that Gelasius is claiming a divine sanction for Rome's preeminence.

[48]Leo III, P.L. 214, 292, as quoted in R. W. Southern, *Western Society and the Church in the Middle Ages* (Grand Rapids: Eerdmans, 1970), 105.

[49]This was the "Papal Schism" of the late fourteenth century.

It is also true that two recent bishops of Rome, John Paul II (reigned 1978–2005) and Francis (2013–present), are persons who have cultivated warm relationships with evangelical Protestants. But it does not follow from any of this that the evangelical Protestant is obliged to accept as true what the papacy has itself in recent times acknowledged as proving to be an obstacle to closer relationships:[50]

- the insistence on the divine origin of the papacy with Peter as the first to hold the office;
- the insistence that the supremacy of Rome and of its bishops in world Christianity is similarly the divine intention;
- the insistence that the bishop of Rome is the representative of Jesus Christ on earth and, consequently, the focus of Christian unity; and
- the insistence that the bishop of Rome stands as a temporal head of a permanent state, the Vatican.

Christian charity requires that we acknowledge the first realities. It does not require us to assent to any of the second.

QUESTIONS FOR DISCUSSION

1. Have you ever witnessed a papal visit? Of the many activities connected with such a visit, which struck you as most constructive and which as least? Do evangelical Protestants reap any benefits when the pope visits a country or a city?
2. For Christians concerned about disunity in the global church, what can the pope offer, and what lies beyond his reach?
3. Does it in the end matter to the claims of the papacy that Rome's first-century house churches had no bishop and that Rome's eventual first recorded bishop was not Peter but Linus?
4. Some of the pope's claims infringe on what belongs to Christ alone; some of his claims infringe on what belongs equally to other Christian leaders. Discuss this difficulty.

[50]Note the document "Ut Unum Sint," referred to above.

14

Is Justification as Protestants Teach It the Historic Faith of the Church?

"JUSTIFICATION" IS ONE OF A SELECT NUMBER of metaphors used in the Scriptures to describe the transferal of a fallen individual from a state of lost-ness or liability to divine judgment to one of restoration and acceptance before God.[1] Jesus used the metaphor in telling the story of an outcast tax collector who appeared at the temple begging for God's mercy; it was not the proud Pharisee (who was also there, praying) but *this* man who went home justified (Lk 18:14). Paul reminded his Galatian readers that the justification before God that they possessed by virtue of their having heard the gospel with faith (Gal 3:5) was the same justification as that granted earlier to Abraham, whose belief in God's promise to him was "credited to him as righteousness" (Gal 3:6). Later, writing to the Romans, the same apostle insisted that those presently in possession of this divine gift of justification enjoyed peace with God (Rom 5:1). Justification is a

[1]Other such images found in the NT would include being "found" after first being "lost" (Lk 15), re-creation (2 Cor 4:6; 5:16), and redemption (1 Cor 1:30; 1 Pet 1:18).

standing entered into by faith-dependence on Jesus Christ, whom God has provided as our once-for-all sacrifice of atonement (Rom 3:25). We enjoy justification by reliance on Christ and not as a consequence of our personal moral exertion. Personal exertion *follows* the receipt of justification without being the prerequisite for it.

THE WIDE-ANGLE VIEW

In the age of the Reformation, the claim was made that this gospel principle of justification had been allowed to fall into obscurity. Classic expression was given early on to this important principle (claimed to be recovered) in the Augsburg Confession (1530), the doctrinal articles summarizing the common faith of German-speaking Protestants who were seeking recognition and toleration from the Holy Roman Emperor, Charles V (1500–1558).

> It is also taught among us that we cannot obtain forgiveness of sin and righteousness before God by our own merits, works, or satisfactions, but that we receive forgiveness of sin and become righteous before God by grace, for Christ's sake, through faith, when we believe that Christ suffered for us and that for his sake our is sin is forgiven and righteousness and eternal life are given to us. For God will regard and reckon this faith as righteousness, as Paul says in Romans 3:21-26 and 4:5.[2]

Now the insistence that in preceding centuries there had been an obscuring of how salvation is obtained was met with a strong countercharge. This countercharge asserted that the "by faith alone" championed by Luther and other early Protestants was a doctrinal novelty, standing without any precedent in earlier Christianity.[3] The classic expression of this objection (which is still heard today) was provided by the Council of Trent (1545–1563), which was summoned to provide an authoritative Roman Catholic response to the perceived dangers posed by such Protestant teachings.

Trent prefaced all its assertions (both regarding justification and other doctrinal topics) with an insistence that the Vulgate (Latin) translation of

---

[2]Augsburg Confession, art. 4, cited from Theodore G. Tappert, trans. and ed., *The Book of Concord* (Philadelphia: Fortress, 1959), 30.

[3]See the elaboration of this counter-charge in Alister McGrath, *Iustitia Dei: A History of the Doctrine of Justification*, 3rd ed. (Cambridge: Cambridge University Press, 2005), 211.

the Scriptures be accepted as foundational for theology.[4] The books of Scripture that the council enumerated as constituting Holy Scripture included the intertestamental writings.[5] Trent also claimed for the Roman Catholic teaching office alone the ability to interpret these Scriptures in a way consistent with "the unanimous consent of the Fathers."[6] Yet assertions of this kind begged important questions that the assembled council was not prepared to consider at that time.[7]

As for the assertion the German Protestants had made about justification itself, the Council of Trent replied that rather than being received primarily by "hearing with faith," justification could not be received "without the laver of regeneration [baptism] or the desire thereof." And as to the suggestion that justification was full and total at the time of receiving it, Trent insisted that "justification is not remission of sins merely, but also the sanctification and renewal of the inward man, through the voluntary reception of the grace, and of the gifts whereby an unjust man becomes just."[8] Here were evidences of strong difference of emphasis as to how justification was entered into and of how (if at all) justification ought to be distinguished from growth in holiness (sanctification), which is intended to characterize all who are restored to fellowship with God. The Council of Trent pronounced "anathemas" (i.e., condemnations) on the contrary opinions they believed Protestants to hold.[9]

---

[4]The Vulgate had been produced by the improving of the Old Latin Bible; the project was brought to completion by Jerome (347-420), working with encouragement given to him by Pope Damasus I in 382. It was to Jerome's credit that he worked to correct the Old Latin version in light of his classical Greek training acquired in his adolescence and the Hebrew instruction received in his adult life. Terrence G. Kardong, s.v. "Vulgate," in *Encyclopedia of Early Christianity*, ed. E. F. Ferguson (New York: Garland, 1990), 932-34.

[5]This viewpoint had previously been endorsed at the Council of Florence (1438–1445). See John W. O'Malley, *Trent: What Really Happened at the Council* (New Haven, CT: Yale University Press, 2013), 91. O'Malley indicates that the council, while acknowledging that the right of the intertestamental books to be included in the canon was a question being freshly aired by Christian humanists (and not simply by committed Protestants), chose to reiterate the earlier position of Florence to streamline their proceedings.

[6]"Council of Trent, Fourth Session: Decree Concerning the Edition, and the Use of the Sacred Books," in *Creeds of Christendom*, ed. Philip Schaff, vol. 2, *The Greek and Latin Creeds* (1877; repr., Grand Rapids: Baker, 1977), 82-83.

[7]The two most important questions were the accuracy of the Vulgate as a translation of the NT and the actual ability of the Council to gauge what the actual "consent of the Fathers" entailed.

[8]Council of Trent, Sixth Session, chaps. 4 and 7, in Schaff, *Creeds of Christendom*, 2:91, 94.

[9]See, for example, Canons 8-14 in Schaff, *Creeds of Christendom*, 2:112-13. It is a matter of current ecumenical discussion whether the "errors" that Trent attributed to contemporary Protestants were in fact maintained by them.

Unsurprisingly, the Council of Trent was faulted by Reformation-era Protestants for these assertions and condemnations. John Calvin of Geneva rapidly produced his own *Acts of the Council of Trent with the Antidote* in 1547. Calvin did a thorough job of evaluating the initial printed proceedings of the council that were available at that early stage.

As for the question of justification itself, Calvin insisted:

> The whole dispute is as to the cause of justification. The Fathers of Trent pretend that it is twofold, as if we were justified partly by forgiveness of sins and partly by spiritual regeneration; or, to express their view in other words, as if our righteousness were composed partly of imputation, partly of quality.[10]

At stake was the council's insistence that there can be no confidence or certainty of one's justification until there is corroboration of it provided in subsequent moral renovation. But Calvin, drawing support from Augustine (354–430) and Bernard of Clairvaux (1090–1153),[11] urged that since salvation is in the end chiefly a matter of divine mercy, certainty that one is forgiven can really only be drawn from the completeness of what Christ has done rather than from one's imperfect steps toward fuller obedience.

A somewhat younger Protestant observer, German theologian Martin Chemnitz (1522–1586), amplified the kinds of concerns first articulated by Calvin. Chemnitz had at his disposal the totality of the documents produced by the Roman Catholic council through to its conclusion in 1563; he produced a compendium of responses extending to four volumes.[12] Chemnitz's argument was not that the majority of early Christian writers understood justification just as he did—in fact, he acknowledged that he could not assemble such a majority.[13] Yet he maintained that if one asked of the Fathers the related question of "how and why a person is reconciled to God, receives the remission of sins and the adoption, and is accepted to life eternal," he

[10]John Calvin, "Acts of the Council of Trent with an Antidote" (1547), in *Calvin's Tracts and Treatises*, vol. 3, *On the Doctrine and Worship of the Church* (Edinburgh: Calvin Translation Society, 1851), 116.

[11]Ibid., esp. 113, 119, 121, 127. Augustine and Bernard are also the fathers whom Calvin regularly cites in support of his understanding of justification in the *Institutes of the Christian Religion* (1536 edition), trans. Ford Lewis Battles (Grand Rapids: Eerdmans, 1975), 3.11.22; 3.12.3, 8; 3.13.4.

[12]Martin Chemnitz, *Examen Concilii Tridentini* (1565–1573) [Examination of the Council of Trent] (St. Louis: Concordia, 1971).

[13]Ibid., 1:468.

would find that many Fathers gave answers comparable to those of Protestants in his own day.[14] How could all this be true?

Chemnitz insisted that the root of the discrepancy lay in translation decisions made far in the past. The Greek verb for "justify" (*dikaioun*), whether in secular or biblical literature, customarily bore the meaning of "to judge or to pronounce something just" or (consistent with the first) "to judicially punish." Early Christian translators had misjudged the matter in rendering *diakaioun* and its cognates by the Latin term *justificare*, meaning "to make righteous" through a transformation from unrighteousness to righteousness. Chemnitz insisted, therefore, "Among Greek authors, therefore, the word 'justify' is not used in that sense for which alone the papalists contend."[15]

Church fathers in the west Mediterranean, reliant on the Latin version of the Bible, "usually follow the analogy of the Latin composition in the word 'justify' (yet) they are nevertheless often compelled by the evidence of the Pauline argumentation to acknowledge the proper and genuine meaning which we have shown."[16] In proof of this assertion, Chemnitz brought forward examples from Augustine, Hilary, Cyril, and Oecumenius.[17]

The pattern of Catholic-Protestant argumentation had now been set in the age of Trent. From the Roman Catholic side, the argument from an alleged unbroken testimony of Christian antiquity about justification continued to be made by such apologists as Jacques-Bénigne Bossuet (1627–1704). In his *History of the Variations of the Protestant Churches* (1688) he insisted, as regards justification,

> Next to the question of the Eucharist, the principal one of our controversies is that of justification, in relation to which the gravity of the Church's decisions may be easily understood in that she did but repeat in the Council of Trent what the Fathers and St. Austin had decided formerly.[18]

---

[14]Ibid.

[15]Ibid., 471.

[16]Ibid., 475.

[17]Ibid. Chemnitz's deep familiarity with the church fathers is surveyed by Carl Beckwith in "Martin Chemnitz's Use of the Church Fathers in His Locus on Justification," *Concordia Theological Quarterly* 68, no. 3 (2004): 271-90.

[18]Jacques Bénigne Bossuet, *The History of the Variations of the Protestant Churches* (1688; English trans., 1742; repr., Dublin: Richard Coyne, 1836), 1:372.

And from the Protestant side, theologians such as James Ussher (1581–1656), Protestant archbishop of Armagh (Ireland), continued to stress the forensic or judicial import of justification. No mean patristics scholar, Ussher produced a dozen patristic supports for his understanding of justification in his *Answers to a Jesuit.*[19] Later, Francis Turretin (1623–1687) of Geneva continued to maintain that *dikaioun*, a forensic term, had been mistakenly rendered by *justificare.*[20]

The issue had not been let slip away in the eighteenth century either. Church of England evangelical chronicler Joseph Milner (1744–1797)[21]—determined not to let it be thought that the renewed preaching of justification by faith in the decades spoken of collectively as the "Evangelical Revival" represented a novelty—took up the question in his multivolume *History of the Church of Christ* (1794–1809).[22] His *History* sought to show that long before justification by faith was ever preached by Luther, it had been proclaimed by Clement of Rome and Origen of Alexandria.[23] His efforts were augmented by those of another Anglican evangelical, G. S. Faber (1773–1854).[24] Faber's treatise, *The Primitive Doctrine of Justification*, was able to demonstrate, by excerpt, a total of twenty-eight writers between Clement of Rome (ca. 96) and Bernard of Clairvaux (1090–1153) who had upheld the importance of justification by faith in distinction from justification by contributed merit.[25]

In sum, from a somewhat tentative beginning in the age of the Reformation itself, the Protestant argument for antiquity gradually expanded

---

[19]James Ussher, *Answers to a Jesuit* (Dublin, 1621).

[20]Francis Turretin, *Institutes of Elenctic Theology*, trans. Charles Musgrave and ed. James T. Dennison, 2 vols. (1679–1685; Phillipsburg, NJ: P&R, 1994), 2:634-35.

[21]On whom, see Arthur Pollard, "Milner, Joseph," in *Blackwell Dictionary of Evangelical Biography*, ed. Donald M. Lewis, 2 vols. (Oxford: Blackwell, 1995), 2:776.

[22]The work was brought to completion in five volumes at the death of Joseph Milner in 1797 by his younger brother Isaac Milner (1750–1820). I have utilized the five-volume edition of T. Caddell (London, 1827).

[23]Joseph Milner, *History of the Church of Christ*, 5 vols. (1794–1809; repr., London: T. Cadell, 1827), 1:130, 467. Milner took the view that the confusion between justification as forensic and justification as a process eventuating in divine acceptance set in during the second century. See ibid., 2:238.

[24]On whom, see Arthur Pollard, "Faber, George Stanley," in Lewis, *Blackwell Dictionary of Evangelical Biography*, 1:374-75.

[25]George Stanley Faber, *The Primitive Doctrine of Justification*, 2nd ed. (London: Seeley and Burnside, 1839), 387-92. In this second edition, Faber incorporated material of which he had been previously unaware, available in James Ussher's treatise of 1621, *Answer to a Jesuit.*

from maintaining only that there had been *some* witnesses to the doctrine of justification by faith prior to the age of Luther to maintaining that there had been witnesses in every century through the twelfth. Writing in 1867, the Scots theologian James Buchanan (1804–1870) articulated this view by maintaining that there was

> a mass of testimonies extending from Apostolic times down to Bernard, the last of the Fathers, abundantly sufficient to prove that the doctrine of justification by grace through faith alone had some faithful witnesses in every succeeding age of the Church. It was never universally received any more than it is at the present day; it was always opposed by the spirit of self-righteousness, often corrupted by human inventions,—sometimes perverted and abused by Antinomian license; but it was then as it is now, the doctrine of many true believers, and the very "joy and rejoicing of their hearts."[26]

This Protestant confidence in the "pedigree" of their understanding of justification held firm so long as clear familiarity with the theology and practice of pre-Reformation Christianity was maintained. We saw earlier that this familiarity was maintained until the period of the Great War (1914–1918), and afterward declined.[27]

A CLOSER LOOK AT THE REFORMATION-ERA CONTROVERSY

This may be the story in broad outline. But on closer inspection this story displays a certain irony: Roman Catholic theologians and bishops present at the Council of Trent were not, in fact, in an unassailable position when they maintained that the teaching on justification that they defended at Trent had "the unanimous consent of the Fathers." What in fact constituted the "consent of the Fathers" was very much up for debate in that period of time.

Earlier in this book, we have shown that carefully edited versions of the patristic writings were only gradually becoming available in that age through the advent of the mechanical printing press. As careful Christian editors did their work, they determined that some patristic writings had suffered by repeated copying, while others had been wrongly attributed to authors to whom they had no connection.[28] Diarmaid MacCulloch has described the

---

[26]James Buchanan, *The Doctrine of Justification* (1867; repr., Grand Rapids: Baker, 1977), 92.

[27]See chapter 5.

[28]It was Erasmus who, in preparing the various writings of Ambrose for publication, determined

extended process, begun at Basel in 1490 and extending sixteen years, of bringing out a complete edition of the writings of Augustine.[29] Other such critical editions followed in steady succession. The question soon became that of who would most profit by this abundance of riches.

In that age of cultural Renaissance we still today associate with great painting, sculpture, poetry, and literary style, there was also a parallel appropriation of certain key emphases bearing on the question of the renewal of Christianity. It appeared to a growing number of thoughtful Christians that the Scriptures and the writings of the church fathers could themselves, once recovered in authentic form, assist in the purification of the church. As historian Robert Linder has put it, "What exactly did Christ and the Apostles teach and what did they really intend Christianity to be like? This approach was common to every Christian humanist, whether Erasmus, Colet, Reuchlin, Lefevre d'Etaples or . . . Calvin."[30]

But the cultural Renaissance did not all at once give birth to this "Christian humanism." Historian Lewis W. Spitz Jr. described "three generations of humanism" and applied the term not only to German-speaking lands (his chief concern) but also to other nations.[31] The earliest of these stages commenced circa 1350 and showed itself concerned for the improvement of style in the writing of Latin or vernacular documents. A second phase was in evidence after 1490; this showed itself in a heightened concern to distinguish the rising humanism of Europe's regions from the similar (and preexistent) movement afoot in Italy. But the "third generation"

> was the rise of the new young generation of humanists who rallied around Luther and became the defenders and builders of the Protestant Church. The renewal of religious life within Catholicism produced also within the old Church a third generation of humanists who were more successful than their elders had been.[32]

---

that the commentary on thirteen letters of the apostle Paul, which had long been attributed to Ambrose, were not in fact his work. "Ambrosiaster" was the name provided by Erasmus for the unknown commentator. See Ferguson, *Encyclopedia of Early Christianity*, 323.

[29]Diarmaid MacCulloch, *The Reformation: A History* (New York: Viking, 2003), 108.

[30]Robert Linder, "Calvinism and Humanism: The First Generation," *Church History* 44, no. 2 (1975): 168-69.

[31]Lewis W. Spitz Jr., *The Religious Renaissance of the German Humanists* (Cambridge, MA: Harvard University Press, 1963), 6-7.

[32]Ibid., 7.

This third generation of younger scholars had acquired the mastery of classical Latin, classical Greek, and the early Christian (patristic) writers, which enabled them to take up the New Testament with a view to asking questions about the correspondence between the current teaching and practice of the church and the foundational New Testament writings.[33] Prior to 1521 the aim of these Christian humanists was one of bringing the church of western Europe back into living contact with these sources that bore so directly on Christian origins.[34] In the period up to the 1540s, one could participate in this movement of shared concern while, gradually, the movement was bifurcating into early Protestant and continuing Roman Catholic expressions.

Such Christian humanists familiarized themselves with the first mechanically printed New Testament offering Greek and Latin texts side by side, the "Novum Instrumentum," produced by Erasmus in a first edition at Basel in 1516.[35] Soon thereafter, there followed a still more elaborate multilingual edition of the Bible: the Complutensian Polyglot, produced by a team of translators at the Spanish University of the Alcalá under the leadership of Cardinal Jiménez de Cisneros (1436–1517).[36] Each of these publishing projects enabled the adequately prepared reader to make comparisons between the Latin text (reflecting the efforts of Jerome circa AD 400) and the Greek text in its then best-available form.[37] And there were conclusions to be drawn.

---

[33]This path had initially been blazed by the Italian humanist Lorenzo Valla (c. 1407–1457), who having acquired Greek, went on to compose "Annotations on the New Testament." His manuscript was published posthumously by Erasmus in 1506. In the work he highlighted the shortcomings of the Latin Vulgate when compared with Greek manuscripts of the New Testament. See Myron P. Gilmore, *The World of Humanism* (New York: Harper & Row, 1952), 199-200.

[34]The work of these Christian humanists is helpfully explored by Lucy E. Wooding in "Christian Humanism: From Renaissance to Reformation," *History Review* 64 (September 2009): 13-18.

[35]A second, improved edition followed in 1519.

[36]What was then the University of Alcalá is today known as the Complutense University of Madrid. The New Testament volume of the six-volume Complutensian Bible was printed in 1514, but as the entire project was not brought to completion until 1517, and as Erasmus had secured an imperial and papal endorsement of his own version for the four years up to 1520, the Polyglot was only offered for sale subsequently. The OT Polyglot volumes featured Hebrew, Latin, Greek, Syriac, and a new Latin translation; the NT volume featured Greek and the Latin Vulgate in parallel columns. A description of the task entailed in producing the Polyglot edition is provided in Erika Rummel, *Jiménez de Cisneros: On the Threshold of Spain's Golden Age* (Tempe, AZ: Center for Medieval and Renaissance Studies, 1999), chap. 4. See also Basil Hall, "Cardinal Jiménez de Cisneros and the Complutensian Bible," in *Humanists and Reformers* (Edinburgh: T&T Clark, 1990), chap. 1.

[37]F. J. Crehan, "The Bible in the Roman Catholic Church from Trent to the Present Day," in *The*

To take just two prime examples, it was soon observed that the command of John the Baptist (in his ministry preparatory to the dawn of Jesus' public career), "Produce fruit in keeping with repentance" (Mt 3:8), had been rendered by the Vulgate as "in keeping with penitence." Yet the Greek word (*metanoias*) pointed not to the compliant actions of a penitent person (pious actions prescribed by the priest to whom one made confession) but to a decisive action in turning away from earlier evil. And in the story Jesus had told about the tax collector who cried out for divine mercy when praying at the temple, the point was not (as the Vulgate had it) that he had returned home "made just" (*justificatus*) but that he had returned home justified in the forensic sense (Greek, *dikaiomenos*) (Lk 18:14). Who could draw such distinctions, and who did draw such distinctions?

The emergence of a Roman Catholic "justification by faith alone" party. Christian humanists could and did draw such distinctions in every European setting where they existed and had access to the "Novum Instrumentum" of Erasmus or the "Complutensian Polyglot" associated with Cardinal Jiménez. And without any intent whatsoever to disrupt the church or to introduce upheaval, those with such linguistic skills began to reconsider whether "to be justified" did not occur in a punctiliar way, the consequence of God's having mercy on a particular sinner at a particular time. Roman Catholic as well as Protestant historians now acknowledge that this was becoming the common understanding of scholars such as France's Lefèvre d'Étaples;[38] Italian cardinals Contarini, Seripando, and Morone;[39] England's Cardinal Pole (1500–1558),[40] who was resident in Italy after 1532; and

---

Cambridge History of the Bible, ed. W. L. Greenslade (Cambridge: Cambridge University Press, 1963), 3:204-5, helpfully explains how the release of the *Novum Instrumentum* by Erasmus in 1516 engendered heated discussion of whether the Greek manuscripts he had relied on were in fact a satisfactory standard against which to compare the Vulgate.

[38]Both P. E. Hughes, *Lefèvre: Pioneer of Ecclesiastical Renewal in France* (Grand Rapids: Eerdmans, 1984), 74-78, and Guy Bedouelle, "Jacques Lefèvre d'Etaples," in *The Reformation Theologians*, ed. Carter Lindberg (Oxford: Blackwell, 2002), 25-26, allow that Lefèvre's understanding of justification approximated the eventual Protestant emphasis on appropriation by faith, yet in combination with a fairly conventional Catholic understanding of a second subsequent and final justification to come.

[39]The stance of the four Italian dignitaries is described in the entry for each in Hans Hillerbrand, ed., *Oxford Encyclopedia of the Reformation*, 4 vols. (New York: Oxford University Press, 1996). The entry for Contarini (1:419) makes plain that his own "breakthrough" in the understanding of justification occurred in 1511. On Seripando, note especially John W. O'Malley, *Trent*, 104.

[40]Reginald Pole had studied at Oxford and Padua and served King Henry VIII until he concluded

the Spaniard (resident in Naples after 1535) Juan de Valdés.[41] And this is to speak purely of those who remained Roman Catholic, all the while modifying their understanding of justification from that of being "made righteous" to that of being "declared righteous." Overlapping circles of earnest Italian Christians—some designated "Spirituali"[42] and others known as "Valdesian" (after Juan de Valdés)—had in common a debt to the burgeoning of Christian humanism, to Renaissance Platonism, and to the emphasis on the study of the Greek New Testament.[43] By 1536, Valdés was circulating from Naples his *Christian Alphabet,* in which he explained:

> You ought to know that the law is very needful to us, for if we had not the law, we would not have conscience, and if without conscience, sin would not be known and if sin were not known, we should not humble ourselves, and if we did not humble ourselves, we should not obtain grace, if we did not obtain grace we should not be justified and not being justified, our souls would not be saved. And this, I believe, St. Paul wishes to be understood where he says that the law is as a schoolmaster who leads and conducts us to Christ, although by means of faith we are justified.[44]

It is only once this reality (the existence of a "justification by faith" party) is acknowledged within early sixteenth-century Roman Catholicism that we are able to properly understand a range of phenomena that unfolded in ensuing years. The current pope, Paul III, drew on this circle

that he must oppose Henry's assumption of the headship of the English church. Both by his flight to the Continent and his authoring a treatise on the unity of the church (which Henry had helped to rupture) he brought danger and persecution on his family, which remained in England.

[41]Valdés is popularly thought to be the primary author of the devotional work *The Benefits of Christ.* He was certainly associated with the work. Clearly attributable to him are two other works, *Diálogo de doctrina Cristiana* (1529) and *Alphabeto Christiano* (1536). See A. Gordon Kinder, "Valdes, Juan de," in *Oxford Encyclopedia of the Reformation*, vol. 4, ed. Hans Hillerbrand (Oxford: Oxford University Press, 1996), 213.

[42]Research on this movement, centering on Cardinal Reginald Pole, is summarized by Elizabeth G. Gleason in "Evangelism," in Hillerbrand, *Oxford Encyclopedia of the Reformation*, 2:82, 83. See also MacCulloch, *Reformation*, 208-9.

[43]Massimo Firpo, "The Italian Reformation and Juan de Valdes," *Sixteenth Century Journal* 27, no. 2 (1996): 362. This story is elaborated more fully by Firpo in *Juan de Valdes and the Italian Reformation* (Burlington, VT: Ashgate, 2015), esp. chap. 3.

[44]Juan de Valdés, "The Christian Alphabet," in *Spiritual and Anabaptist Writers*, ed. George H. Williams and Angel M. Mergal (Philadelphia: Westminster, 1957), 366-67. One finds this teaching present in germinal form in Valdés's 1529 work, "Dialogue on Christian Doctrine," which is an exposition of the Lord's Prayer. See the "Dialogue" in ibid., 325-26.

(as on others) in 1536 to form a commission that would report to a council he intended to call the next year in Mantua. Of nine commission members that drew up the document "*Consilium de Emendanda Ecclesia*" in preparation for this council (which, in the end, was postponed), we can identify at least two individuals who were identified with the "Spirituali" cause: Contarini and Pole.[45]

The concord achieved on justification at the Catholic-Protestant Colloquy of Regensburg (1541). When Pope Paul III was thwarted in 1537 in his desire to see a pan-European council assembled to deal with the danger posed by emergent Protestantism, Holy Roman Emperor Charles V became increasingly motivated to see a conciliation achieved between his Protestant and Catholic subjects. To that end, after secretly setting carefully chosen Catholic and Protestant theologians to work in preparation, he convoked the Colloquy of Regensburg in April 1541. Cardinal Contarini, a "Spirituali" sympathizer, was named by the pope to represent him as his legate at Regensburg.[46] While the Catholic-Protestant consultation that took place there was eventually abandoned over unresolvable differences over the Eucharist and papal authority, there had been a quite impressive concurrence achieved between Catholic and Protestant delegates over justification.

One Catholic theologian in particular, Johannes Gropper (1503–1559), who was associated with the reform of the Catholic diocese of Cologne, evidently was of the same outlook as the Italian "Spirituali"; we know that he was a Christian humanist follower of Erasmus.[47] As part of the secret team (which included Martin Bucer [1491–1551] and Wolfgang Capito [1478–1541] of Strasbourg) working to prepare a conciliatory draft document to be presented for discussion at Regensburg, Gropper had lent his

---

[45]Elisabeth G. Gleason, "Consilium de Emendanda Ecclesiasia," in Hillerbrand, *Oxford Encyclopedia of the Reformation*, 1:415.

[46]A. N. S. Lane, *Justification in Catholic-Protestant Dialogue: An Evangelical Assessment* (Edinburgh: T&T Clark, 2002), 51. A good overview of the transactions of this colloquy is provided by Basil Hall in the essay "Colloquies Between Catholics and Protestants 1539–1541" in his *Humanists and Protestants*, chap. 5. Contarini's role at Regensburg was earlier helpfully described by Heinz Mackensen in "Contarini's Theological Role at Ratisbon," *Archiv für Reformationsgeschicte* 51 (1960): 36-57.

[47]John Patrick Donnelly, "Johann Gropper," in Hillerbrand, *Oxford Encyclopedia of the Reformation*, 2:197.

hand to a draft regarding justification that, after deliberation by delegates at Regensburg, affirmed,

> It is a reliable and sound doctrine that the sinner is justified by living and efficacious faith, for through it we are pleasing and acceptable to God on account of Christ. And living faith is what we call the movement of the Holy Spirit by which those who truly repent of their old life are lifted up to God and truly appropriate the mercy promised in Christ.[48]

And this assertion regarding the punctiliar nature of justification was then stated in its relation to the need for the demonstration of the advance of charity in the life of the believing one: "Every Christian should learn that this grace and this regeneration have not been given to us so that we might remain idle in that stage of our renewal which we at first obtained, but so that we might grow in everything into him who is the head."[49]

The contested principle had been granted by Catholic and Protestant delegates alike: Christian salvation is by divine mercy; pardon and acceptance are granted to the one who believes in Christ; growth in grace is expected and will be rewarded.

News of this concurrence reached at Regensburg regarding justification did not impress Martin Luther, nor did it please Pope Paul III. Luther felt that the agreed statement was not stringent enough;[50] Pope Paul (knowing that there were other outstanding issues about which no concurrence would be gained at Regensburg) determined to hold out for the prospect of the General Council, which he had been advocating since 1536.[51]

The Roman Catholic "justification by faith alone" party was represented at the Council of Trent. Now as we acknowledged earlier in this chapter, the Council of Trent, which commenced meeting in 1545, dealt with the theme of justification among its most urgent topics. We should not be surprised then to learn that there were present in the council individual theologians, bishops,

---

[48]"The Regensburg Agreement (1541) Article 5," as printed in appendix A in Lane, *Justification by Faith*, 234. This document is reproduced in appendix A of this current work.

[49]"The Regensburg Agreement (1541) Article 5," 236.

[50]By contrast, Lane (56) is able to demonstrate that John Calvin, who attended but did not enter debate at Regensburg, indicated his clear satisfaction with what had been arrived at regarding justification. See his n44. Luther was not present at this colloquy as his safe travel could not be assured. He was represented by Melanchthon, who took a very active part.

[51]Lane, *Justification by Faith*, 52-54.

and cardinals who, because they were in step with the Christian humanist movement and earlier influenced by the overlapping influence of the "Spirituali" and the teachings of Juan de Valdés, would arrive at Trent prepared to contend for a doctrine of justification that would take seriously its forensic or judicial character. Present at Trent were Cardinals Pole (initial session only), Contarini, and Seripando and the German theologian Gropper.[52] At Trent, we find this advocacy carried on quite openly, though not successfully.[53]

Cardinal Pole, present only for the council's opening discussions regarding justification, made a most interesting plea on June 21, 1546, for moderation on the part of the council. The books of those deemed to be "adversaries" must be read; no one should conclude prematurely that because Luther held a certain opinion, it must therefore be wrong. Every alleged "heresy" contained some element of truth.[54] Yet having made such a suggestive speech, Pole left the council within a week and did not return. Another dignitary, Tommaso Sanfelice, the bishop of La Cava, openly advocated "justification by faith alone" on July 8. When he did so a second time on July 17, a bishop of diametrically opposite conviction, Dionisio de Zanettini of Chironissa and Melopotamus, openly disparaged him, and they came to blows. Sanfelice was required to absent himself for a week; he did not return to the sessions of the council.[55]

It fell to one particular cardinal, Girolamo Seripando (1493–1563),[56] to be the unrelenting advocate of a position like the one that was endorsed at Regensburg in 1541. Yet despite Seripando's ongoing work as a major drafter of the final decree on justification, his repeated interjections, both spoken and written, on behalf of the conviction that even the best efforts of the believer must in the end be covered by divine mercy were disregarded. Some,

[52]The presence in Trent of those inclined to a Lutheran-style understanding of justification is acknowledged by Lane (60) and buttressed by Hubert Jedin, *History of the Council of Trent* (St. Louis: Herder, 1957 and 1961), 167-71. O'Malley, *Trent*, mentions particularly Cardinal Seripando (104) and Bishop of La Cava, Tommaso Sanfelice (109). Marvin W. Anderson discusses how this Roman Catholic approximation of the Protestant doctrine of justification was reflected in some commentary writing inside Italy in the 1540s. See "Luther's Sola Fide in Italy," *Church History* 38, no. 1 (1969): 25-42.

[53]McGrath, *Iustitia Dei*, chap. 4.

[54]O'Malley, *Trent,* 107-8.

[55]Ibid., 109.

[56]On whom, see Giuseppe Alberigo, "Girolamo Seripando," in Hillerbrand, *Oxford Encyclopedia of the Reformation*, 4:47-48.

such as the Jesuit theologian Diego Laínez, dismissed Seripando's opinion as a "Lutheran novelty."[57] The Trent decree on justification was therefore published to the world in January 1547 with no concession to the convictions articulated by representatives of this "justification by faith alone" party.

But these voices had been represented within the council, just as they had been articulated at Regensburg and in the Roman Catholic Christian humanist circles known variously as "Spirituali" and "Valdesian." It was this Roman Catholic Christian humanist point of view (rather than the majority at Trent) that was most informed by the renewed study of the Greek New Testament and the church fathers. Two conclusions seem to follow.

First, the council's determination to treat the Latin Vulgate as decisive for its deliberations—whatever benefits this ensured in terms of ready appeal to the Bible best known—effectively ruled out of court any exegetical appeals to the Greek text of the New Testament. Yet, on what other basis might a fresh examination of the doctrine of justification have proceeded? Second, the mere existence, advocacy, and continuance of this "justification by faith alone" party within the Roman Catholic Church and the Council of Trent in the period to 1563 seriously undermined Trent's claim that its decree on justification was nothing other than a restatement of the patristic understanding. On the contrary, the existence of the "justification by faith alone" party argued strongly that prior to Trent there had been *no single* perspective on this question within Roman Catholicism. Trent's hard-line position therefore utilized a strong element of "bluff."[58]

RECKONING WITH OUR NOW CHANGED CIRCUMSTANCES

We have established two things so far in this chapter. First, Protestants have always pointed to at least *some* precedents in Christian antiquity for their

[57]Lane, *Justification*, 62-63. Klaas Runia, "Justification in Roman Catholicism," in *Right with God: Justification in the Bible and the Church*, ed. D. A. Carson (1992; repr., Eugene, OR: Wipf & Stock, 2002), 205, indicates that when the voting delegates were asked to indicate whether they supported the concept of justification by "infusion" or "imputation," the balloting in favor of "infusion" ran 32 to 5.

[58]There is some evidence that though the "party" within Roman Catholicism supportive of forensic justification expired with the generation of those who advocated it up until Trent, the point of view did not entirely disappear. Francis Turretin, writing in the period 1679–1685, found evidence of its continuation in the writings of Robert Bellarmine (1542–1641) and Cornelius á Lapide (1567–1637). See Turretin's *Institutes of Elenctic Theology*, 2:634-35.

understanding of justification by grace through faith alone. The number of known patristic precedents expanded from a few in the sixteenth century to many by the nineteenth century. Second, Roman Catholic theology since the Council of Trent has insisted that it has always maintained (with the unbroken support of the early Christian fathers) that an initial justification received in baptism must be augmented by a final justification granted in light of "faith working through love." Rome utilized this argument from antiquity in spite of having permitted a statement of concurrence with the Protestant view endorsed at Regensburg (1541) and the advocacy of the "by faith alone" position within Trent by cardinals, bishops, and theologians sympathetic with the "Spirituali." It was this loose alliance that, because it was caught up in the Christian humanist movement of the sixteenth century, was most likely of all Roman Catholics to reengage with the church fathers. But though this is where the matter still stood as we entered the twentieth century, it is assuredly not the place where things stand in the opening decades of the twenty-first. We may speak of three main factors contributing to a change of perspective from the Roman Catholic side.

"Nouvelle Theology." First was the emergence from the mid-1930s onward of a different orientation in Catholic theology that has come to be known by the terms "ressourcement" or "nouvelle theology." Associated with such names as Henri de Lubac, Yves Congar, and Jean Daniélou,[59] this movement stood in self-conscious distinction to the Thomist and Aristotelian focus that dominated much of Roman Catholic theology since the late nineteenth century. Advocates of the "nouvelle theologie" (actually a term coined by their detractors, who portrayed them as modernists) believed that the Vatican-led embrace of Thomism in late nineteenth century had been a defensive strategy by Catholic thinkers who were determined to resist unsettling critical trends surfacing at that time.

Advocates of the "nouvelle theology" urged the laying of far greater stress on the fresh exegesis of the Scriptures employing the original languages and new study of the early church fathers with a view to rethinking a range of modern questions. The powerful critique raised against this outlook in the immediate aftermath of World War II led to the temporary silencing of some

[59]David Grummett, "Nouvelle Theology," in *Cambridge Dictionary of Christian Theology*, ed. Ian MacFarland (New York: Cambridge University Press, 2011), 348-49.

of its most identifiable leaders, notably de Lubac. But by the mid-1950s, these individuals began to be rehabilitated under the papacy of Pope John XXIII and had a strong influence through the following decade.[60] The present writer finds it intriguing that it was this movement that promoted a fresh study of the church fathers after an era in which they had been neglected; this movement is chronologically parallel to the resurgence of Protestant interest in the patristic period since WWII.[61]

Catholic reengagement in the wider world of biblical and theological studies. In the same period, a second influence was encouraged within Roman Catholicism: a reengagement with the wider world of biblical and theological studies. Catholic biblical scholar Joseph A. Fitzmyer singled out an action by Catholic cardinal and biblical studies professor Augustin Bea in 1962 as holding special significance. In that year, Bea inserted an endorsement within the German-language edition of the *Theological Dictionary of the New Testament* urging Roman Catholic scholars and pastors to make use of this biblical-theological resource.[62] The work, which is still in print, was very extensively the work of German Lutheran scholars. Fitzmyer noted that this encouragement to engage with non-Roman Catholic scholarship coming in the period of Vatican II (where such encouragements would be augmented) was especially noteworthy, serving as a kind of bellwether of things to come.[63] Taking the long view, one could say that such encouragements, given in the early 1960s, put spurs to Catholic biblical exegesis, using Greek and Hebrew, on a scale not seen since the age of Christian humanism in the sixteenth century.

There was also in these decades increasing evidence of Roman Catholicism's theological investigation of Protestantism and Protestant

---

[60]The influence was certainly felt at the Second Vatican Council.

[61]A theme explored in chapter 5 of this book.

[62]This multivolume work, originally appearing in German as *Theologische Wörterbook zum Neuen Testament*, is known in English as *Theological Dictionary of the New Testament.* Bea's endorsement appeared in the 1964 German edition, volume 7.

[63]Joseph A. Fitzmyer, "Justification by Faith and 'Righteousness' in the New Testament," in *Justification by Faith: Lutherans and Catholics in Dialogue VII*, ed. H. George Anderson and T. Austin Murphy (Minneapolis: Augsburg, 1985), 78. Fitzmyer points, in illustration of the new openness to collaboration in biblical studies, to the production of the ecumenical project *Righteousness in the New Testament*, edited by John Reumann (1982). Fitzmyer's own commentary in the Anchor Bible series, *Romans* (New York: Doubleday, 1992) makes plain that his own understanding of justification as forensic and majoring on acquittal has been influenced through this engagement with wider biblical studies. See, for example, his comment on Romans 3:24 (347).

theology. But more was to come. A fresh assessment of Martin Luther was undertaken, and a growing Roman Catholic impression formed that he had had substantial foundation for his Reformation protest.[64] The Protestant doctrine of justification found a sympathetic Roman Catholic appraisal in Hans Küng's *Justification: The Doctrine of Karl Barth and a Catholic Reflection.*[65]

Vatican II and ensuing ecumenical dialogues. The Second Vatican Council (1962–1965) impacted Roman Catholic thinking in two specific ways bearing on the justification question. First, the council broke with past reluctance to employ anything other than the Latin Vulgate for study and liturgical use: it encouraged the reading of Scripture by the faithful in vernacular translations sanctioned and approved for Catholic use.[66] In short order, two English-language Catholic versions of the Scriptures—the *Jerusalem Bible* (1966) and the *New American Bible* (1970)—were produced for Catholic use. Catholic bishops had at the same time (1966) similarly approved an ecumenical edition of the *Revised Standard Version* (1946) for Catholic use. An understanding of justification more compatible with the understanding of Protestantism was promoted by this initiative.[67]

Second, Vatican II placed a higher premium than ever before on exploring commonalities with non-Roman Catholic churches and believers. Whereas prior to Vatican II, the stated view of Catholicism regarding non-Roman Catholic Christianity was provided in the condemnations of the Council of Trent, Vatican II taught differently. Protestants, with other

---

[64]This reevaluation is described in both James Atkinson, *Martin Luther: Prophet to the Church Catholic* (Grand Rapids: Eerdmans, 1983), chaps. 1 and 2, and Johann Heinz, "Martin Luther and His Theology in German Catholic Interpretation Before and After Vatican II," *Andrews University Seminary Studies* 26, no. 3 (1988): 253-65. See Harry McSorley, *Martin Luther: Right or Wrong?* (Minneapolis: Augsburg, 1969) and Jared Wicks, ed., *Catholic Scholars Dialogue with Luther* (Chicago: Loyola University Press, 1970).

[65]Hans Küng, *Justification: The Doctrine of Karl Barth and a Catholic Reflection* (Toronto: Thomas Nelson, 1969). The place of Küng's contribution in the larger theological reassessment taking place within Roman Catholicism is helpfully discussed by Runia, "Justification and Roman Catholicism," chap. 11.

[66]This priority is set out in the "Dogmatic Constitution on Divine Revelation," chap. 6 in *Documents of Vatican II*, ed. Austin Flannery (New York: Guild, 1996), 125-28. In fact, an earlier pope, Pius XII, had sounded a similar appeal in the encyclical *Divino Afflante Spiritu*, in October 1943.

[67]A comparison of these versions at passages such as Luke 18:14 and Romans 3:26 and 5:1 demonstrates that by 1966, Catholic translators were rendering the passages in a way indistinguishable from the work of Protestant translators.

non-Roman Catholic Christians, were now designated "separated brethren."[68] Consistent with this perspective, Protestant theologians were present as observers in all sessions of the council.

In ensuing decades, there followed a range of doctrinal consultations between theological representatives of the Roman Catholic Church and their counterparts in the Church of England, the Methodist World Council, and the Lutheran World Federation.[69] The cumulative effect of these consultations was encouraging and provided evidence of a growing convergence between the understandings of justification held within Roman Catholic and various Protestant bodies. Roman Catholic theology eventually agreed that its old objection to the Protestant insistence that justification is by faith *alone* needed to be set aside.[70]

These demonstrations of increasing convergence have continued, culminating most fully in the 1999 *Joint Declaration on the Doctrine of Justification* of the Lutheran World Federation and the Roman Catholic Church.[71] That document affirmed,

> Justification is the forgiveness of sins (Rom 3:23-25; Acts 13:39; Luke 18:14), liberation from the dominating power of sin and death (Rom 5:12-21) and from the curse of the law (Gal 3:10-14). It is acceptance into communion with God—already now, but then fully in God's coming kingdom (Rom 5:1ff). It unites with Christ and with his death and resurrection (Rom 6:5).[72]

Yet the question nevertheless arises as to what this encouraging statement of consensus changes. Importantly (for the purposes of this chapter) it contains no acknowledgement (from the Roman Catholic side) that important witnesses to the truth of justification by faith alone preceded Luther. This has, after all, been the bone of contention for centuries.[73] There is an

---

[68]Flannery, *Documents of Vatican II*, para. 20, 362, "Decree on Ecumenism."

[69]A. N. S. Lane in *Justification in Catholic-Protestant Dialogue* has provided in his third chapter, "The Eight Documents," an evaluation of what these ecumenical dialogues have produced.

[70]Lane, *Justification in Catholic-Protestant Dialogue*, 122.

[71]I have consulted the English translation (Grand Rapids: Eerdmans, 2000).

[72]*Joint Declaration on the Doctrine of Justification* (Grand Rapids: Eerdmans, 2000), I.11, 13.

[73]On the contrary, in the important work of 1974, *Justification by Faith: Lutherans and Catholics in Dialogue VII*, Robert Eno summarizes (129) pre-Reformation teaching on the subject as supporting what has long been the Roman Catholic teaching that there is both a *first* justification of the sinner "by faith" (on the Catholic understanding, through the administration of baptism) and a *second* justification required at the day of judgment.

acknowledgement made by Roman Catholic signatories that the "anathemas" (condemnations) pronounced at Trent against the Protestant understanding of justification cannot any longer apply to their conversation partners.[74] But this begs the question of whether the anathemas delivered at Trent *ever* accurately typified the views of *any* actual Protestants of that day or since.

Rome and Protestants did not disagree in the sixteenth century that justification before God, at his *initial* reception of us, was a divine gift of the righteousness of Jesus Christ to be accepted in faith;[75] they do not disagree about this today.[76] Where they disagreed in the sixteenth century and have agreed (by this document) to continue to disagree in the twenty-first century is over whether a *subsequent* second justification of the individual is required in light of the admitted fact that sin recurs inside the life of the Christian. Roman Catholicism still affirms this, and historic Protestantism denies it. The Lutheran endorsers of the "Joint Declaration," with their Roman Catholic counterparts, agreed to emphasize their commonalities, leaving disagreements like this unresolved.[77] One thinks, at this point, of the proverbial water glass, partly full. Is it half full or half empty?

A. N. S. Lane has aptly cautioned that Protestants are prone to suppose that justification plays as large a role in Catholic theology as it does within Protestantism.[78] But in fact, Roman Catholicism insists that Christian salvation is sacramentally received, whereas Protestants stress that it comes "from hearing" (Rom 10:17). This being so, Protestant and Catholic dialogue partners do not attach exactly the same weight to the doctrine of justification about which they claim a growing consensus. The current teaching of the Roman Catholic communion, summarized in its *Catechism of the Catholic Church* (1994), indicates that considerable changes in biblical-theological study and ecumenical dialogue notwithstanding, the outlook of Trent and the Vulgate still rules.

---

[74]*Joint Declaration on the Doctrine of Justification*, V.41, p. 26.

[75]Trent at the same time affirmed that this initial justification was transmitted in the act of baptism.

[76]Having said this, it does not follow that Protestants affirm (as does Rome) that justification is initially given through baptism.

[77]This writer endorses the cautious evaluation provided by Douglas Sweeney in "Taming the Reformation: What the Lutheran-Catholic Justification Declaration Really Accomplished—and What It Did Not," *Christianity Today* 44, no. 1 (January 10, 2000): 63-64.

[78]Lane, *Justification by Faith*, 83-84.

> The first work of the grace of the Holy Spirit is *conversion*, effecting justification in accordance with Jesus' proclamation at the beginning of the Gospel, "Repent for the kingdom of heaven is at hand." Moved by grace, man turns toward God and away from sin, thus accepting forgiveness and righteousness from on high. "Justification is not only the remission of sins but also the sanctification and renewal of the inner man."[79]

The idea of second, subsequent justification is still clearly maintained:

> Since the initiative belongs to God in the order of grace, so no one can merit the initial grace of forgiveness and justification at the beginning of conversion. Moved by the Holy Spirit and by charity, *we can merit* for ourselves and others the graces needed for our sanctification, for the increase of grace and charity and for the attainment of eternal life.[80]

DEVELOPMENTS IN THE EVANGELICAL PROTESTANT WORLD

In the same post–World War II decades as we have just been surveying, there were strikingly parallel developments in the world of evangelical Protestantism. For reasons explored in chapter five of this volume, the first half of the twentieth century was a fairly barren period for study of the early church in almost all expressions of Western Christianity. Evangelical Protestantism began to move beyond this period of neglect of early Christianity with the help of Anglican scholarship, with Anglican evangelicals well represented. Some have consulted with profit the important compact work of H. E. W. Turner, *The Patristic Doctrine of Redemption.*[81] More will recall utilizing the handbook of J. N. D. Kelly, *Early Christian Doctrines,* as a first text introducing them to the teaching of the church fathers.[82] There followed such stimulating works as Maurice Wiles's *The Divine Apostle: The Interpretation of St. Paul's Epistles in the Early Church.* This demonstrated that while the Pauline letters had found very wide acceptance in the Mediterranean churches by the late second century, systematic study of them was only

[79] *Catechism of the Catholic Church* (Rome: Libreria Editrice Vaticana, 1994), section 1989, 482. Words within quotation marks (original) are meant to indicate direct quotation from the decrees of Trent.

[80] *Catechism*, section 2010, 487. Emphasis original.

[81] H. E. W. Turner, *The Patristic Doctrine of Redemption* (1952; repr., Eugene, OR: Wipf & Stock, 2004).

[82] J. N. D. Kelly, *Early Christian Doctrines* (New York: Harper & Row, 1959). A second edition followed in 1960. Kelly became equally influential through subsequent biographies on Jerome (1975) and Chrysostom (1995).

belatedly undertaken.[83] This was also the era when the late Geoffrey Bromiley (d. 2009) pointed to the urgency of evangelicalism's correcting its relative neglect of early Christianity. He did this through a 1971 essay, "The Promise of Patristic Theology," and in his important text *Historical Theology.*[84] Gerald Bray provided a similar stimulus for the study of the early church by English-speaking evangelicals with his study of Tertullian, *Holiness and the Will of God,* and a survey of theological developments in early Christianity, *Creeds, Councils and Christ.* There followed his important history of biblical interpretation across the centuries, *Biblical Interpretation: Past and Present.*[85] But perhaps of greatest significance for our current discussion was the appearance in 1986 of the work of yet another Anglican evangelical, Alister McGrath. His *Iustitia Dei: A History of the Christian Doctrine of Justification* was rapidly recognized at its release as the most ambitious treatment of this theme in the English language in the twentieth century.[86]

With this Anglican stimulus to return to the study of the early church (in general) and the history of the doctrine of justification (in particular), the last quarter century has witnessed both a proliferation of fresh evangelical Protestant scholarly interest in the early church and in the history of justification. It is as if the energetic quest to demonstrate that rootedness of the evangelical understanding of justification in the patristic era demonstrated by such nineteenth-century writers G. S. Faber and James Bannerman has been resumed and surpassed.[87]

[83]Maurice Wiles, *The Divine Apostle: The Interpretation of St. Paul's Epistles in the Early Church* (Cambridge: Cambridge University Press, 1967). The obituary for Wiles (d. 2005) in the *Daily Telegraph* indicates that at the time of writing *The Divine Apostle*, Wiles was still reckoned to be affiliated with the evangelical wing of Anglicanism. In subsequent publications, he distanced himself from this earlier outlook. See his obituary at www.telegraph.co.uk/news/obituaries/1491502/The-Rev-Professor-Maurice-Wiles.html, accessed July 8, 2015.

[84]Bromiley, an Anglican evangelical, left St. Thomas Episcopal Church, Edinburgh, in 1957 to become professor of church history at Fuller Theological Seminary. His essay on patristic theology was published in the 1971 volume edited by David F. Wells and Clark F. Pinnock, *Towards a Theology for the Future* (Carol Stream, IL: Creation House, 1971). *Historical Theology* was released by Eerdmans in 1978.

[85]*Holiness and the Will of God* (Atlanta: John Knox, 1979); *Creeds, Councils and Christ* (Downers Grove, IL: InterVarsity Press, 1984); and *Biblical Interpretation: Past and Present* (Downers Grove, IL: InterVarsity Press, 1996).

[86]Alister McGrath, *Iustitia Dei: A History of the Christian Doctrine of Justification* (Cambridge: Cambridge University Press, 1986). Further editions followed in 1998 and 2005.

[87]Faber, incorporating patristic references employed by James Ussher in a 1617 work of controversy into his own researches, listed twenty-eight church fathers ranging from Clement (ca. 96) to Bernard of Clairvaux (ca. 1130).

In addition to McGrath's thorough treatment, *Iustitia Dei*, we have now seen that the Methodist scholar Thomas F. Oden's *A Justification Reader* has displayed a wide range of pre-Reformation writers who largely anticipated Luther's emphasis.[88] Nick Needham has provided a recent competent chapter-length survey of the early fathers' teaching on justification,[89] and a recent dissertation has found numerous witnesses to justification by faith within a century of the death of the apostle Paul.[90] And we are steadily witnessing a surge of scholarly writing about the elaboration of justification by faith in the writings of individual church fathers: the author of the *Epistle to Diognetus*,[91] Hilary of Poitiers (ca. 315–367),[92] Basil of Caesarea (330–379),[93] Ambrosiaster (ca. 366),[94] Chrysostom (347–407),[95] Augustine (354–430),[96] and most fully Bernard of Clairvaux (1090–1153).[97]

In these same decades, evangelical Protestants have—with others—been drawn into a discussion generated in the field of New Testament studies about the actual place of justification by faith in the overall theology of the apostle Paul. Century-old arguments that Paul's emphasis on justification was merely part of a polemical argument against the Judaizers of the first century (intended to demonstrate that Gentile converts had gained full participation in God's covenant with Israel) have been revived. There has been

[88]Oden in *A Justification Reader* (Grand Rapids: Eerdmans, 2002) claimed wider success than McGrath in finding pre-Reformation antecedents of Luther's teaching.

[89]Nick Needham, "Justification in the Early Fathers," in *Justification in Perspective: Historical Developments and Contemporary Challenges*, ed. Bruce McCormack (Edinburgh: Rutherford House, 2006), chap. 2.

[90]Brian John Arnold, "Justification One Hundred Years After Paul" (PhD dissertation, The Southern Baptist Seminary, Louisville, Kentucky, 2013). In this connection, see also the work of Andrew Daunton-Fear, *Were They Preaching "Another Gospel"? Justification by Faith in the Second Century* (London: Latimer Trust, 2015).

[91]Matthew R. Crawford, "'Oh the Sweet Exchange': Grace and Justification in the Epistle to Diognetus" (unpublished conference paper, 2010).

[92]D. H. Williams, "Justification by Faith: A Patristic Doctrine," *Journal of Ecclesiastical History* 57, no. 4 (2006): 649-67.

[93]Michael A. G. Haykin, *Rediscovering the Church Fathers* (Wheaton, IL: Crossway, 2011), chap. 6.

[94]Dongsun Cho, "Ambrosiaster on Justification by Faith Alone in His Commentaries on the Pauline Epistles," *Westminster Theological Journal* 74 (2012): 277-90. See also Gerald Bray, "Ambrosiaster," in *Reading Romans Through the Centuries*, ed. Jeffrey P. Greenman and Timothy Larsen (Grand Rapids: Baker, 2005), chap. 2, esp. 25-29.

[95]Douglas Hall, "Chrysostom," chap. 3 in Greenman and Larsen, *Reading Romans*, esp. 45-47.

[96]D. F. Wright, "Justification in Augustine," chap. 3 in McCormack, *Justification in Perspective*.

[97]A. N. S. Lane, *Bernard of Clairvaux: Theologian of the Cross* (Collegeville, MN: Liturgical Press, 2013), esp. chap. 12.

a similar reconsideration of the century-old notion that justification by faith is a relatively minor theme, among others, used by Paul to elucidate the doctrine of Christian salvation. Such germinal ideas, once associated with scholars Wilhelm Wrede (1859–1906) and Albert Schweitzer (1875–1965), have gained new circulation in recent times.[98]

This movement, particularly as represented by its broadly evangelical interpreters, J. D. G. Dunn and N. T. Wright, has served to stimulate fresh consideration of such questions as what were the "works of the law" (Rom 3:20) Paul dismissed as being incapable of securing salvation. There has also been fresh reflection given over to the question of whether justification by faith, as traditionally conceived by Protestants, has given sufficient recognition to the fact that the one who is justified before God through faith in Christ is justified in company with all other believers. But strong reservations remain about this approach to justification by faith, and it does not yet appear that the doctrine of justification by faith as traditionally conceived by Protestants will give way to what has been proposed.[99]

COMING FULL CIRCLE

The Reformation-era controversy regarding justification revolved extensively around how various Scriptures bearing on justification had been understood in Christian antiquity. It was not early Protestantism but Roman Catholicism that insisted that Christian antiquity spoke with only one voice on this subject and in such a way that rendered the early Protestant position

---

[98]The discussion referred to here was engendered by the publication in 1963 of an essay by then Harvard professor Krister Stendahl, "The Apostle Paul and the Introspective Conscience of the West," *Harvard Theological Review* 56 (1963): 199-213, and in E. P. Sanders's *Paul and Palestinian Judaism* (Philadelphia: Fortress, 1977). This and Sanders's subsequent publications gave impetus to what came to be called the "new perspective on Paul." That designation came into wide use after an important published lecture of J. D. G. Dunn, "The New Perspective on Paul," *Bulletin of the John Rylands Library* 65 (1983): 95-122. N. T. Wright's approach to these questions is set out in his *Justification: God's Plan and Paul's Vision* (Downers Grove, IL: InterVarsity Press, 2009).

[99]Note especially the cautionary overviews of the "new perspective" view provided at the space of a decade by Peter T. O'Brien, "Justification in Paul and Some Crucial Issues of the Last Two Decades," in *Right with God: Justification in Bible and Church*, ed. D. A. Carson (Eugene, OR: Wipf and Stock, 2002), 51-68, and Peter Stuhlmacher, *Revisiting Paul's Doctrine of Justification: A Challenge to the New Perspective*, with an essay by Donald A. Hagner (Downers Grove, IL: InterVarsity Press, 2001). The appended Hagner essay deserves as close a reading as the Stuhlmacher lectures, which constitute the main body of the work.

a novelty. The early Protestant position that there were at least *some* clear witnesses in antiquity supporting the "faith alone" view was clearly the more modest. Over time, the Protestant argument from antiquity has only been strengthened by the discovery of numerous additional witnesses—among them important Catholic voices from the early sixteenth century. There is therefore no reason for evangelical Protestants to fly the white flag of surrender over justification by faith alone.

QUESTIONS FOR DISCUSSION

1. In your mind, what is the single largest difference between the Roman Catholic and Protestant understanding of justification?
2. The fault lines between the mainstream Roman Catholic understanding of justification and other understandings opened not because of the Reformation but because of the earlier Christian Renaissance. Discuss.
3. Since Roman Catholic biblical scholars and Bible translators no longer object to explaining justification to mean a court-like remission of sin in this life, what hinders the Roman Catholic Church from not just tolerating but teaching this understanding of the gospel?
4. What has the Roman Catholic Church meant by the phrase "a second justification"?

15

Why Are Younger Evangelicals Turning to Catholicism and Orthodoxy?

SINCE THE MID-1980S, the North American evangelical movement has regularly observed a striking phenomenon: departures for Roman Catholicism and expressions of Eastern Orthodoxy by individuals considered to have possessed stature within evangelicalism. In 1985, the headlines belonged to Thomas Howard, a professor of English literature who, in being received into the Roman Catholic Church, also came to a parting of the ways with his evangelical Protestant employer, Gordon College.[1]

Many North American observers might suppose that the reaffiliation of Howard—who had been raised by evangelical parents who were missionaries to Belgium and who had first migrated to the Episcopal Church USA in his twenties (before his reception to Roman Catholicism in 1985)—marked the turning of a kind of tide in the direction of such reaffiliations. In fact, Howard's reaffiliation to Roman Catholicism had been anticipated by another significant development, six years previous. This—though not so widely reported at the time—proved to be a bellwether of the same trend.

[1]Howard's reaffiliation warranted extensive coverage in the May 1985 issue of *Christianity Today* magazine.

This was the 1979 recasting of the nascent "New Covenant Apostolic Order" (earlier known as the "Christian World Liberation Front"—a movement that had emerged from Campus Crusade in 1973) as the "Evangelical Orthodox Church."[2] By 1987, seventeen congregations and two thousand adherents of what they still understood to be an evangelical Protestant movement were received into the Antiochian Orthodox Church of North America.[3] Thus, by the late 1980s, North American evangelical Christians were starting to become accustomed to news reports of defections of prominent individuals to *both* Roman Catholicism and Orthodoxy.[4]

PRIMARILY A NORTH AMERICAN PHENOMENON

It is clearer today than it was then that this trend is observable *primarily* among North Americans. One can learn that there were some reaffiliations from the Church of England to Antiochian Orthodoxy in the 1990s, spurred by a worrisome relaxing of the theological boundaries in the English national church.[5] Recently, we have read of a prominent Swedish Pentecostal leader who caught his congregation and wider movement off guard by his reaffiliation to Rome in March 2014.[6] Some reports indicate that a similar trend can be observed in South Korea.[7] But such stories, from outside

---

[2]The best account available of this chain of developments, led by ex-staffers of Campus Crusade such as Jack Sparks (d. 2010) and Peter Gillquist (d. 2012), is provided in D. Oliver Herbel, *Turning to Tradition: Converts and the Making of an American Orthodox Church* (New York: Oxford University Press, 2014), chaps. 4 and 5.

[3]A special report in *Christianity Today* 29, no. 8 (1985): 45 reported on early attempts by the Evangelical Orthodox Church to explore affiliation with forms of Eastern Orthodoxy. Herbel, *Turning to Tradition*, 120-23, reports that in the 1984–1986 period, the EOC had applied (unsuccessfully) for membership in the National Association of Evangelicals. That its application was rejected propelled it further in the direction of actual linkage with one of the forms of Orthodoxy.

[4]It needs to be noted that Howard, up to the time of his 1985 reception by the Roman Catholic Church, had been a participant with Robert E. Webber (1933–2007) in drawing attention to the attractions of the Anglican tradition, represented by the Episcopal Church USA. Webber's book, *Evangelicals on the Canterbury Trail* (Nashville: Word, 1985), did not include Howard among the six contributing "pilgrims."

[5]This at least is the account of one UK Anglican evangelical who, with others, was received into Antiochian Orthodoxy in the early 1990s. See Michael Harper, *The True Light: An Evangelical's Journey to Orthodoxy* (London: Hodder & Stoughton, 1997).

[6]See the accounts in Ruth Moon, "Conversion of Sweden's Most Influential Pastor Causes Pain and Disillusion," *Christianity Today*, March 14, 2014, www.christianitytoday.com/gleanings/2014/march/sweden-pentecostal-converts-catholicism-ulf-ekman-word-life.html.

[7]There are reports of a movement of some South Korean evangelicals in the direction of Roman Catholicism. I am grateful to Dr. Chung Won Shu of Chongshin Theological Seminary, Seoul, for alerting me to this trend. See "Catholicism, Not Protestantism, Captures Minds of Koreans," *The*

North America, are unusual and rare. Inquiries I have made of contacts in Europe, West Africa, and Southeast Asia confirm my opinion that this is extensively a "made in North America" development. That is to say that it tells us something about questions asked and uncertainties experienced *inside* North American Christian culture.

It is important to acknowledge, at the same time, that this chapter will explore only *one* of two expressions of the "drift" to Roman Catholicism and Orthodoxy: that pursued by evangelical Protestants. The last quarter century has witnessed a parallel and distinct "turn" to Rome and Orthodoxy by disheartened mainline Protestants. Troubled at the steady slide away from an authoritative Scripture and the ecumenical creeds, a succession of mainline Lutherans, Methodists, and Episcopalians have sought "refuge" in Roman Catholicism and Orthodoxy.[8] In a word, they have been motivated by the theological disarray they have encountered.[9] In passing, it can be said that while motivated by quite different concerns emerging from their own denominational contexts, the power of the example of these individuals has been duly noted by evangelical Protestants whose own restlessness has distinct motivations.

Now, as to self-consciously evangelical Protestants' reaffiliations to Rome and Orthodoxy, we are confronted by the fact that the scene is much more complicated than the vast range of testimonial literature would suggest. This literature has been produced in vast quantity by those who have traveled on the road marked out by Howard and Gillquist. Taken collectively, it would lead us to believe that evangelical Protestantism is tottering "on the brink," that it is inherently unstable, incurably prone to division, that its theology

---

Hankyoreh, December 1, 2006, english.hani.co.kr/arti/english_edition/e_national/175532.html; and Jonathan Cheng, "South Korea's Protestants Struggle as Catholics Grab Spotlight," *Wall Street Journal*, August 16, 2014, blogs.wsj.com/korearealtime/2014/08/16/south-koreas-protestants-struggle-as-catholics-grab-spotlight/.

[8]It needs to be noted that not all such concerned Episcopalians have done so. The existence of the growing Anglican Church in North America bears witness to the approach of those who have sought a still-Protestant remedy to this malaise.

[9]This move of mainline Protestants is described by Jason Byasee, "Going Catholic: Six Journeys to Rome," *Christian Century*, August 22, 2006, www.christiancentury.org/article/2006-08/going-catholic. See also the June 2014 article by R. R. Reno (himself a convert) in *First Things*, "Why Do People Become Catholic? Eight Reasons," www.firstthings.com/web-exclusives/2014/06/why-do-people-become-catholic. An interesting example of testimonial literature from within this movement is Frederica Matthewes-Green, *Facing East: A Pilgrim's Journey into the Mysteries of Orthodoxy* (New York: HarperOne, 1997).

is mongrelized, and its worship threadbare. Most of all, it is also said to be substantially out of step with Christian antiquity. And so, various Christian publishing houses in North America continue to churn out volumes reflecting as much.[10] Yet this literature, produced by disaffected evangelicals, is not entirely aboveboard.

CLAIMS ABOUT THE ATTRACTIONS OF ROME AND ANTIOCH ADMIT NO CONTRARY TRENDS

Trends within American Catholicism and Orthodoxy. The information we have indicates that since at least 1950, the "traffic" of those leaving Roman Catholicism for forms of Protestantism *far* exceeds the traffic of those moving in the opposite direction. *Time* magazine reported research in 1954 indicating that over the preceding decade, four million Roman Catholics had left to join Protestant churches, while only about one million Protestants had journeyed in the opposite direction to Roman Catholicism.[11]

What *Time* magazine reported as true in 1954 is still prevalent across North America if we take seriously contemporary reports furnished by journalists, commentators, and polling organizations. While so many individual and group testimonials are published extolling Protestant reaffiliations to Catholicism and Orthodoxy, all the while, Roman Catholic as well as trade journalists continue to draw attention to the fact that the flow of traffic is

---

[10]Thomas Howard, *Evangelical Is Not Enough* (San Francisco: Ignatius, 1984); Peter Gillquist, *Becoming Orthodox* (Ben Lomond, CA: Conciliar, 1989) and *Coming Home: Why Protestant Clergy Are Becoming Orthodox* (Ben Lomond, CA: Conciliar; 1995); Scott and Kimberly Hahn, *Rome Sweet Home: Our Journey to Catholicism* (San Francisco: Ignatius, 1993); Charles Bell, *Discovering the Rich Heritage of Orthodoxy* (Minneapolis: Light and Life, 1994); Frank Schaeffer, *Dancing Alone: The Quest for Orthodox Faith in an Age of False Religion* (Brookline, MA: Holy Cross, 1994); David Currie, *Born Fundamentalist, Born-Again Catholic* (San Francisco: Ignatius, 1996); Steve Ray, *Crossing the Tiber: Evangelical Protestants Discover the Historic Church* (San Francisco: Ignatius, 1997); Thomas Howard, *Lead Kindly Light: My Journey to Rome* (Steubenville, OH: Franciscan University Press, 1994; repr., San Francisco: Ignatius, 2004); Francis Beckwith, *Return to Rome: Confessions of an Evangelical Catholic* (Grand Rapids: Baker, 2009); Christian Smith, *How to Go from Being a Good Evangelical to a Committed Catholic in Ninety-Five Difficult Steps* (Eugene, OR: Cascade, 2011); Devin Rose, *The Protestant's Dilemma* (n.p.: Catholic Answers, 2014); John Beaumont, *The Mississippi Flows into the Tiber: A Guide to Notable American Converts to the Catholic Church* (South Bend, IN: Fidelity, 2014); and Douglas M. Beaumont, *Evangelical Exodus: Evangelical Seminarians and Their Paths to Rome* (San Francisco: Ignatius, 2016).

[11]"Religion: Catholics into Protestants," *Time*, April 5, 1954, content.time.com/time/magazine/article/0,9171,819765,00.html, accessed October 29, 2015.

massively in the opposite direction. In a much-quoted essay of 2006, Father Gerald Mendoza, writing in the *Homiletics and Pastoral Review,* indicated that 100,000 American Catholics reaffiliate to forms of evangelical Protestantism every year. He ventured the estimate that "up to 30% of American evangelical or Pentecostal Christians are first or second-generation former Catholics."[12] Such information as we have regarding trends in Orthodox Christianity in the United States indicates a definite though not so spectacular decline. Over a decade, Orthodoxy has declined from 0.6 percent to 0.5 percent of the American population.[13]

As regards the Roman Catholic decline, Thomas J. Reese, writing in the *National Catholic Reporter* in 2011, described the American Roman Catholic church as "hemorrhaging members." Reese acknowledged that while a good number leave Catholicism to become persons of no religious profession, and others leave because of Catholicism's conservative stance on moral and ethical questions (these tend to reaffiliate with mainline Protestant denominations), a far larger number—usually those under age twenty-four—are turning evangelical or Pentecostal because they did not find their "spiritual needs being met within Catholicism."[14] In light of these daunting trends (with one-third of those raised Catholic in the United States no longer identifying as Catholic), Reese called for drastic changes: more flexible liturgies (with less deference to "rubrical purists"), more exposition of Scripture from Catholic pulpits, and more "Bible education."[15]

The shortcomings within American Catholicism highlighted by Reese that incline Roman Catholics to consider evangelical Protestantism have also been observed by the Protestant writers Scot McKnight and Hauna

---

[12]Gerald Mendoza, OP, "Why Do Catholics Become Evangelicals?," *Homiletics and Pastoral Review*, December 2006, 8-17.

[13]Information about Orthodox Christian trends are harder to come by as Orthodox Christianity, aggregately, constitutes a much smaller segment of the American religious public than does Roman Catholicism. To put the decline of Orthodoxy in perspective, one might consider that the cultic Jehovah's Witnesses represent a larger portion of the American population than all forms of Orthodoxy combined. See "Brazil's Changing Religious Landscape," Pew Research Center, July 18, 2013, www.pewforum.org/2015/05/12/americas-changing-religious-landscape/.

[14]Thomas J. Reese, "The Hidden Exodus: Catholics Becoming Protestants," *National Catholic Reporter*, accessed October 31, 2015, at ncronline.org/print/news/faith-parish/hidden-exodus-catholics-becoming-protestants.

[15]Ibid.

Ondrey. They enumerate three main issues commonly cited by Roman Catholic converts to evangelical Protestantism: (1) a yearning for assurance of salvation, (2) a settling on the primacy of biblical authority, and (3) a flight from an "anemic parish life."[16] Their research also highlighted the role played by such megachurches as greater Chicago's Willow Creek Church in facilitating the evangelical conversion of myriads of American Roman Catholics.

This large-scale "hemorrhaging" of Roman Catholic adherents is also detected by analysts *outside* the churches. The *Pew Religious Census* of 2015 notes that this communion in the United States is currently losing six persons who were raised in Catholicism for every convert that it gains.[17] The *National Review* reported in 2015 that the diocese of New York, which in 1970 would have counted 903,000 Catholics attending weekly mass, today counts only 336,000. The explanation lies not in any simple reduction of those self-identifying as Roman Catholic, for in the same period the nominally Catholic population of greater New York has risen from 1.85 million to 2.8 million.[18]

Trends within Hispanic American Catholicism. At the same time, American Catholic journalists are acknowledging that Hispanic immigrants to the United States (on whom the Roman Catholic Church in America is increasingly dependent to fill the pews being vacated by nonobservant American Catholics) are *themselves* reaffiliating to evangelical and Pentecostal Protestantism in a similar massive shift. Mendoza, writing in 2006, described a realignment of five million Hispanic Americans to forms of evangelicalism within the United States in the preceding decade.[19]

While loyalty to the Roman Catholic tradition continues to characterize 55 percent of Hispanic Americans, this proportion is declining steadily. The proportion of the Hispanic American population now identifying with

[16]The third chapter of McKnight and Ondrey's *Finding Faith, Losing Faith* (Waco, TX: Baylor University Press, 2008) is titled "Leaving Rome: Finding Wheaton." Ondrey is the primary researcher of this material.

[17]"Chapter 2: Religious Switching and Intermarriage," Pew Research Center, May 12, 2015, www.pewforum.org/2015/05/12/chapter-2-religious-switching-and-intermarriage/.

[18]Nicholas Frankovich, "In New York, a Smaller, Shrinking Catholic Church Greets Pope Francis," September 24, 2015, www.nationalreview.com/article/424552/new-york-smaller-shrinking-catholic-church-greets-pope-francis-nicholas-frankovich.

[19]Mendoza, "Why Do Catholics Become Evangelicals?"

evangelical or Pentecostal Protestantism has risen to 16 percent.[20] And with such statistical evidence readily available, comment and interpretation has been rapidly forthcoming in the public press. *Time* magazine, abreast of the ongoing findings of the Pew Religious Census, devoted a major cover story in 2013, "Evangelicos! The New Latin Reformation," in which attention was paid to the breadth and diversity of what is now a major trend. In fact, this trend had been under observation for more than two decades. *Christianity Today* had already given extensive coverage to the trend in a 1991 article, "Viva Los Evangelicos!"[21]

Trends within Latin American Catholicism. What is more, the departure of Hispanic Roman Catholics for expressions of evangelical Protestantism *inside* the United States strongly mirrors trends long under way in the Central and South American homelands from which they have transitioned to the United States. In the countries constituting Central and South America (with Puerto Rico added), adherence to Roman Catholicism has declined markedly. While 84 percent of Latin Americans acknowledge being raised as Roman Catholics, only 69 percent reckon themselves as Roman Catholic now. Conversely, while a mere 9 percent acknowledge being raised as Protestant, 19 percent reckon themselves Protestant today.[22] Since 1970, the percentage of Latin Americans self-identifying as Roman Catholic has declined from 92 percent to the current 69 percent, whereas the percentage self-identifying as Protestant has risen from 4 percent to the current 19 percent. These trends are most pronounced in Colombia, Paraguay, Peru, Ecuador, Bolivia, and Venezuela. The single most frequently cited reason for the reaffiliation of Latin American Roman Catholics is that they were "seeking a personal connection with God."[23] Authors of a recent history of global evangelicalism concur: up to ten thousand

[20]"The Shifting Religious Identity of Latinos in the United States," Pew Research Center, May 7, 2014, www.pewforum.org/2014/05/07/the-shifting-religious-identity-of-latinos-in-the-united-states/. An additional 5 percent of the Hispanic American population now identifies with mainline Protestantism.

[21]"Viva Los Evangelicos!," *Christianity Today* 35, no. 12 (October 28, 1991): 16-22.

[22]"Religion in Latin America: Widespread Change in a Historically Catholic Region," Pew Research Center, November 13, 2014, www.pewforum.org/2014/11/13/religion-in-latin-america/.

[23]*Christianity Today* magazine "mined" the Pew survey and characterized its findings in an article in November 2014: Morgan Lee, "Sorry Pope Francis: Protestants Are Converting Catholics Across Latin America," November 13, 2014, www.christianitytoday.com/gleanings/2014/november/sorry-pope-francis-protestants-catholics-latin-america-pew.html.

Latin Americans are turning Protestant each day.[24] In Brazil, the proportion of citizens adhering to Roman Catholicism has declined since 1970 from 92 percent to 65 percent today.[25]

In sum, North Americans who turn *from* evangelical Protestantism to embrace Roman Catholicism or Eastern Orthodoxy are leaving a movement that is at least stable as to its size and is growing observably by the enfolding of Hispanic Americans of Roman Catholic heritage. They are turning *to* churches that are in observable numerical decline and (in the case of Roman Catholicism) experiencing definite "angst" over steady losses among both the native-born and the immigrant population. Meanwhile, Roman Catholic leaders are taking steps toward the incorporation of evangelical Protestant worship styles and spiritual emphases into their church services as a means of stanching their losses.

We must assume that evangelical Protestant recruits to Roman Catholicism and Eastern Orthodoxy have noted these trends and have pondered what they portend as to the future.[26] Yet only a fraction of the converts to Catholicism and Orthodoxy who write testimonial literature are willing to share any "angst" at the unsettling trends encountered in their new ecclesiastical settings.[27] Alongside these factors, or perhaps even in spite of them, they have found a home in their new communions. What has propelled them?

REASONS BEHIND THE DRIFT

Statistical trends for North American Roman Catholicism and the branches of Eastern Orthodoxy may well be unsettling, but they provide no basis for

---

[24]Mark Hutchinson and John Wolffe, *A Short History of Global Evangelicalism* (Cambridge: Cambridge University Press, 2012), 233.

[25]"Brazil's Changing Religious Landscape."

[26]No evangelical convert to Roman Catholicism has acknowledged these issues so fully as has Thomas Howard. Imperturbably, he has dismissed these trends as of little significance. See his *Lead Kindly Light* (1994; repr., San Francisco: Ignatius, 2004), 61. Note also his candor in the afterword, 97-105. More candid is Bradley Nassif, "Will the 21st Be the Orthodox Century?," *Christianity Today*, December 2006, 40-43.

[27]The recent public chastisement of the progressive theologians within Catholicism by *New York Times* columnist and Pentecostal convert to Catholicism Ross Douthat creates the impression that Douthat did not properly estimate the range of Catholic theological and ethical opinion at the time of his reaffiliation. See Douthat, "The Plot to Change Catholicism," October 17, 2015, www.nytimes.com/2015/10/18/opinion/sunday/the-plot-to-change-catholicism.html.

complacency on the part of evangelical Protestantism. The paradoxical fact remains: many hundreds of intelligent younger adult believers are voting with their feet and reaffiliating to these churches. The reasons for their doing so are many and varied, but they group themselves into six broad major categories.[28] On close inspection, we will find that no individual has been motivated by any single reason; the motivations seem to function in clusters.

For some, a return to the church of one's upbringing. In some cases, individuals have made an actual *return* to the Roman Catholicism or Orthodoxy of their upbringing. Over time, individuals such as Francis Beckwith (of Baylor University) and Bradley Nassif (of North Park University) found that their genuine and continuing loyalty to evangelical Protestantism came to be overshadowed by the heritage and gravitational "pull" of the church of their upbringing. Beckwith had been converted to Christ and nurtured within charismatic evangelicalism; he returned to the Catholicism of his upbringing only once he was well established in his academic career.[29] Bradley Nassif, though raised in the Antiochian Orthodox tradition, traced his conversion to an evangelical outreach ministry in his high school years.[30] It is noteworthy that each has tried to function astride the two ecclesiastical worlds they have experienced, disparaging neither and conscious of the strengths and weaknesses of each.[31]

The search for the "historic church" as a haven from sectarianism. The statement is sometimes made that evangelicalism lacks an ecclesiology, or a thorough doctrine of the church.[32] The idea is too broad-brush to be genuinely helpful, but it does highlight an ongoing deficiency in certain strands of evangelicalism that have tended to glory in their separation and

[28]See Ed Stetzer's reflections on the reasons contributing to the withdrawal of Hank Hanegraaff and others to Eastern Orthodoxy: "Hank Hanegraaff's Switch to Eastern Orthodoxy, Why People Make Such Changes, and Four Ways Evangelicals Might Respond," *Exchange* (blog), *Christianity Today*, April 13, 2017, www.christianitytoday.com/edstetzer/2017/april/how-should-we-respond-to-hank-hanegraaffs-switch-to-orthodo.html. Stetzer pinpoints four contributing factors.

[29]Beckwith, *Return to Rome*.

[30]Nassif, "Will the 21st Be the Orthodox Century?," 40-43.

[31]Note this especially in ibid., 43. See also Nassif's contribution to the anthology volume *Three Views on Eastern Orthodoxy and Evangelicalism*, ed. James Stamoolis (Grand Rapids: Zondervan, 2004).

[32]See this argument pressed in the essay of Bruce Hindmarsh, "Is Evangelical Ecclesiology an Oxymoron? A Historical Perspective," in *Evangelical Ecclesiology: Reality or Illusion?*, ed. John G. Stackhouse Jr. (Grand Rapids: Baker Academic, 2003).

"other-ness" relative to the rest of the Christian movement. Particularly, thoughtful believers from independent, Bible church, and Pentecostal backgrounds can initially be thrown into confusion when asked to join in affirming the existence of "one holy catholic" church (in the words of the Nicene Creed). Such an affirmation can provoke the question of where this global, visible, and continuous church can be located across the centuries leading up to our own.[33] Even less-sectarian evangelical Christians have a "default" inclination to prize the experience and the position of the individual believer above the corporate and collective life of believers, past and present, in visible expressions of the church. This is at the very least odd, inasmuch as for every generation of Christians—other than the first—the church's existence preceded their own.

The more isolationist, independent, and separatist the stream of evangelicalism one has stood in, the greater the attraction of the idea of an unbroken, historic, visible church.[34] Charles Bell sensed this while still a pastor of a California congregation in the Vineyard Fellowship and wishing, with his people, to be fully conformed to the pattern of a "New Testament Church" (that is, *beyond* the Vineyard). He gradually came to realize that there were "1500 years that were unaccounted for."[35] He claimed to find them accounted for in Antiochian Orthodoxy.

The desire for liturgical and doctrinal stability. Vast swathes of evangelical Christianity have functioned with a very slender theological or creedal foundation. This is partly due to evangelicalism's strong tendency to activism—the valuing of action above reflection. Evangelicalism is also wedded to pragmatism—the appraising of methods or strategies based, above all, on their ability to deliver desired results. It is due as well to evangelicalism's

---

[33]Robert L. Plummer, ed., *Journeys of Faith: Evangelicalism, Eastern Orthodoxy, Catholicism and Anglicanism* (Grand Rapids: Zondervan, 2012), 225n3 reports "The Pew Foundation Religious Landscape Survey of 2008 found that 10% of persons raised as non-denominational evangelicals eventually adhere to a non-Protestant religious tradition." This report is accessible at www.pewforum.org/files/2013/05/report-religious-landscape-study-full.pdf (chap. 2).

[34]This is, in effect, the "lateral factor" highlighted in this book's preface.

[35]M. Charles Bell, *Discovering the Rich Heritage of Orthodoxy* (Minneapolis: Light and Life, 1994), 10. It seems clear that the claim of Roman Catholicism and Orthodoxy to represent this kind of unbroken continuity is also highly attractive to mainline Protestants who have reluctantly come to the conclusion that the Reformation—for whatever its genuine merits—has finally collapsed in a concessive liberal Protestantism. For such sentiments, see R. R. Reno, "Why Do People Become Catholic?"

laudable tendency to achieve cooperation by emphasizing select key biblical teachings (for example, the bodily resurrection of Jesus or biblical inspiration) and leaving secondary doctrinal matters unaddressed. The unintended consequence of this activism, pragmatism, and doctrinal minimalism, however, is that large portions of the evangelical movement are left especially vulnerable to what can only be called "faddishness."

In the 1980s, there was too great a fascination with the programs of the Institute for Basic Youth Conflicts. Promise Keepers stadium rallies and accountability groups followed in the next decade, along with the WWJD? craze; since then we have observed the debacle stirred up by Harold Camping (1921–2013), founder of the Family Christian Radio network, who caught the attention of mainstream media with his erroneous predictions that the second advent would occur in May 2011.[36] Now it has struck some observers that evangelicalism is vulnerable to these "pendulum swings" in direct proportion to its disinterest in the great statements of Christian doctrine found in the ecumenical creeds of the early church. Wilbur Ellsworth, former pastor of Wheaton's First Baptist Church, began a quest that led him eventually to Antiochian Orthodoxy when the worship life of his congregation was upended by the introduction of an aggressive youth ministry program. Reverence went out the window.[37]

Attraction to a style of worship that is "objective." In a strong reaction to the tendency of some evangelical Protestant worship services to emphasize the maudlin and the creation of a suitable "mood," a proportion of those raised within the evangelical tradition have learned both to question it and to seek out forms of worship that neither assume the emotional engagement of the worshiper nor seek to cultivate it. It is not that they wish for emotional austerity as such; they in fact admire liturgical beauty and take pleasure in what can be called the "aesthetic" aspect of divine worship. But they wish to be neither besieged nor plied while

---

[36]Robert McFadden, "Harold Camping, Dogged Forecaster of the End of the World, Dies at 92," *New York Times*, December 17, 2013, www.nytimes.com/2013/12/18/us/harold-camping-radio-entrepreneur-who-predicted-worlds-end-dies-at-92.html. Though on a trajectory leading from the Episcopal Church USA into Orthodoxy, Frederica Matthewes-Green (with her husband) struck out on a journey seeking a church that "had never, could never, apostatize." *Facing East*, xi.

[37]Wilbur Ellsworth, "A Journey to Eastern Orthodoxy," in Plummer, *Journeys of Faith*, 23-53.

gathered for worship. Christian Smith, the former evangelical Protestant and now Roman Catholic sociologist, writes, "Church is about a shared identity in Christ, sacramental life, and formation in right Christian living. It does not require that everyone know each other well, much less experience 'intimacy' together. It does require that people participate in the liturgy, worship God, celebrate the sacraments, and do good in Christ's name."[38]

An admiration for the Catholic intellectual and theological tradition. Thirty years ago, Mark Noll gently chided North American evangelicalism for the cumulative neglect of the intellectual life over the twentieth century that led to what he described as "the scandal of the evangelical mind."[39] In contrast to the nineteenth century, when evangelical Protestants were prominent in academia, public service, and intellectual life, the century that followed showed too many signs of retreat from these spheres. Thanks in part to the stimulus Noll provided in his 1994 book, a generation of younger evangelicals have gained academic doctorates, entered academia and public office, and a range of professions in which they were earlier under-represented. And yet, in literature, philosophy, law, and theology it remains true that so many of the "greats" were representatives of the "great tradition" most closely associated with Roman Catholicism.

One finds, on inspection, that evangelical Protestants who turn to Catholicism and Orthodoxy have had this issue very much on their minds. Where are the evangelical Protestant equals of J. R. R. Tolkien, Dorothy Sayers, and Flannery O'Connor? Christian Smith drew attention to the "fact that six of the current nine Supreme Court judges are Roman Catholic while there has never been a modern evangelical on the court."[40]

A strong tendency, long present in American evangelicalism, to aim at recovering the "primitive," yet in eclectic fashion. The early nineteenth century spawned a number of "Restorationist" movements, some of which are still with us. The Plymouth Brethren and the Churches of Christ are

---

[38]Smith, *How to Go from Being*, 155-56.

[39]Mark Noll, *The Scandal of the Evangelical Mind* (Grand Rapids: Eerdmans, 1994).

[40]Smith, *How to Go from Being*, 78-79. One also finds strong reference to the attraction of the Roman Catholic intellectual tradition in R. R. Reno, "Why Do People Become Catholic?," though he is in fact describing the reaffiliation of mainline Protestants. Since that time, one such admired Supreme Court Justice, Antonin Scalia, passed away in February 2016.

simply the two best-known examples of a determination to recover the simplicity of Christian faith and life thought to be reflected in the Acts of the Apostles. Those ex–Campus Crusade leaders who founded what would become the Evangelical Orthodox Church in 1979 were, by their own admission, hunting for "the New Testament Church."[41] Yet according to the thoughtful analyst D. Oliver Herbel, the dynamic being pursued by modern American Restorationists (who convert to both Roman Catholicism and Orthodoxy) is that they are in fact "anti-tradition traditionalists." They wish to embrace what *they* deem to be elements of the Christian past on their *own* terms.[42] Significantly, in recent times both Roman Catholicism and Antiochian Orthodoxy have become aware of the need for the "de-conversion" of evangelical Protestant converts who have assumed that, upon entering their new ecclesiastical settings, they can continue in eclectic "pick and mix" fashion to assimilate old with new.[43]

The North American context, in which every family's roots contain an immigration story from some past era, is one in which many people (and by extension, Christian congregations) have been shorn of important elements of the Christian tradition as part and parcel of the immigrant experience. Many forms of American Christianity—especially those that are self-consciously independent, nonaligned, or nondenominational—have had it gradually dawn on them that they need to reassemble things lost.

We must acknowledge that hunger for recovering a past that has been lost is affecting not only those who depart from evangelical Christianity for Roman Catholicism and Orthodoxy but also a far-larger number of evangelical Christians who remain in their existing settings. We see a wide range of evidence of this desire. The late Robert Webber (1933–2007) addressed this sense of restlessness with a whole series of books, beginning with *Common Roots: A Call to Evangelical Maturity* and extending to *Ancient-Future Worship.*[44] *Christianity Today* magazine in February 2008 featured a cover story,

---

[41]Gillquist, *Becoming Orthodox*, 28.

[42]Herbel, *Turning to Tradition*, 146-57.

[43]Ibid., 150-51 uses the term "de-conversion" to describe Orthodoxy's "reining in" of the Restorationist streak in converts of this type.

[44]Robert E. Webber, *Common Roots: A Call to Evangelical Maturity* (Grand Rapids: Zondervan, 1978) and *Ancient-Future Worship* (Grand Rapids: Baker, 2008). Note, however, the insight of

"Lost Secrets of the Ancient Church: How Evangelicals Started Looking Back to Move Forward."[45] So many more evangelical individuals and congregations now observe the season of Lent, when only a generation ago doing so marked one out as leaning to high church ways.[46] A congregation at Rock Harbor, Cape Cod, Massachusetts, has intentionally incorporated fresco, mosaic, sculpture, and stained glass into its sanctuary in the hope of reflecting Christian antiquity.[47] Dallas Seminary professor Michael Svigel has authored *Retro-Christianity: Reclaiming the Forgotten Faith* (2012) to assist an already Restorationist-leaning "free church" or "Bible church" constituency to "reassemble" some of the elements of Christian antiquity.[48]

In a similar vein, recent decades have witnessed an upsurge of evangelical interest in appropriating lessons from the history of Christian spirituality. To take just two examples of this, we can consider a pioneering work of Richard Foster, *Streams of Living Water,* and a more recent work of Gerald Sittser, *Water from a Deep Well.*[49] Both books are highly interesting and make edifying reading. But what is significantly absent in the two works is any strong element of theological evaluation of the various periods or epochs into which the history of Christian spirituality can be partitioned. A reader of Foster's *Streams of Living Water* would go away with the impression that the enlightened Christian of today will proceed to appropriate something of value from each of the contemplative (monastic) tradition, the holiness tradition, the charismatic tradition, the social justice tradition, the evangelical (Word-centered) tradition, and the incarnational (sacramental) tradition. The wise Christian

---

Elesha Coffman pointing out that circle of persons who collaborated with Webber exerted an exaggerated influence relative to their numbers. See Coffman, "The Chicago Call and Responses," in *Evangelicals and the Early Church,* ed. George Kalantzis and Andrew Tooley (Eugene, OR: Cascade, 2012), 108-24.

[45]Chris Armstrong, "Lost Secrets of the Ancient Church," *Christianity Today* 52, no. 2 (February 2008): 22-29.

[46]See the author's reflections on this phenomenon in Kenneth J. Stewart, "Much Ado About Something? Nagging Questions About Observing Lent," www.covenant.edu/docs/faculty/Stewart_Ken/Much_Ado_about_Something.pdf.

[47]David Neff, "The Art of Glory," *Christianity Today* 54, no. 10 (2010): 34-36. Article is also viewable at www.christianitytoday.com/ct/2010/october/24.34.html.

[48]Michael Svigel, *Retro-Christianity: Reclaiming the Forgotten Faith* (Wheaton, IL: Crossway, 2012). See the author's review of this book in *Themelios* 37, no. 3 (2012): 546-47, available at themelios.thegospelcoalition.org/review/retro-christianity-reclaiming-the-forgotten-faith#page=.

[49]Richard Foster, *Streams of Living Water* (San Francisco: Harper, 1998); and Gerald Sittser, *Water from a Deep Well* (Downers Grove, IL: InterVarsity Press, 2007).

reader is to avoid any narrow loyalty to or preference of any one over the others. Sittser's more historically informed *Water from a Deep Well*, while following a similar pattern of surveying major epochs, advances beyond the first-named title by focusing more attention on aspects of evangelical Protestant history. We have chapters on the spirituality of Reformers, evangelicals, and missionary pioneers. But in the end, all expressions of Christian spirituality are "refracted light."[50] The evident implication displayed in such works is that evangelical Christianity is but a late manifestation in the Christian tradition, and its insistence on the supremacy of Scripture is not genuinely representative or requisite. Evangelical Christianity stands in need of the kind of "nutritional supplement" that other expressions of the Christian faith can offer.

However, all such efforts at assembling some of the elements of Christian antiquity never quite succeed in producing a true replica of that Christian past that, the Restorationist hopes, can be recovered in a straightforward way. Such efforts are attempts at synthesizing or weaving together things that may not cohere. Taken as a whole, this represents a smorgasbord approach in which the individual congregation or believer picks and chooses which elements of the Christian past to incorporate. For lack of some guiding principle, this approach is idiosyncratic. Two guiding principles, mentioned earlier in this book, are the perpetuity of evangelical movements from earliest times and the steadying effect exercised by regarding biblical authority as supreme.[51] Neither principle exerts a strong influence in these eclectic approaches.

Implications. It is often remarked that evangelical Christianity thrives in direct proportion to its adaptability. It has been in considerable part because forms of evangelical Christianity have favored the introduction of vernacular Scriptures, the rapid training of indigenous leadership, a largely voluntary use of set liturgies, higher degrees of lay participation in church services, and "cell" or "small groups" for accountability and fellowship that this form of Christianity has gained traction in settings subject to cultural

---

[50]Sittser, *Water from a Deep Well*, 281.

[51]The author would point the reader to chapters 3 and 4 of this book, which stress the perpetuity of evangelical movements in Christian history and the recurring principle that Scripture must hold a role as supreme authority. An admirable recent book-length treatment that recognizes the existence of a distinctively evangelical heritage of spirituality is that of Tom Schwanda, *The Emergence of Evangelical Spirituality* (Mahwah, NJ: Paulist Press, 2015).

change. Consistent with this, it is now regularly reported that unaffiliated independent congregations (often of massive size and meeting at multiple sites) represent the shape of things to come in the evangelical future. Most of the one hundred largest North American evangelical congregations are now of this type. Approximately 25 percent of today's North American evangelicals could be categorized as nondenominational.[52]

Yet this final chapter constitutes a discussion about why certain thoughtful younger evangelical Christians are leaving their churches and reaffiliating to Roman Catholicism and Orthodoxy. And the odd fact is that it is the same admirable evangelical Protestant readiness to be adaptable and innovative, to keep denominational tradition and heritage in the background, that is itself a contributing factor in stoking up disaffected attitudes among those motivated by one or more of the six factors just named. The thoughtful evangelical who is seeking the kind of theological stability that could be called "mere Christianity," a way of worshiping God that is less concerned about fostering the right "mood" in the worshiper than on focusing on the objective work of salvation God has wrought in Jesus Christ, and to find and identify with the "one holy catholic" church may well be steadily less likely to find these attributes within our evangelical churches *just because of* our evangelical penchant for adaptation and pursuit of cultural relevance.

Considerations like these raise awkward questions. Should this minority, so intent on locating the "historic church," now be able to restrain the evangelical Christianity that is evidently succeeding at outreach and at enfolding the unchurched through church planting? Instead of catering to their aspirations, why should we not instead dismiss persons of this outlook as the "liturgical fringe" and let them go where they will?

But to even frame the issue this way is to perpetuate a terrible misunderstanding. For the fact seems to be that it is evangelicalism's anti-traditional, pro-adaptability, ready-for-anything mindset (the lateral factor) that is now providing the fertile soil out of which the aspirations and longings of "going

---

[52]Ed Stetzer, "The Rapid Rise of Nondenominational Christianity: My Most Recent Piece at CNN," *Exchange* (blog), *Christianity Today*, June 12, 2015, www.christianitytoday.com/edstetzer/2015/june/rapid-rise-of-non-denominational-christianity-my-most-recen.html; see also Ed Stetzer, "The Rise of the Evangelical 'Nones,'" CNN, June 12, 2015, www.cnn.com/2015/06/12/living/stetzer-christian-nones/index.html.

home to Rome/Antioch" sprout and grow. If one accepts what has been just stated as true, then pragmatic evangelicalism can be understood to be the breeding ground of the "liturgical fringe," and the process that we have watched unfold since the 1980s will go on, indefinitely, as the steady side effect of evangelical pragmatism. When viewed from this perspective, the quest for rootedness of these younger evangelicals is actually performing the service of forcing evangelical Christianity (in its various expressions) to ask overdue questions about itself. One of the chief questions overdue for a hearing is, why has evangelical Christianity let its roots in antiquity wither so badly in recent times?

CONCLUSION

If you have persisted in reading this far, you may be wondering how the important but elusive link with Christian antiquity can be recovered. A good portion of this book has been taken up with what I will call "slamming doors" on dubious proposals about how to recover a lost connection with Christian antiquity. No, evangelical Christianity's claim to authenticity is *not* going to be made or broken by whether or not we carry Bibles that contain the apocryphal books, whether we give monasticism a second look, or whether we belatedly recognize the bishop of Rome as the leader of world Christianity.

My answer to this question is that evangelical Christianity—consistent with its being a Christ-centered, Spirit-empowered, and scripturally guided movement intent on the evangelization of the world—must again become adept at what it was doing until a hundred years ago. In ways consistent with the supreme authority of Scripture, evangelical Christianity was until then regularly drawing on the resources of the early church, assisted by the insights of the Reformation of the sixteenth century. Then, evangelical Protestants took a back seat to no one in studying the church fathers, researching the apostolic fathers of the second century, and gaining fresh insights into liturgical practices such as baptism and the Lord's Supper. So long as evangelical Christianity "mined" early Christianity in such ways at that time, no one dared whisper that it was illegitimate, threadbare, or squatting on turf actually owned by others.

It is only in the last hundred years, when such important pursuits have been ignored, that our movement has become vulnerable to suggestions that we lack the approbation of antiquity. It is implied that this approbation is available to us only if we come to terms with the magisterium of Rome, the legacy of monasticism, and the neglected Apocrypha. Happily, we have so many indications that the pendulum—which, for evangelical and other streams of Christianity, steadily moved away from attending to early Christianity—has recently swung in the opposite direction. However, much of this recovery is being carried out in libraries, classrooms, and in publishing houses. We need to consider how this recovery ought to affect congregations and ordinary Christians. Let me ask three questions.

Your congregation and Christian antiquity. First, in ways consistent with your evangelical Protestantism, what connects your congregation and denomination to Christian antiquity? Charles Bell was surely speaking for many evangelicals in his admitting a desire to find those "missing 1500 years" that his expression of evangelical Christianity had either not mentioned or mentioned only to disparage. Of course, not every church attender or professed believer is that curious about such questions. But if the "home to Rome/Antioch" movement demonstrates anything, it is that there are far more college-educated individuals—fascinated with questions of history, literature, and the history of ideas—wanting to learn about our tie to Christian antiquity than are hearing or observing this being emphasized in their congregations week by week.

The neglect to make the connection with antiquity may have been the greatest in independent evangelical churches, but there is also evidence that denominational churches are neglecting this task as it is more and more widely accepted that *only* generic, nontraditional expressions of Christianity will gain traction in our culture.[53] Evangelical Protestants do not talk openly about historical legacy, and it is time to change that. Perhaps the "lightening of the ship" in the early twentieth-century liberal-fundamentalist struggle, with its wrangling over the defense of foundational Christian doctrines, discouraged this use of heritage as an expendable luxury.[54]

---

[53]The dangers inherent in denominational churches choosing to "go generic" and to downplay their heritage is aptly described in the essay of Patrick Malloy, "Rick Warren Meets Gregory Dix," *Anglican Theological Review* 92, no. 3 (2010): 439-53. The essay is accessible online at www.anglicantheologicalreview.org/static/pdf/articles/malloy.pdf.

[54]Chapter 5 of this book demonstrated that Protestantism did well in maintaining its connection with antiquity until the early twentieth century.

We could begin the process of reacquainting ourselves with early Christianity by taking up popular treatments such as Henry Chadwick's *The Early Church*.[55] It is much better to get our bearings with the help of a dispassionate teacher whose aim is to inform rather than from one whose aim is to recruit. The martyrs of early Christianity were remembered in classic style by John Foxe (1516–1587), whose massive work of 1563 is still available to us in more digestible form in a one-volume condensed edition.[56] The beliefs and practices of the early Christians are ably set out in trusty guides such as Michael G. Haykin's, *Rediscovering the Church Fathers* and Bryan Litfin's *Getting to Know the Church Fathers*.[57]

Your congregation and the holy catholic church. Second, in ways consistent with your evangelical Protestantism, what unites your congregation and denomination to the "one holy catholic" church? Are worship practices of the church of the ages featured in your services? Of course, the inclusion of any practice must be warranted by broad biblical principles. But with this granted, is your congregation incorporating elements such as the reciting of the Apostles' Creed and the Nicene Creed?[58] Is your congregation marking out of the main days of the church year associated with the life of Jesus Christ on earth?[59] Is the Lord's Supper administered with a healthy regularity and is it twinned with the hearty preaching of God's Word?[60] Is Christian baptism insisted on as a "mark"

---

[55]Henry Chadwick, *The Early Church*, vol. 1 of *Penguin History of the Church* (New York: Penguin-Putnam, 1993).

[56]John Foxe, *Acts and Monuments* (1563) is available in such one-volume condensed versions as *Foxe's Book of Martyrs*. The one-volume edition, produced in the Victorian age, is still available and devotes its first three chapters to martyrs in early Christianity.

[57]Michael G. Haykin, *Rediscovering the Church Fathers* (Wheaton, IL: Crossway, 2011); and Bryan Litfin, *Getting to Know the Church Fathers* (Grand Rapids: Brazos, 2007).

[58]In recommending the use of the Apostles' Creed, I am fully cognizant that this creed does not achieve total doctrinal clarity on all points, such as the "descent into hell," and that there have been justifiable efforts made to alter the wording so as to avoid confusion. There are also several versions of the Apostles' Creed set to music that are well suited to congregational singing. A thoughtful rationale for restoring the use of creeds in evangelical worship is provided by Scot McKnight in "Evangelicals and the Public Use of Creeds," in Kalantzis and Tooley, *Evangelicals and the Early Church*, 140-53.

[59]As I stand in the Presbyterian and Reformed tradition, I note with interest the measured approach of the Second Helvetic Confession (1566) XXIV.4: "If in Christian liberty the churches religiously celebrate the memory of the Lord's nativity, circumcision, passion, resurrection, and of his ascension into heaven, and the sending of the Holy Spirit upon his disciples, we approve of it highly. Be we do not approve of feasts instituted for men and for saints." This is an excellent example of how the Reformation "sifted" Christian antiquity for our benefit.

[60]The reader is referred to chapter 7 of this book, recounting how the earlier efforts of evangelical

of every Christian? Holy baptism, preceded or followed by catechetical instruction, is a pairing that has to be recovered where it has been lost. There is every bit as much reason why those professing faith in Christ in the twenty-first century should be instructed in the Ten Commandments, the Lord's Prayer, and the assertions of the Apostles' Creed as there was in the sixteenth or sixth centuries.[61] This catechetical instruction should be preliminary to one's participating, with understanding, in the Lord's Supper.

And what do you sing? If we are concerned that our worship assemblies would show some connection to Christian antiquity, then our sung praises to God should include hymns and songs of the church at all times and places. A good hymnal and a good church music director will familiarize Christians with praises from all ages. Out of curiosity, I examined the hymnal used within my congregation's traditional service; I was delighted to find that it included thirty-five selections authored by sixteen hymn writers who wrote prior to AD 1400. What a resource, especially for Christmas, Good Friday, Easter, Pentecost, and Ascension Day! How does your hymnal fare? We could make greater use of these resources than we do. If your church uses no hymnal, there are still hymns of all ages waiting to be drawn on under copyright licenses. What is called blended worship can easily incorporate elements both ancient and modern, provided that we are determined to identify with believers of all ages when we worship God.[62]

Your congregation and the global church. Third, in ways consistent with your evangelical Protestantism, do those welcomed into your church family understand that they are being welcomed into the church of all ages and the global church of Jesus Christ? Or, to put it another way, does your congregation acknowledge to being an "outpost" of the church of all times and all places? It is right and proper to emphasize the importance of the "local" church, but no local church exists other than by being a concrete expression of the vast community of believers assembling in many places.

---

leaders to increase the regularity of observance met with resistance. It was not weekly observance that they aimed at.

[61]The best such catechetical guide available to evangelical Protestants is surely that of J. I. Packer, *I Want to Be a Christian* (Carol Stream, IL: Tyndale House, 1985), republished as *Growing in Christ* (Wheaton, IL: Crossway, 2007).

[62]*Trinity Hymnal* (Suwanee, GA: Great Commission, 1990). This wonderful hymnal is representative of those that encompass great hymns and creeds of all ages. In it, I have found thirty-six hymns originating before the year 1000.

What actions and policies within your congregation bind you to common action with Christians beyond your walls and beyond your denomination (if you are in a linked congregation)? If your congregation is independent, how do you close the gap that can make it appear that your assembly of believers is aloof from other evangelical congregations?

These emphases, if energetically pursued, would go a long way toward demonstrating "small c" catholicism across our evangelical churches, the absence of which currently confirms too many in the inclination that they should look outside our evangelical Protestant tradition in order to find historic Christianity. Evangelical Protestantism is not the problem; evangelical Protestantism that has severed its roots in early Christianity is a problem.

QUESTIONS FOR DISCUSSION

1. If you have spoken to a former evangelical Protestant who is now Roman Catholic or Eastern Orthodox about his or her reason for reaffiliating, did this person mention any one (or more) of the six reasons identified in this chapter? Were there other noteworthy reasons also?
2. Do you accept that evangelical Protestantism shares some responsibility for the loss of such individuals from our churches? If you say yes to this question, do you agree that these losses will continue, or can they be averted?
3. In your opinion, do those who leave for Roman Catholicism or Eastern Orthodoxy have a romanticized or a realistic conception of the church they are now entering?

APPENDIX

The Colloquy of Regensburg (1541) on Justification

THE JUSTIFICATION OF MAN[1]

1. No Christian should doubt that after the fall of our first parent all men are, as the apostle says [Eph. 2:3], born children of wrath and enemies of God and thereby are in death and slavery to sin.

2. Likewise, no Christian should question that nobody can be reconciled with God, nor set free from slavery to sin, except by Christ the one mediator between God and men, by whose grace, as the apostle said to the Romans [6:17-18], we are not only reconciled to God and set free from slavery to sin, but also made sharers in the divine nature [2 Pet. 1:4] and children of God.

3. Likewise, it is quite clear that adults do not obtain these blessings of Christ, except by the prevenient movement of the Holy Spirit, by which their mind and will are moved to hate sin. For, as St Augustine says, it is impossible to begin a new life if we do not repent of the former one. Likewise, in the last chapter of Luke [24:47], Christ commands that

[1]Translated from G. Pfeilschifter (ed.), *Acta Reformationis Catholicae*, vol. 6 (Regensburg: F. Pustet, 1974), 52-54. The paragraphs are not numbered in the original text. I have made use of a translation from Calvin's French edition (CO 5:524-27) made by Dr. Pierre Landry, though the present translation is very different. I am grateful to David Wright for some helpful suggestions.

repentance and forgiveness of sin should be preached in his name. Also, John the Baptist, sent to prepare the way of the Lord, preached repentance, saying [Matt. 3:2]: "Repent [*Poenitentiam agite*], for the kingdom of heaven is drawing near." Next, man's mind is moved toward God by the Holy Spirit through Christ and this movement is through faith. Through this [*faith*] man's mind believes with certainty all that God has transmitted [*tradita*], and also with full certainty and without doubt assents to the promises made to us by God who, as stated in the psalm [144:13], is faithful in all his words. From there he acquires confidence [*fiduciam*] on account of God's promise, by which he has pledged that he will remit sins freely and that he will adopt as children those who believe in Christ, those I say who repent of their former life. By this faith, he is lifted up to God by the Holy Spirit and so he receives the Holy Spirit, remission of sins, imputation of righteousness, and countless other gifts.

4. So it is a reliable and sound doctrine that the sinner is justified by living and efficacious faith, for through it we are pleasing and acceptable to God on account of Christ. And living faith is what we call the movement of the Holy Spirit, by which those who truly repent of their old life are lifted up to God and truly appropriate the mercy promised in Christ, so that they now truly recognize that they have received the remission of sins and reconciliation on account of the merits of Christ, through the free [*gratuita*] goodness of God, and cry out to God: "Abba Father." But this happens to no one unless also at the same time love is infused [*infundatur*] which heals the will so that the healed will may begin to fulfil the law, just as Saint Augustine said. So living faith is that which both appropriates mercy in Christ, believing that the righteousness which is in Christ is freely imputed to it, and at the same time receives the promise of the Holy Spirit and love. Therefore the faith that truly justifies is that faith which is effectual through love. Nevertheless it remains true, that it is by this faith that we are justified (i.e., accepted and reconciled to God) inasmuch as it appropriates the mercy and righteousness which is imputed to us on account of Christ and his merit, not on account of the worthiness or perfection of the righteousness imparted [*communicatae*] to us in Christ.

5. Although the one who is justified receives righteousness and through Christ also has inherent [righteousness], as the apostle says [I Cor. 6:11]: "you are washed, you are sanctified, you are justified, etc." (which is why the holy fathers made use of [the term] "to be justified" even to mean "to receive inherent righteousness"), nevertheless, the faithful soul depends not on this, but only on the righteousness of Christ given to us as a gift, without which there is and can be no righteousness at all. And so by faith in Christ we are justified or reckoned to be righteous, that is we are accepted through his merits and not on account of our own worthiness or works. And on account of the righteousness inherent in us we are said to be righteous, because the works which we perform are righteous, according to the saying of John [1 John 3:7]: "whoever who does what is right is righteous."
6. Although fear of God, patience, humility and other virtues ought always to grow in the regenerate, because this renewal is imperfect and enormous weakness remains in them, it should nevertheless be taught that those who truly repent may always hold with most certain faith that they are pleasing to God on account of Christ the mediator. For it is Christ who is the propitiator, the High Priest and the one who prays for us, the one the Father gave to us and with him all good things.
7. Seeing that in our weakness there is no perfect certainty and that there are many weak and fearful consciences, which often struggle against great doubt, nobody should be excluded from the grace of Christ on account of such weakness. Such people should be earnestly encouraged boldly to set the promises of Christ against these doubts and by diligent intercession to pray that their faith may be increased, according to the saying: "Lord increase our faith" [Luke 17:5].
8. Likewise, every Christian should learn that this grace and this regeneration have not been given to us so that we might remain idle in that stage of our renewal which we at first obtained, but so that we may grow in everything into him who is the head. Therefore, the people must be taught to devote effort to[2] this growth which indeed happens through good works, both internal and external, which are commanded and

[2]Reading *det* for *de*.

commended by God. To these works God has, in many passages from the Gospels, clearly and manifestly promised on account of Christ a reward—good things in this life, as much for the body as for the soul (as much as seems right to divine providence) and after this life in heaven. Therefore, although the inheritance of eternal life is due to the regenerate on account of the promise, as soon as they are reborn in Christ, nevertheless God also renders a reward to good works, not according to the substance of the works, nor because they come from us, but to the extent that they are performed in faith and proceed from the Holy Spirit, who dwells in us, free choice concurring as a partial agent.

9. The joy of those who have performed more and better works will be greater and more abundant, on account of the increase of faith and love, in which they have grown through exercises of that kind. Now those who say that we are justified by faith alone should at the same time teach the doctrine of repentance, of the fear of God, of the judgement of God and of good works, so that all the chief points of the preaching may remain firm, as Christ said: "preaching repentance and the remission of sins in my name" [Luke 24:47]. And that is to prevent this way of speaking [i.e., *sola fide*] from being understood other than has been previously mentioned.

General Index

Scripture Index